MW01256128

The Legisl[
Edward M. Kennedy

The Legislative Legacy of Edward M. Kennedy

Eleven Milestones in Pursuit of Social Justice, 1965–2007

CRAIG A. HOROWITZ

McFarland & Company, Inc., Publishers

Jefferson, North Carolina

LIBRARY OF CONGRESS CATALOGUING-IN-PUBLICATION DATA

Horowitz, Craig A., 1961–
    The legislative legacy of Edward M. Kennedy : eleven
milestones in pursuit of social justice, 1965–2007 /
Craig A. Horowitz.
        p.   cm.
    Includes bibliographical references and index.

    ISBN 978-0-7864-7873-6 (softcover : acid free paper) ∞
    ISBN 978-1-4766-1401-4 (ebook)

    1. Kennedy, Edward M. (Edward Moore), 1932–2009—
Influence.   2. Legislators—United States—Biography.
3. United States. Congress. Senate—Biography.   4. United
States—Politics and government—1945–1989.   5. United
States—Politics and government—1989–   I. Title.

    E840.8.K35H66   2014
    328.73'092—dc23
    [B]   2013051366

BRITISH LIBRARY CATALOGUING DATA ARE AVAILABLE

Front cover: Official Senate photograph of Edward Kennedy

Manufactured in the United States of America

McFarland & Company, Inc., Publishers
    Box 611, Jefferson, North Carolina 28640
    www.mcfarlandpub.com

To my wife, Cathy Seidman,
who put up with stacks of books and research materials
in our living room and bedroom, as well as my researching
and writing during evenings and weekends.
Her encouragement, draft after draft, to not give up
made this book possible.

Table of Contents

Acknowledgments

Writing a book of history, first and foremost, requires endless research. For help on finding primary sources, I wish to thank Bobby Griffith, a research librarian I have never met but who promptly responded to my many inquiries. Mr. Griffith routinely emailed me bills and committee reports after I could not personally locate them.

It also takes considerable guidance—particularly for someone like me, a practicing lawyer who has not written history in over 30 years—for a book such as this to achieve success. My thesis mentor at Brown University, eminent historian James T. Patterson, read early chapters of this book and with his characteristic style, asked many probing questions and provided incisive edits. Steve Gillon, long ago my teaching assistant at Brown and now also an eminent historian, steered me toward focusing on specific major pieces of legislation rather than trying to describe Kennedy's role in so many of the bills he championed over his 47-year Senate career.

Through chance I received tremendous help from a Kennedy insider, Nick Allard, who worked on his staff from 1983 to 1986. I found Nick through Darryl Nirenberg, whom I grew up with. Darryl, a friend from Facebook, saw a post regarding my book and put me in touch with his law partner, Nick Allard. Nick provided great insight and assisted me in placing this book. So too Michael Waterstone, Associate Dean of the Loyola School of Law, read my ADA and FMLA chapters and helped me immeasurably.

I am grateful to my law partner, Wayne D. Clayton, for his time in listening to my thoughts on the book, as well as for his careful editing.

I write my books the old fashioned way—with a pen and a pad of paper. I cannot fully express my gratitude to my legal secretary, Elda Salazar, for typing this entire book and all the many revisions. Elda even personally proofread each and every page before I sent the book out for review and ultimately publication.

My family encouraged me to keep working on this book even when I had "writers block." I thank my children, Nicole, Jake, and Jordan, for their optimism. Finally, I owe so much to my wife, Cathy. She believed I could write this book and gave me the time to do it. I spent countless Sunday afternoons in our living room and evenings in our bedroom writing this book. She understood my passion in doing this, and I truly appreciate her patience and support.

Introduction

In 1962, when Edward M. ("Ted") Kennedy became the junior senator of Massachusetts, many Americans reveled in the Camelot era. John F. Kennedy won the presidency by the narrowest of margins over Richard M. Nixon. The televised Nixon-Kennedy debates had captivated a nation. Robert ("Bobby") Kennedy, a key member of JFK's cabinet, served aggressively as the attorney general. The Kennedy dynasty expanded with Ted Kennedy's Senate victory.

Just one year later the nation witnessed and mourned the assassination of JFK in Dallas, Texas, as he rode in an open motor car. Few alive during that time fail to remember where they first learned the tragic news. The funeral, nationally televised, displayed an elegant Jackie Kennedy in mourning and the unforgettable photograph of then young "John John" in a suit, saluting his fallen father.

Then, only five years after, in 1968, Sirhan Sirhan assassinated Bobby Kennedy at the Ambassador Hotel in Los Angeles, California, following Bobby's dramatic Democratic primary victory in California. Rosie Greer, then a prominent athlete and actor, tackled Sirhan Sirhan, but Bobby did not survive. Once again, a nation mourned the passing of a Kennedy. The timing of Bobby's assassination coincided with the fracturing of a society beset by the Vietnam War, the prior assassination of the Reverend Martin Luther King, Jr., and a divisive presidential campaign, leading to the unexpected rebirth and ascendency of Richard M. Nixon to the White House.

Most would not have expected in 1962 that the youngest Kennedy brother, Ted Kennedy, of all the Kennedys, would have the longest political career. Indeed, Ted Kennedy already had a tarnished reputation with his cheating scandal while in college at Harvard University. By the time he succumbed to cancer in 2009, Ted Kennedy had served 37 years in the Senate. He entered the Senate at the minimum Constitutional age of 30; few could have predicted what impact this inexperienced politician would have in the Senate.

On May 21, 2008, the *Boston Globe* and the *Seattle Times* hailed the following nine major pieces of legislation as highlights of Edward M. "Ted" Kennedy's career in the Senate.

Immigration (1965). Kennedy managed a successful floor battle to pass the Hart-Cellar Act that abolished quotas and lifted a 1924 ban on immigration from Asia.

Cancer (1971). After rising to the position of majority whip in 1969, Kennedy and Rep. Paul Rogers, D-FL, passed legislation establishing a federal cancer research program that quadrupled the amount spent fighting cancer.

Women's Sports (1972). Kennedy was a key Senate backer of Title IX, a 1972 amendment requiring colleges and universities to provide equal funding for men's and women's athletics.

Campaign Finance (1974). Joining with Sen. Hugh Scott, R-PA, Kennedy sponsored the sweeping overhaul of ethics rules after Watergate, limiting political donations and establishing public financing for presidential candidates.

Anti-Apartheid (1986). After President Ronald Reagan vetoed economic sanctions banning the purchase of gold, coal, iron, and other goods from the apartheid government of South Africa in 1986, Kennedy spearheaded the bipartisan effort in both houses to override the veto.

Family Leave (1990). Kennedy and Sen. Christopher Dodd, D-CT, authored the Family and Medical Leave Act, requiring businesses to provide unpaid leave for family emergencies or after the birth of infants. It was signed by President Clinton in 1993.

Health Care (1996). Kennedy joined with Sen. Nancy Kassebaum, R-KS, in 1996 to pass the Kennedy-Kassebaum Act, which allowed employees to keep health insurance after leaving their job and prohibited health insurance companies from refusing to renew coverage on the basis of preexisting medical conditions.

Minimum Wage (1996). Kennedy was the lead Senate sponsor of legislation increasing the minimum wage from $4.25 to $5.15. He reprised this role in 2007, after Democrats retook Congress, quarterbacking the effort to raise the minimum wage from $5.15 to $7.25 by 2009.

Education (2001). Over the objections of some fellow Democrats, Kennedy helped pass President Bush's No Child Left Behind Act in 2001.[1]

A recent biography of Ted Kennedy, in a chapter titled "A Master Legislator," glowingly describes Ted Kennedy's legislative accomplishments in the Senate.

> Ted had compiled a legislative record unsurpassed by any living senator. Among the scores of bills bearing his name or imprint, he could take credit for the Civil Rights Act of 1964; The Voting Rights Act of 1965; the expansion of the voting franchise to eighteen years old; the 1992 Kennedy-Hatch law providing health insurance to children; the 1982 Voting Rights Act extension; the 1996 Kennedy-Kassebaum bill, which made health insurance portable for workers; the 1998 law that allocates billions for aids testing, treatment and research; the 1990 Americans with Disabilities Act; the 1993 Family Medical Leave Act; and the 2001 No Child Left Behind Act.[2]

This book analyzes the nine pieces of legislation described in the *Boston Globe* article as major achievements, as well as the 1990 Americans with Disabilities Act (ADA) and failed efforts at Immigration reform with Senator John McCain from 2005 to 2007, from both a legal and historical perspective. It not only critically examines the political negotiations behind the passage of eventual legislation and text of the actual bills, but also addresses the path of the acts following their passage, which sometimes resulted in unintended consequences. In that regard, this book tests the enthusiastic description of Kennedy's role, in an even-handed basis. Moreover, this book identifies a common theme among much of Kennedy's legislative efforts—eradicating discrimination. The Immigration Act of 1965, Kennedy's first sponsored bill passed into law, ended a racist quota system. The Title IX amendment to the Education Act in 1972 prohibited discrimination in education, and had a profound impact on the rise of women's collegiate sports. The Comprehensive Anti-Apartheid Act of 1986 sought to eliminate the most serious type of insidious discrimination by policing strict sanctions on the racist South African regime. It culminated two years later with the freeing of political prisoner Nelson Mandela after well over 25 years. Mandela, in fact, visited the United States with much fanfare and a noteworthy meeting with Ted Kennedy. The ADA, passed in 1990, sought to provide opportunities to America's many disabled, with the initial purpose of eradicating discrimination in the workplace based on disability. The Family Medical Leave Act of 1993 provided women and men caring for their babies with serious illnesses with equal opportunity (with some unanticipated problems) in the workplace. And Immigration reform efforts from 2005 to 2007 with Republican Senator John McCain sought to address the problems raised by undocumented immigrants' presence in the United States and the poverty afflicting many of them due to illegal compensation below the minimum wage.

However, this book also debunks myths that inflate Kennedy's actual role in the passage of these ten pieces of legislation. Indeed, as this book describes, between the Immigration Act of 1965 and the Healthcare legislation of 1996, no single piece of major legislation passed into law bore the name of Ted Kennedy. Nonetheless, such legislation as the ADA, passed in 1990, no doubt reflected Kennedy's ceaseless efforts following his sister Rosemary's tragic disability (called retardation back then), his own son Teddy's cancer, which resulted in amputation of his leg, and his persistent desire to combat discrimination in the work-place.

But while he certainly backed other legislation and played his role in the Senate in assisting passage of ultimate compromise legislation, his sponsored bills routinely met defeat and often did not even make it out of Committee. Kennedy's ultimate legacy may well be measured by his attempts, time and again, to reach across the aisle and accept com-promise legislation, which if fully known to his liberal backers, may have angered them.

Kennedy, as noted, entered the Senate in 1962. A year following the inauguration of John F. Kennedy as president in 1961, Ted Kennedy won JFK's vacant Senate seat in Massachusetts with 54 percent of the vote, and at age 30 became the junior senator from Massachusetts.[3] He served 47 years in the Senate before his death, the third longest tenure in the Senate ever.[4] The evaluation of Ted Kennedy's legacy depends largely on the political affiliation of the individual assessing him. To the liberal left, Kennedy represents the best of Democratic party values—a social reformer ceaselessly standing up for the poor and disenfranchised.[5] The ardent Republican right, however, views Kennedy as a morally bankrupt politician undeserving of serving in the Senate.[6] The late Republican National Chairman Lee Atwater described Kennedy as "the man in American politics Republicans love to hate."[7] By his death in 2009, a fractured American citizenry and Senate, faced with President Obama's health care reform efforts, surely wished Kennedy's presence to weigh in on attempts to heal the partisan divide. In fact, as this book describes, while Ted Kennedy held decidedly liberal views, his ultimate Legislative record reflects a much more moderate approach, such as that of his older brother, JFK. (Bobby was plainly much more liberal than both JFK and Ted.)

To be sure, the Chappaquiddick incident in 1969, originally reported on a small corner of the front page of a newspaper describing American's first launch to the moon with the headline "Man Walks on the Moon,"[8] along with Kennedy's frequent public bouts with alcohol, has tarnished his reputation with some Americans. Others, though, deem the senior senator as the savior of liberal ideals and principles and look past his personal flaws. This book seeks to set aside such facile partisan judgment and present the reader with the details of Kennedy's legislative career so as to enable the reader to reach an informed assessment of Kennedy's accomplishments and limitations.

In truth, Kennedy's time in the Senate presents a record of legislative accomplishments that differ from the black and white viewpoints of Kennedy espoused by the liberal left and the Republican right. In fact, as demonstrated by Kennedy's attempt at immigration reform before his passing, frequently the Massachusetts senator has reached across the aisle in an effort to enact laws. Working with Republican presidential candidate John McCain, Kennedy co-authored a bill to address the country's immigration problems. Derisively referred to as "amnesty" legislation for *illegal* immigrants by many on the right,[9] the bill that stalled in Congress actually sought to fortify the border, crack down on employers with illegal immigrant undocumented workers and at the same time provide a path to citizenship for those illegal immigrants productively working in the United States.[10] To date, comprehensive immigration legislation still remains stuck in Congress.

The fact that Senator McCain, in the midst of his presidential bid, would work assiduously with Kennedy in an attempt to reach consensus in Congress on an immigration bill highlights the respect Kennedy earned in his years in the Senate, even with his Republican counterparts. While the bill ultimately failed to pass, the consensus-building efforts of Kennedy (and McCain) provide a much different concrete example of Senator Kennedy's skills as a legislator than those typically depicted by the Republican right and liberal left. Indeed, during the highly partisan debates on health care reform in 2009, Senator McCain lamented that his friend and colleague, Ted Kennedy, could not participate to bring consensus and raise the confidence level of many skeptical Americans.

Senator Kennedy even bewildered members of his own Democratic party. In a move that shocked many, Kennedy did not endorse Hillary Clinton, but instead heartily embraced the unlikely candidacy of Barack

Obama.[11] Kennedy's January 29, 2008, endorsement of Obama—two days after Obama's primary victory in South Carolina and just eight days before Super Tuesday—angered the Clinton camp and some party regulars.[12] Those on the right, fast to portray Kennedy as a party hack, could scarcely make such accusations after Kennedy split ranks with the party faithful. And the confused Democratic party stalwarts had trouble coming to grips with the fact that Kennedy would risk a volatile party fissure by straying from the Clinton campaign. Kennedy, though, as this book will show, departed from conventional liberal Democratic positions to try to achieve pragmatic results. Surely, he viewed Obama as having the best chance for victory, and decided after eight years of George W. Bush's regime not to have the nation placed in yet another debate about the morality of the Clintons.

Nonetheless, in the wake of the sudden diagnosis of a terminal brain tumor and surgery, nobody other than those so radically right could not appreciate Senator Kennedy's dedication to the country. A severely weakened and ill Kennedy flew to Denver for the Democratic National Convention. He immediately went to the hospital. The Obama camp did not know whether Kennedy could attend the convention and give his speech. Following his release from the hospital, Kennedy arrived to the convention site and proceeded in a wheelchair to the back of the stage. Unwilling to speak while in a wheelchair, Kennedy walked himself to the podium and delivered a short but powerful speech. Evoking the presidency of his deceased brother, Senator Kennedy spoke.

> We are told that Barack Obama believes too much in an America of high principle and bold endeavors, but when John Kennedy called of going to the moon, he didn't say it's too far to go there... Yes we are all *Americans*. This is what we do. We reach the moon. We scale the heights. I know it. I've seen it. I've lived it. And we can do it again.[13]

Kennedy also referred to a goal that he repeatedly emphasized during his long tenure as a senator: "Barack Obama will close the book on the old politics of race and gender and group against group and straight against gay."[14]

Few compare Ted Kennedy's actual political accomplishments to the policies of JFK, nor have many probed into how a man of such privilege made individual rights and programs for the poor a centerpiece of his governance. Ted Kennedy, truly a patrician, ceaselessly lobbied during his 47-year tenure in the Senate for equal rights for all. Yet, by reaching across the aisle on so many occasions on compromise legislation,

Kennedy also embraced some of the moderate stances of his deceased brother JFK. Indeed, a fair share of Republicans now look to JFK's presidency as a time of conservative policymaking.

JFK stood for a balanced budget,[15] supported increased spending on foreign policy,[16] and "embodied the spirit of racial moderation."[17] Many on the right would have us believe that Ted Kennedy ventured far away during his career from the policies of his brother.[18] In truth, as this book demonstrates, Ted Kennedy's bipartisan efforts led to the passing of many bills that the liberal left would view as watered down. While other historians have described these approaches to reaching across the aisle, none have, as in this book, examined the specifics of the legislation originally proposed by Ted Kennedy and the final version passed into law.

Many on the left, on the other hand, harbor the sentiment that Senator Kennedy's policies were far more liberal than the policies of his deceased older brother.[19] In truth, though, historians agree that Ted Kennedy forged a middle road in his Legislative efforts and willingness to compromise. Thus, apart from strident politicians' rhetoric either on the Senate floor or stump speeches, Ted Kennedy's politics assuredly bore more resemblance to his brother JFK's moderation than to such liberal proponents as George McGovern.

Putting aside partisan political myths, the only way to assess Senator Kennedy's true political accomplishments involves a legal and historical assessment of the actual legislation he spearheaded and the path of these laws since their passage. Therefore, this book, as noted, examines nine major pieces of legislation, listed by the *Boston Globe* and the *Seattle Times* as Kennedy's major legislative accomplishments: (1) the Immigration Act of 1965; (2) the National Cancer Act of 1971; (3) Title IX, eliminating discrimination in college education; (4) 1974 Campaign Finance Reform; (5) Anti-Apartheid Legislation in 1986; (6) the Family and Medical Leave Act (FMLA) of 1993; (7) Health Care Continuation Coverage of 1996; (8) Minimum Wage Legislation in 1996; and (9) the No Child Left Behind Act of 2001. It also assesses the Americans with Disabilities Act landmark legislation that has since been trimmed by a conservative majority of the United States Supreme Court, as well as Immigration Reform efforts from 2005 to 2007.

This account therefore differs from previous works by unabashed Kennedy admirers, such as Theo Lippman, Jr., who states on page x of his Author's Note in his book *Senator Ted Kennedy: The Career Behind the Image*, that Kennedy's career in the Senate "has been as commendable as it has been full." In addition, a review of the style Kennedy displayed in the Senate and the relationships he forged provides useful information to perform this objective examination. For example, this book analyzes the relationships Senator Kennedy developed, for many have written on the embittered confrontations his brother Bobby created in his short time in the Senate.[20] Central to such an analysis, Kennedy's involvement on Legislative Committees also informs a nonpartisan judgment of his actual legislation. Kennedy's spirited relationships with Republicans such as Orrin Hatch, Nancy Kassebaum and John McCain deserve particular attention. For looking at their relationships, particularly in this unprecedented era of partisanship, where vote after vote goes along strictly partisan lines, should provide insight into a method for producing needed legislation in the future. With budget woes and painful economic decisions in the forefront, hopefully this study can shed some light on parties with different ambitions reaching a bipartisan consensus to achieve goals helpful to our country and now, in this era, to the entire global economy. As this book shows, Ted Kennedy enabled legislation to pass into law under both Democratic presidents and Republican presidents, often by reaching consensus and compromise. Thus, interestingly, several of Ted Kennedy's ardently supported legislations passed under the likes of Nixon, Ronald Reagan, and George W. Bush.

This book presents, in historical and legal perspective, ten actual major pieces of legislation embraced or sponsored by Kennedy, as well as his 2005–2007 Immigration Reform efforts. It also chronicles Kennedy's interactions with fellow senators both during periods of Democratic congressional majorities and minorities. While no doubt the contents of this book will not sway perceptions of Senator Kennedy by the fringes of both parties, nonetheless many Americans may well gain insight into Kennedy's efforts and achievements in the Senate from 1962 to 2009. Hopefully, by looking at the past, we can create a blueprint for successful cooperation in the House and Senate for the difficult future we face.

1

Entrance into the Senate and the National Immigration Act of 1965

In 1965, Senator Ted Kennedy made his first big splash in the Senate by sponsoring the National Immigration Act. Its purpose, to eliminate racism in the immigration system, has precursors in Kennedy's early years in the Senate as described herein. So too this chapter explores the unintended consequences of the act over the last 48 years.

To explore Kennedy's reasons for sponsoring the act requires an understanding of his election to the Senate in 1962 and his early years forging relationships with his elders in both parties. Ted Kennedy's Senate career flows, of course, from his brother's election as president. On January 20, 1961, John F. Kennedy took the presidential oath in the freezing cold of Capitol Plaza. According to Kennedy advisor and friend Arthur Schlesinger, Jr.,

> the Kennedy Presidency began with incomparable dash. The young President, the old poet, the splendid speech; the triumphant parade, the brilliant sky and the shining snow: it was one of the most glorious of inaugurals. And the new President himself obviously savored every moment of it.[1]

Ted Kennedy attended the inauguration, listening to his brother's famous statement: "Ask not what your country can do for you, but what you can do for your country."[2] Ted Kennedy at this time felt unsure about his future. After coordinating the Western states for JFK during the 1960 campaign, Ted, only 28 years old at the time, had thought about making a career for himself in the Rocky Mountains. However, the Kennedy brothers' power-craving father, Joseph Kennedy, had other ideas for Ted. According to historian Doris Kearns Goodwin, it was Joseph Kennedy, hurrying to finish up his work before the inaugura-tion, who insisted that the family clear the way for Teddy to run for Jack's seat in the Senate.[3]

Ted, only 28 at the time, had little political ambition. "The person who was primarily interested in having him run was my father," Bobby said later. "He just felt that Ted had worked all this time on the campaign and sacrificed himself for the older brother and ... he should have the right to run."[4] Ted Kennedy himself disputes that he ever had any doubts about running for the Senate. "Of course I wanted to make that run.... Elective office had been on my mind as early as my days at Milton."[5]

But Ted could not hold JFK's vacant senate seat until he turned 30 in 1962, the minimum age required by the Constitution. While the gov-ernor of Massachusetts technically held the selection call for the interim senator, JFK lobbied for Benjamin A. Smith, a college friend, who vowed to stand aside for Ted after two years.[6]

Ted Kennedy announced his candidacy for the Senate in March 1962,[7] one month after his thirtieth birthday (Ted Kennedy shares George Washington's February 22 birthday.) Ted Kennedy distanced himself from JFK in the primary, but clearly the president had a strong interest in Ted's election. JFK "made it clear that a defeat would not be just Ted's loss, but his own too, and would not be tolerated."[8] With Bobby as Attorney General, JFK clamored for Ted to become the next senator from Massachusetts. Therefore, JFK had a pronounced influence at the local level in lobbying behind the scenes for Ted's campaign. While not a stump speaker, JFK called on party stalwarts and those who owed favors to back his young brother's nascent candidacy. The nephew of the House Majority Leader, Massachusetts Attorney General Edward McCormick, challenged Kennedy in the primary, but to no avail. Ted Kennedy won by a landslide, leaving little drama for election night.

Thus, a reluctant Ted Kennedy, unsure of where he fell under the spotlight of his president brother and prominent Attorney General Bobby, began a 47-year career in the Senate in 1962. From 1962 until JFK's death in November 1963, the Kennedys held unprecedented famil-ial positions of power. With JFK as president, Robert Kennedy in the Cabinet post as Attorney General, and Ted Kennedy a senator from Mas-sachusetts, the Kennedys had every opportunity to push their agenda. But as a junior senator, Ted Kennedy predictably needed time to settle into the hierarchical Senate tradition. Indeed, Kennedy respected and abided by the Senate honors and customs. In contrast to his brother

Robert F. Kennedy, who would become the senator from New York in 1964 following JFK's death, "Ted Kennedy was a more cautious and canny politician than Bobby, and more inclined to adhere to Senate party rules and customs."[9] Not until 1965 would Kennedy make his first major imprint with the passage of his National Immigration Act.

Still, Kennedy joined the Senate Judiciary Committee upon his entry into the Senate, and ultimately held a Committee membership until he stepped down voluntarily in December 2008 to focus on health care reform. In these early days, Ted Kennedy seemed awed by the political life he had embraced. Although he would later run a spirited campaign in the 1980 Democratic primary against incumbent Jimmy Carter, Ted Kennedy in these early years expressed skepticism about ever seeking the high office. Speaking about his brother JFK, Ted remarked, "After seeing the cares of office on you, [I] wasn't sure [I'd] ever be interested in being the President. I wonder if you [JFK] ... had to do it over again, would you work for the presidency and whether you can recommend the job to others."[10] Throughout the years, both before and after Chappaquiddick, Kennedy would decline political office, even the Vice Presidency in 1968, because of the toll the presidency took on JFK before his assassination. While he ultimately challenged Jimmy Carter in the 1980 election, Ted Kennedy's prime years for election, particularly in 1972 or 1976, had long passed him.

Contrary, then, to some accounts, Ted Kennedy entered the Senate not seeking political aggrandizement but in a cautious manner. Even harsh Kennedy critics acknowledge that Ted Kennedy began his Senate career learning the ropes.

> For the past two years [1962–63] he had done an apprenticeship to work his way through Senate protocols and take care of his own political business and that of his home state—notably legislation favorable to New England fisheries and airlines.[11]

Accordingly, even partisan opponents concede that Ted Kennedy's "good nature and hard work had won him grudging respect from colleagues."[12]

Yet, the description of Ted Kennedy's home state legislation in the 1962–63 time frame ignores important behind-the-scenes work that would plant the seeds for future battles. As a frequent attendee of the Judiciary Committee, Kennedy came aboard after the appointment and confirmation of Byron "Whizzer" White as an associate justice of the United States Supreme Court. The former football star and Yale law graduate worked on JFK's campaign and played a prominent role thereafter. He turned out to become a conservative voice on the United States Supreme Court.

White's appointment in the spring of 1962 displays the lack of scrutiny provided by the Senate to judicial nominees in those days.

> White had been a dashing figure of John F. Kennedy's New Frontier. When he was appointed to the Court in 1962, the Senate was giving little scrutiny to Supreme Court nominees, and his hearing before the Judiciary Committee lasted fifteen minutes and consisted of eight questions. He had never been a judge, had spent most of his career in private law practice in Colorado, and was far better known for his exploits as a college and professional football star than for his brief tenure as Kennedy's deputy attorney general. By far the best-known fact about White was his nickname, Whizzer, which he hated. At the time of his appointment, White's views on constitutional issues was a mystery.[13]

JFK had fully expected to appoint several other Supreme Court justices. As Ted Kennedy diligently attended the Judiciary Committee meetings, he thought he would take part in that process. But White turned out to be JFK's lone nominee, due to his early and unexpected assassination.

Ted Kennedy, of course, would use these early days and the White example to more critically scrutinize future Supreme Court nominees. Few would have predicted, back in 1962–1963, that the cautious Massachusetts senator would play a prominent role in derailing Ronald Reagan's attempted appointment of the arch conservative Robert Bork more than two decades later. Indeed, Kennedy's vitriolic attack on Bork caused even some of his supporters pause. Kennedy alienated many supporters by his unprincipled assault on Bork. Indeed, many expected an experienced senator such as Kennedy to make his points in a much more professional fashion. Perhaps, Kennedy thought, he had no other option but to viciously deride Bork given the ardent conservative presidency of Reagan. But Kennedy miscalculated. In fact, Kennedy's all out frontal attack on Bork, including on the abortion issue, had the unintended effect of causing future Supreme Court nominees to refuse to comment about such issues or to provide evasive answers. This has backfired for liberals, for current Supreme Court Chief Justice Roberts scrupulously avoided the vetting process sufficient to expose his doctrinaire views. Even his role as William Rehnquist's clerk received little scrutiny.

In any event, while learning the ways of the Judiciary Committee, Kennedy also did more than simply sponsor local legislation for Massachusetts fisheries. In the fall of 1963 Senator Kennedy supported a treaty banning nuclear tests in the atmosphere.[14] While numerous other senators also did so, this does display Kennedy's foray from local to international politics. Every senator, of course, devotes considerable efforts to pork barrel projects important to his or her constituents. Yet in the short time Ted Kennedy served in the Senate prior to JFK's assassination on November 22, 1963, Senator Kennedy planted the seeds for more sweeping legislative efforts—including his initial major piece of legislation, the Immigration Act of 1965. Acting in a restrained manner, in stark contrast to the brash efforts of his brother Robert F. Kennedy when elected senator of New York in 1964,[15] Ted Kennedy supported JFK's unfinished efforts, largely conservative, of a balanced budget and increased spending on foreign policy.[16] In so doing, Ted Kennedy had begun to forge relationships in the Senate that would increase his political clout in later years.

Ted Kennedy's relationship with then Vice President Lyndon Baines Johnson provides a prime example on this point. Unlike Bobby, Ted Kennedy kept a cordial, indeed, productive relationship with LBJ. Johnson respected Ted Kennedy's knowledge of the Senate, for that was what he liked about Ted—the youngest Kennedy had dedicated himself to becoming a first class senator.[17] Of course, Kennedy also vigorously supported LBJ's Civil Rights Act of 1964, which endeared him to the president. In a speech given on January 17, 1969, LBJ's last full weekend as president, Ted Kennedy rose on the floor of the Senate to praise LBJ,

> The circumstances which brought President Johnson to the office he has held made it inevitable that there would be speculation about strained relations between him and my family … [any disputes between RFK and LBJ] came not from personal grievances but from the obligation of men in public life to discharge their responsibilities to the people of the United States as they saw them and from what at the time were fundamental differences over important public policies, I know.[18]

Ted Kennedy avoided such personal disharmony with LBJ and, as discussed within, worked with the president from 1964 to 1968 in passing sweeping domestic legislation.

JFK's assassination, coming just 1,000 days into his presidency, resulted in a lack of concrete legislative accomplishments. However, with Ted Kennedy learning the tools of his trade, he stood in a unique position to make a difference when LBJ took the solemn oath of the presidency in November 1963. Speaking years later upon receiving an honorary degree at Harvard, Kennedy explained his legislative philosophy:

And along the way, I have also learned lessons in the school of life, that we should take issues seriously, but never take ourselves too serious, that political differences may make us opponents, but should never make us enemies, that battles rage and then quiet.[19]

JFK's death marked a profound change in Ted Kennedy's ambitions and influence in the Senate. Remember, Senator Kennedy had served less than a year in the Senate before JFK's death. In addition, accounts vary as to Ted Kennedy's "ambition" prior to the tragic events of November 22, 1963.

One Kennedy biographer, Adam Clymer, portrays Kennedy as ready and willing to become the youngest constitutionally allowed senator at age 30: "By textbook standards, his ambition was breathtaking."[20] Doris Kearns Goodwin, to the contrary, paints a compelling picture of Ted Kennedy acceding to his father Joe Kennedy's wishes.[21]

No doubt the truth lies somewhere in between these two accounts. On the one hand, Ted Kennedy, only 28 at JKF's election, and with the Harvard cheating scandal still haunting him, wished to avoid public life. Back in 1951, Kennedy, then a freshman, cheated on an exam. He had trouble with Spanish, and fearing not getting at least a C- he had a friend, Bill Frate, take the exam for him. Harvard expelled both of them, but after a year-long military stint, he returned to Harvard in the fall of 1953 under probation.[22] Given the scandal and widespread rumors that political opponents would use the cheating scandal to derail any political campaign, accounts abound about Ted Kennedy wishing to move to a Midwest state to gain a fresh start. On the other hand, with Bobby becoming Attorney General and the Massachusetts Junior Senate seat up for grabs, Kennedy eventually seized his opportunity. Regardless of whether Ted Kennedy ran in 1962 reluctantly or due to ambition, historians agree that following JFK's death he took on a decidedly more visible presence in the Senate.

Previously content, for the most part, to press for local Massachusetts bills for his constituents, Ted Kennedy now forged ahead on a national platform. Whereas JFK had preached racial moderation, Senator Kennedy in April 1964, as the Senate debated the civil rights bill, hearkened back to LBJ's reaction to JFK's late efforts to pass real civil rights reform:

No memorial or eulogy could more eloquently honor President Kennedy's memory than the earliest possible passage of the civil rights bill for which he fought so long.[23]

In fact, in the summer of 1963, JFK had voiced enthusiasm for comprehensive civil rights legislation. With little headway made, Ted Kennedy took LBJ's cue in pressing for an anti-discrimination bill.

Historians have long chronicled the passage of the momentous Civil Rights Act of 1964. Viewed in the context of the times, the Civil Rights Act of 1964 represents a watershed in American history.[24] The Act endured the longest filibuster in Congressional history. "As strengthened it promised to attack racial discrimination in employment as well as to banish Jim Crow in public accommodations."[25] Particularly in view of the fact that little had occurred during the 12 years following the landmark desegregation decision by the United States Supreme Court in *Brown v. Board of Education*,[26] and the passage of the Civil Rights Act of 1964, the bill stands as a shining moment in the history of laws passed by Congress. As described by a historian of the civil rights movement,

> on July 2, President Lyndon Johnson signed the act which prohibited discrimination in most places of public accommodation, authorized government to withhold federal funds to public programs practicing discrimination, banned discrimination by employers and unions, created an Equal Opportunity Commission, established a Community Relations Service and provided technical and financial aid to communities desegregating the schools.[27]

Still, despite these remarkable innovations, the 1964 bill omitted key concerns. Most prominently, the 1964 Civil Rights Act did not secure the right to vote for blacks.[28]

As a junior senator, Ted Kennedy neither authored the legislation nor played a major part in its passage. No doubt he wholeheartedly supported the Civil Rights Act of 1964 and touted its passage as the cornerstone of his early achievements in the Senate.[29] Yet, putting his speeches aside, Kennedy grossly overstates his role in the passage of the Act. While plainly in support of the bill, Kennedy as such a young senator held little clout. The House passed the bill in February 1964, but when it came to the Senate a long filibuster ensued,

> Ending prolonged debate would require the vote of the 67 Senators. That meant that most Republicans would be needed. Everett Dirksen of Illinois, a florid orator and the minority leader, was the key player. But in April he was just beginning to show his hand. *No Republicans heard Kennedy's speech, because they were caucusing to hear the amendment Dirksen was suggesting to get their support*[30] [emphasis added].

Kennedy's claim in his book *America Back on Track*, obviously written by his "collaborator" Jeff Madrick, the editor of *Challenge Magazine*, exaggerates the senator's involvement in the passage of the Civil Rights Act of 1964. In the Senate, President Johnson relied heavily on Senator Hubert Humphrey of Minnesota, who would become his vice presidential running mate in the 1964 election.[31] A three-month filibuster in the Senate ensued. Johnson courted minority leader Dirksen, who eventually persuaded Republicans to vote for cloture, leading to the passage of the landmark bill.[32]

In assessing Kennedy's influence on the passage of the Act, the record presents the inescapable conclusion that Senator Kennedy did not play an important part in breaking the Senate filibuster—a necessary step for the legislation's enactment. President Johnson, Humphrey and Dirksen played instrumental roles in the bill becoming the law. While Kennedy's maiden speech, as reported in the Congressional record, could arguably support a position of his increased involvement, even Kennedy biographer Adam Clymer concedes Republicans did not listen to it, and it had no persuasive effect.[33] Nor could anyone have expected that a first term senator would have such a major impact on this type of groundbreaking legislation. It does not work that way. In the annals of history few, if any, senators had an immediate effect in bills they sponsored. In recent years, neither President Obama nor former Secretary of State Hillary Clinton can point to any such bills in their early years in the Senate.

On the other hand, a nascent senator, lacking power due to the hierarchical emphasis in the Senate on seniority, can certainly state claim to political victory based on his vote. And, no doubt, Kennedy voted in favor of the Civil Rights Act of 1964. However, Kennedy, in his own book, takes far more credit than he deserves for the passage of the Act. While a staunch supporter of civil rights, Kennedy had little to do with the behind-the-scenes dynamics of passing the bill. Still, with now over nearly 50 years of hindsight, Ted Kennedy's unwavering support of sweeping antidiscrimination legislation deserves considerable attention. With lynching and riots in the south, and the National Guard called in, Ted Kennedy took a definitive stance. On the Civil Rights Act of 1964, Ted Kennedy did not waver. Indeed, he also championed rights of women, decried by many. His viewpoints on this subject would come to the forefront in his ardent support of Title IX, ensuring equality to women in education.

While breathtaking in its passage at the time, historians writing about the act have frequently overlooked its limitations. Nor does Ted

Kennedy's soaring rhetoric about his part in "the great battle for equality" accurately portray the reach and effect of the Civil Rights Act of 1964. Although supposedly banning discrimination, the act notably did not outlaw other insidious forms of discrimination, such as for the disabled.[34] In addition, while the act included a prohibition against sex discrimination, its inclusion as a category was by Republican House Chairman Howard Smith, who sought to jettison the bill. Smith miscalculated and his cynical "amendment" became the law.

The other feature of the bill, the creation of the Equal Employment Opportunity Commission (EEOC), has more symbolic value than real results. To begin, the EEOC, designed to investigate and enforce discrimination laws, does nothing in reality of the sort. Lawyers, frankly, seek to avoid EEOC involvement and simply obtain a "Right to Sue" letter. This means the aggrieved employee can bypass an EEOC investigation and simply proceed to court with his or her own lawyer. The EEOC takes an exceedingly long amount of time to investigate a case, and often does not even get to a true investigation, simply advising the complainant of a right to go to court. One flaw of Title VII of the Civil Rights Act of 1964 stems from the ability of the president, not the Congress to appoint the head of the EEOC. Simply put, the head of the EEOC (including ironically at one time now United States Supreme Court Justice Clarence Thomas), over the years, simply obtained the position as a result of political favoritism and acted as an uninvolved figurehead at best. While one cannot fault Kennedy for this dysfunctional system, nonetheless in subsequent years Kennedy did not sponsor legislation to rectify this obvious flaw in Title VII. Unfortunately, then, the EEOC has become a joke among experienced employment lawyers, particularly those in states where the antidiscrimination laws have more teeth.

More importantly, the EEOC has over the years served as a bureaucratic obstacle, rather than a stimulus, for real discrimination reform. For example, informed California employment lawyers representing discrimination victims will never file a charge of discrimination with the EEOC; rather under more expansive state antidiscrimination laws seasoned plaintiff employment lawyers bypass the federal legislation and EEOC entirely.[35] So has the EEOC suffered in reputation since its enactment. Designed to come to the aid of aggrieved victims, the EEOC has a scarce record of obtaining true reform for those discriminated against, leaving the battles for private lawyers on contingency fees to obtain just results. Unfortunately many individuals who go to the EEOC for an investigation cannot obtain legal representation. Thus, such individuals must rely on the EEOC investigator without the benefit of true legal advice. In addition, the EEOC now presses hard for early mediation, where an EEOC representative looking more to ease the workload than to achieve a just result often cajoles an unrepresented individual into a low settlement.

Currently, savvy employment defense lawyers relish the task of responding to an EEOC investigation. Typically defense lawyers write and submit a detailed position statement. This often ends the investigation. Sometimes the EEOC will follow up with a request for information, seeking voluminous and often irrelevant documentation. The best defense tactic is to inundate the EEOC investigator with documents, as they typically will then punt the investigation and close the "investigation" without making a determination. Claiming an overburdened staff, hundreds of discrimination victims each year cannot even get the EEOC to conduct an investigation, the primary reason Congress created the agency in the first instance. The EEOC, a byproduct of Title VII, thus has failed seriously in fostering the sweeping antidiscrimination laws envisioned by Title VII.

Aside from bureaucratic ineptitude resulting in interminable delay, the well publicized tenure of Clarence Thomas as head of the EEOC has stained the agency. To begin, Thomas' hostility toward affirmative action[36] and consistent efforts to narrow the reach of discrimination laws has sullied the agency. Then, Anita Hill's shocking allegations against Thomas during his soap-operatic Supreme Court nomination hearings further raised questions about the EEOC's effectiveness. How could the EEOC do its job when, according to Hill, Thomas engaged in the very conduct the EEOC sought to prohibit?[37]

Certainly, Hill's belated accusations brought forth only as Thomas awaited Senate confirmation for a United States Supreme Court associate justice position, describing purported conduct years earlier, raise suspicion as to the veracity of her claims. On the other hand, there is no question the Thomas/Hill saga created a setback for the EEOC and antidiscrimination enforcement at the Federal level.[38] Simply stated, antidiscrimination lawyers do not find the EEOC of any help, in most cases, in prosecuting offending employers. Justice Thomas' subsequent 2009 decision by a slim 5–4 United States Supreme Court majority also demonstrates his disdain for discrimination laws, confirming that Reagan appointing him as the head of the EEOC was a mockery. Indeed, as will be described later, Justice Thomas in 2009 wrote a shocking decision, cutting back on the rights of older workers to secure jury verdicts. Indeed, Justice Thomas has now set a standard never contemplated by Senator Kennedy of providing workers over 40 fewer rights than others subject to discrimination based on race, sex and other protected categories.

Still, in assessing Kennedy's efforts in the Senate in 1963–64 on the civil rights bill, critics unfairly look at the later amendments and limitations placed on the act. Most of these limitations came under Republican presidents and Republican-dominated Congresses. At the time, however, America had no laws governing discrimination in employment. Ted Kennedy, a two year senator, openly supported the Civil Rights Act of 1964. While not an author or sponsor of the bill given his lack of seniority in the Senate, Kennedy clearly forged a position in 1964 as a staunch civil rights advocate. In essence the question becomes whether Ted Kennedy can be judged by later limitations to the Act while he served as a senator. This raises an important question as to the effectiveness of a senator in general and Kennedy in particular. As will become increasingly apparent as this book analyzes specific pieces of legislation, the passing of a bill into law only starts the process. Thereafter, Congress enacts detailed regulations interpreting the law. If a senator does not monitor these regulations, unanticipated changes to the original intent of the law inevitably occur. This plainly is the case with the Civil Rights Act of 1964.

In fact, events following passage of the Civil Rights Act of 1964 would soon turn Kennedy to other topics as he steadily gained influence in the Senate. The year 1965 ushered in a new era for the Kennedy family. For the first time, two brothers simultaneously sat in the Senate, comprised of only 100 individuals.[39] Bobby Kennedy had defied many political advisors and run for the Senate in New York, not his true home state of Massachusetts. Called by some a carpetbagger, Bobby's choice to run for the Senate baffled many of his supporters. Bobby, many felt, would not transition smoothly from his Attorney General position, where he held unfettered power, to the role of a freshman senator.

This created an uneasy situation. Bobby, the older brother and Attorney General for JFK, suddenly under the Senate's seniority system, held a lower-level office than his younger brother. Ted Kennedy biographer Adam Clymer wrote: "Ted Kennedy walked stiffly into the Senate with his brother Robert, and they took the oath together on January 4, 1965."[40]

Yet, the evidence does not support the view of any rift between Bobby and Ted. To be sure, Ted initially cautioned Bobby against a Senate run and advised he either remain as Attorney General under LBJ or take stock in his future. By all accounts, though, once Bobby made up his mind, Ted Kennedy stood not only behind Bobby's New York Senate run, but actively supported it. Therefore, Clymer's reference to Ted Kennedy walking "stiffly" with Bobby as they took their Senate oath appears odd indeed.

Perhaps the reference reflects the different styles of the two men. While Ted in 1963 and 1964 acted with caution and shaped his initial efforts at local legislation, Bobby had other ideas,

> When Robert Kennedy entered the United States Senate in January 1965 he was already impatient. He had little love for the Senate; it was, he said, a hell of a place to get anything done. It was a deliberative body, and though Bobby Kennedy was a deliberative man he was always rather quick about it: target the problem, consult this man and read the report, craft a solution, get it done. He had been spoiled by the rapidly deployed power of the executive branch, by its speed and autonomy.[41]

Ted Kennedy, by 1965, "began to be noticed in the Senate for more than knowing a freshman's place."[42] Ted Kennedy set his sights on two legislative goals for 1965: voting rights that the Civil Rights Act of 1964 did not cover, and immigration reform. Bobby, on the other hand, had grandiose ideas far beyond the reach of a freshman senator: "No junior senator, not even a Kennedy, [could] expect in his first few months in office to propose anything huge or historic."[43] Yet on an education bill, Bobby Kennedy antagonized President Lyndon Baines Johnson. "Kennedy's substantive badgering was an affront to Lyndon Johnson's legislative strategy: pass now, ask questions later."[44] To the contrary, Lyndon Baines Johnson "looked on Ted Kennedy as a friend."[45]

Rather than confronting Johnson, Ted Kennedy took up his causes in a collaborative fashion. Ted Kennedy focused on voting rights, seeking legislation to eliminate the poll tax.[46] In his memoir, Ted Kennedy describes his early legislative achievements in glowing terms:

> A century after the Civil War ended, we outlawed racial segregation, eliminated the poll tax that barred many African Americans from voting, guaranteed equal access to public accommodations, outlawed job discrimination because of race and gender, and passed the Fair Housing Act.[47]

On the issue of outlawing racial segregation, the United States Supreme Court in *Brown v. Board of Education* had a decade earlier outlawed segregation in schools.[48] Yet, the very checkered history of delayed implementation of *Brown*'s mandate has received considerable historical attention. Surely, Kennedy's soaring rhetoric that "we outlawed" segregation, while technically true, ignores repeated efforts by Southern judges to blunt the intended holding of *Brown*. Indeed, far more than a decade would pass before real progress in desegregating schools occurred. On his claim that the Senate "eliminated the poll tax," Kennedy simply misstates the events. In truth, despite Ted Kennedy's legislative efforts in 1965, Congress did not eliminate the poll tax.

The actual Legislative record reflects that Ted Kennedy's well-intentioned efforts failed. Poll taxes, primarily in Southern states, kept poor blacks and many poor whites from voting. Kennedy, serving on the Judiciary Committee, enlisted an array of experts to assist him in crafting legislation.[49] The bill first needed to get through the Judiciary Committee. Over the objection of conservative Everett Dirksen, Kennedy prevailed by a 9–5 margin.[50] While Kennedy championed the elimination of the poll tax, his efforts fell short. Indeed, his failure illustrates his lack of effectiveness in his early years in the Senate of sponsoring and getting enacted meaningful legislation. Despite reaching across the aisle and following Senate protocol—respecting your elders—Kennedy lost this battle.

Once the bill came out of committee, Kennedy amplified his concerns. He argued that "the history of the poll tax is so entwined with racial discrimination that it could never be separated from racial discrimination."[51] However, even President Johnson sided with conservatives, arguing that the issue of the poll tax's legality needed a decision by the Supreme Court. Kennedy plowed ahead, and the matter went to vote in the full Senate. He lost 49–45.[52]

The Supreme Court vindicated Kennedy's viewpoint regarding the poll tax by finding it unconstitutional in 1966.[53] In assessing Kennedy's efforts, we should not underestimate his impact on the eventual elimination of the poll tax. While losing in the Senate, Kennedy kept on his cause, albeit through seasoned lawyers, to ultimately gain vindication of his position. This proves a good lesson: well-intended legislation often does not come to fruition without help from other branches of government and considerable follow up. Thus, Kennedy did not allow his initial loss in Congress to thwart his intentions. But it is noteworthy that Kennedy's first major legislative effort in the Senate failed, albeit by just four votes.

Ted Kennedy did achieve his first major legislative achievement later in 1965, however. The following is from a recent article in the *Boston Globe*:

> In his first major legislative accomplishment, the 32-year-old Kennedy managed the successful floor battle to pass the Hart-Cellar Act, a reform of immigration policy that abolished quotas and lifted the 1924 ban on immigration from Asia.[54]

Kennedy chose immigration reform due to his view that the existing system fostered racism. A natural outgrowth of his commitment to civil rights, the Immigration Act of 1965 provided Kennedy his first real chance of sponsoring legislation aimed at eliminating racism. What spurred Kennedy to the cause and his active sponsorship of the bill was a deeply held desire to address a racist quota system.

Kennedy, buoyed by bipartisan support for his bill, ushered the immigration legislation through the Senate. Under the old system, admission to the United States depended upon an immigrant's country of birth. The United States allotted 70 percent of all immigrant slots to just three countries—the United Kingdom, Ireland and Germany.[55]

The new system eliminated nationality criteria and substituted a system primarily based on family reunification.[56] According to the nonpartisan Congressional Research Service,

> these amendments abolished the 40-year-old national origin quota system as the primary control on U.S. Immigration replacing it with an annual ceiling on Eastern Hemisphere Immigration of 170,000 and a 20,000 per country limitation. Within these restrictions immigration visas were distributed on a first-come first-served basis according to a seven category preference system. The 1965 amendments also provided for a ceiling on Western Hemisphere immigration for the first time in our history, limiting total immigration from other countries in this Hemisphere to 120,000 a year.[57]

The bill received little opposition in the House and passed by a 318–95 vote.

In the Senate, the long-honored practice of consensus building and give and take proved necessary for its passage.[58] With Dirksen and Sam Ervin of North Carolina threatening to block the bill in the Senate Judiciary Committee, Kennedy agreed to an annual quota of 120,000 Western Hemisphere immigrants.[59] The concern stemmed from a belief that elimination of quotas would lead to an unrestrained increase in immigration. Senate immigration subcommittee chairman Ted Kennedy reassured his colleagues that such would not occur:

First, our cities will not be flooded with a million immigrants annually. Under the proposed bill, the present level of immigration remains substantially the same.... Secondly, the ethnic mix of the country will not be upset.... Contrary to the charges in some quarters, [the bill] will not inundate America with immigrants from any one country or area, or the most populated and deprived nations of Africa and Asia.[60]

With the benefit of over 35 years of hindsight, Kennedy's assurances to the Senate proved wrong. Still, one cannot discount Kennedy's altruistic motive in enacting the bill—the elimination of racism with respect to immigrants. In this regard the act flowed naturally from his support of Title VII of the Civil Rights Act of 1964 and his attempt at passage of a voting rights act.

To Kennedy, the Immigration bill stemmed directly from the civil rights antidiscrimination legislation. By opening up immigration from Africa, he thought, blacks would increase in population to take advantage of America's new discrimination laws.[61] One must remember that, in 1965, the Civil Rights Movement in America had gained momentum. Increasingly, a majority of Americans detested the racist practices in the South. Lunch counter protests, and efforts by collegians, brought the issue to national attention. As depicted in the popular movie *Mississippi Burning*, three white Northern college students were brutally murdered in their civil rights cause. The nation and Congress stood ready for true reform, thus aiding the passage of Kennedy's immigration bill.

Critics, though, predicted that the bill would dramatically increase, to unsustainable levels, the number of immigrants and rob native-born Americans of jobs. Kennedy retorted, "The bill will not flood our cities with immigrants. It will not upset the ethnicity of our society. It will not cause American workers to lose their jobs."[62]

Ted Kennedy's keen interest in immigration reform stemmed from earlier pronouncements by JFK. President John F. Kennedy's immigration message to Congress on July 23, 1963, assailed the national origin quota system as having no basis in logic or reason:

It neither satisfies a national need nor accomplishes an international purpose. In an age of interdependence among nations, such a system is an anachronism for it discriminates among applicants for admission to the United States on the basis of the accident of birth.[63]

Ted Kennedy echoed these sentiments, noting that "the heart of President Kennedy's bill lay in the elimination of the quota system. The law does eliminate the national origins system ... a period of bigotry and reaffirmed in the McCarthy era. A nation's willingness to ... reform public policy is a measure of its greatness."[64]

Moreover, Kennedy's role in managing the bill on the Senate floor displayed a maturity not before seen in the young senator. Rather than antagonizing opponents to the bill, Kennedy allotted time to answering arguments against the measure. For example, Senator Spessard Holland of Florida expressed shock that the bill would treat people from new African nations just as it treated people from "our mother countries." Kennedy replied by pointing out the principle of the bill:

> This bill really goes to the very central ideals of our country.... We are the land of opportunity. Our streets may not be paved with the promise that men and women who live here—even strangers and newcomers B can rise fast, as far as their skills will allow, no matter what their color is, no matter what the place of their birth. We have never fully achieved this ideal. But by striving to approach it, we reaffirm the principles of our country.[65]

Holland appreciated Kennedy's point, but still disagreed. The bill passed, though, by a 76–18 margin on September 22, 1965.[66]

Regardless of whether the bill had the unintended consequences raised by the Center for Immigration Studies, or worked in the fashion Kennedy envisioned in 1965, Kennedy's handling of the bill sheds light on his effectiveness as a senator as of 1965. Only 32 years old then, Kennedy nonetheless handled debates with elder conservative senators in a restrained and respectful way.[67] Knowing full well he would not change their minds, he heard them out, thereby receiving praise from even his opposition. Kennedy, in this early stage of his career, established a reputation as a consensus builder. In so doing, Kennedy gained the respect of Republican Senate elders, while in stark contrast, Bobby antagonized them.

This style, confirmed by his colleagues, stands in stark contrast to the view, held by some, of Kennedy as a strident liberal catering to the radical left. Even so, given the vast array of legislation the Johnson administration backed through passage of his War on Poverty, the 1965 immigration bill stands as a minor achievement. Laws such as Medicare to provide health care for the elderly, college loans and scholarships and direct aid to elementary and secondary schools overshadowed the immigration bill.

The Hart-Cellar Act of 1965, Kennedy's most important legislative accomplishment to date,

- abolished the national origins quota system while attempting to keep immigration to a manageable level;
- allocated 170,000 visas to countries in the Eastern Hemisphere, and 120,000 to countries in the Western Hemisphere;
- gave preference to relatives of American citizens.[68]

The Center for Immigration Studies, in a September 1995 article, posits that the 1965 bill had the unintended consequences of increasing immigrants by 18 million in the ensuing 30 years as of the time the article appeared.[69] The article criticizes the legislation for many social ills, including an increase in high school drop outs. Moreover, the article states that

> the unexpected result has been one of the greatest waves of immigration in the nation's history—more than 18 million legal immigrants since the law's passage, over triple admitted during the previous 30 years, as well as unaccountable millions of illegal immigrants.[70]

An alternative view, however, argues that the benefit from Asian and African *legal* immigration, during a time of unprecedented economic growth, fostered expansion in many industries.[71] In addition, the number of immigrants admitted to the United States appears quite debatable. The Congressional Research Service provides the following data on immigration during a ten year period in the 1970s:

1970	373,326	1975	386,194
1971	370,478	1976	398,613
1972	384,685	1977	462,315
1973	400,063	1978	601,442
1974	394,861	1979	760,348[72]

Kennedy did appear to miscalculate the number of immigrants who would enter America as a result of the 1965 bill. Nonetheless, while the act had the unintended consequence of increasing immigration, at least as of 1995, it cannot be blamed for all of the ill effects suggested by the Center for Immigration Studies. According to the Center,

> the 1965 changes unwittingly ushered in a new era of mass immigration. The current level of immigration is actually higher ... because illegal immigration is much higher than ever before with a conservative estimate of 300,000 new permanent illegal immigrants each year. The result is an influx of more than one million people a year with no natural end in sight.[73]

Contrary to this view, the 1965 act expressly placed a limit on "special immigrants."[74] Section 21(e) expressly states,

> Unless legislation inconsistent herewith is enacted on or before June 30, 1968 ... the number of special immigrants ... shall not, in the first year beginning July 1, 1968, or in any fiscal year thereafter, exceed a total of 120,000.[75]

Therefore, the description of the bill opening floodgates of new immigrants does not comport with the plain language of the act.

Much of the unintended consequences of the act stem from a flood of *illegal* immigrants. This new "enlarged immigration flow came from countries in Asia and Latin America which heretofore had sent few of their sons and daughters to the United States."[76] Such immigrants, history has shown, developed roots in the United States and ushered in friends and relatives, often illegally. However, Congress subsequently enacted the Immigration Control and Reform Act (IRCA), designed to crack down on illegal immigration. But Republican and Democratic presidents alike failed to utilize strict enforcement against employers, the only way to halt illegal immigration.

The subsequent statistics of *legal* immigration show a higher quantity of legal immigration than envisioned in 1965. The huge increase in illegal immigration, though, while providing harsh consequences, does not flow from any language in the act. It does flow from societal events never contemplated by the original act, such as lax or no enforcement of laws designed to prevent employers from employing illegal immigrants.[77]

To be sure, illegal immigration has resulted in serious problems, particularly in major cities such as Los Angeles and others near the border. School systems have failed given the flood of non–English-speaking students. The health care system, already crippled, now finds itself struggling to care for millions of the uninsured. Gang activity has increased in areas long thought immune from such influences. Many California politicians, including former Governor Arnold Schwarzenegger, embraced the notion of Los Angeles as a "sanctuary city," welcoming illegal immigrants. In a speech, before he relinquished his office due to term limits, Schwarzenegger attributed California's economic strength to illegal immigrants, yet at the same time at least four billion dollars of the state's then budget deficit directly related to illegal immigration. Still, such consequences stem from other sources. To trace illegal immigration problems to the 1965 Immigration Act does not pass muster, either from a critical review of the language of the act or from any subsequent scholarship. To put it bluntly, the act does not allow illegal immigration.

Ted Kennedy sponsored a bill designed to eliminate racism in our immigration system. It achieved that goal. While Kennedy miscalculated the number of legal immigrants subject to the legislation—plainly an unintended and profound side effect—illegal immigration stems from different societal forces. Kennedy and McCain subsequently in 2005–2007 attempted to remedy illegal immigration effects, but a fiercely partisan Congress stalled such efforts. While many times senators fail to follow up on the unintended consequences of their initial legislation, Ted Kennedy tried with respect to immigration. He unfortunately died before further reform could be enacted.

Summarizing Kennedy's role in the Senate as of 1965, then, the young senator had begun to make his mark as an effective senator member. However, the junior senator from Massachusetts had not assumed a leadership position on major legislation. Waiting his turn, Kennedy would soon vault to the forefront on the national issues of the times. Yet, it would take a brash move by his brother Bobby to catapult him into national prominence, not any legislative acts within the Senate.

2

The Tumultuous Late 1960s and the National Cancer Act of 1971

Ted Kennedy's next major Legislative accomplishment occurred six years after the Immigration Act of 1965. In 1971, Kennedy spearheaded the National Cancer Act of 1971. The tumultuous six-year period between these acts, involving Vietnam, his own brother's death, and the Chappaquiddick scandal defined his ultimate future as a politician and most certainly kept him from becoming president.

In August 1974, following Richard M. Nixon's resignation from the presidency, Senator Ted Kennedy insisted that "it was time to terminate America's endless support for an endless war."[1] Years later, writing about Iraq, Senator Kennedy wrote, "The commitment to our military forces cannot be open ended."[2]

To many conservatives, the "Kennedy liberals" reflect an element of the Democratic Party that opposes military force. To these members of the Republican right, Kennedy symbolizes American weakness abroad.

Ardent Kennedy supporters envision Ted Kennedy as a leading voice against militarism. Viewed as an early opponent of Vietnam, they say, Ted Kennedy helped lead the charge to America's disillusionment with the war and ultimate disengagement from Vietnam.

Neither side has it right. As Kennedy turned to foreign policy issues in 1965, he decidedly favored America's involvement in the Vietnam War. His brother Bobby, though sometimes in stumbling fashion, spoke against Johnson's Vietnam policy and eventually emerged as the leading political voice for the end of the war, stirring his 82-day campaign for the presidency in 1968. Back in 1965, though, Ted Kennedy fully supported President Johnson's Vietnam War efforts.[3] Kennedy traveled to

Saigon on October 23, 1965. There Kennedy denounced the antiwar demonstrations that had begun in the United States: "The overwhelming majority of American people are behind the policies of President Johnson in Vietnam."[4] James Carroll, writing for the *Boston Globe* on December 1, 2008, asserted, "Kennedy quickly emerged as a leading voice against the Vietnam War, which sealed his skepticism toward military adventures."[5] Wrong on several fronts, his article does not accurately depict Kennedy's role in the Vietnam War and certainly not in military action in general.[6]

In truth, the Senate did not contain any significant opposition to Johnson's Vietnam strategy in 1965. Kennedy supported Johnson's ill fated Gulf of Tonkin resolution on August 7, 1964, as did the entire House (414–0) and virtually all of the Senate (88–2). Only Senators Wayne Morse of Oregon and Ernest Gruening of Alaska opposed.[7] Neither Ted Kennedy nor Bobby Kennedy called for an inquiry of the Gulf of Tonkin. Ted's reluctance seems explainable: he tried ceaselessly to work with LBJ to form a consensus for major legislative reform, much of which occurred. LBJ fashioned the Great Society, and Ted Kennedy supported the far-reaching domestic efforts. Bobby's silence on the Gulf of Tonkin remains unexplainable.

Indeed, reminiscences of stances 40 years earlier often do not stand up to scrutiny. The Carroll article in the *Boston Globe* exemplifies this point. By the end of 1965 Ted Kennedy had supported the Tonkin resolution and massive bombing of North Vietnam. He supported an increase in troops in 1965 from 23,000 to 175,000. In the face of opposition to the war at Boston University, Kennedy warned that to pull out of Vietnam "would permanently undermine our credit with other nations in the area while we are trying to remain independent of the historic and powerful influence exerted in China."[8] Most decidedly, he did not call for a Congressional inquiry on the Gulf of Tonkin, nor raise any opposition whatsoever. Surely, as a young senator, Kennedy did not want to buck the president who took over for his slain brother.

To describe Senator Kennedy as an early voice against the Vietnam War rings hollow. Not that this condemns Kennedy in any fashion. By vote alone, virtually nobody in political power opposed the war efforts in 1965. Yet, some now so many years later view Ted Kennedy as an early antiwar activist. This, decidedly, does not reflect Ted Kennedy's sentiments at the time. Slowly, though, one voice began to emerge on Vietnam: not Ted's, but Bobby's.

Robert Kennedy sent mixed messages in 1965 about his position on the Vietnam War. But more and more, he leaned toward a negotiated solution, not escalation of the war. In April 1965, in a speech at John Hopkins College, Bobby declared himself open to "unconditional discussions."[9] In November 1965, RFK suggested a mission to Hanoi with Ho Chi Minh, stating, "I am prepared to go anywhere to meet anyone."[10] This met with disdain, both from party regulars as well as LBJ.

Yet, as late as July 13, 1965, Ted Kennedy continued to toe the Johnson administration line. Speaking at a Foreign Relations Committee hearing, Ted Kennedy implored,

> Communist forces are deliberately creating refugee movements to foster confusion and instability in the countryside, to overtax existing relief facilities, and to obstruct the movement of Government personnel and materials.[11]

And on March 6, 1966, Senator Kennedy, despite Bobby's more frequent and clear calls for negotiations, stated, "I support our fundamental commitment in Vietnam…. It is fundamental and it is sound. I believe we have to utilize every resource in our power, whether it is military or diplomatic, to see that this commitment is fulfilled."[12] His was hardly the voice of an antimilitaristic dove.

In retrospect, Ted Kennedy's backing of the Johnson administration's Vietnam bombing efforts in 1965–1966 appears misguided. At the time, though, the majority of Democrats supported the war efforts. Bobby began at this time to emerge as a potent antiwar voice, along with Eugene McCarthy. Ted Kennedy would soon follow suit, but one can scarcely argue that Ted Kennedy stood at the forefront of the antiwar movement. Whether fueled by his hatred of LBJ or by a distinct moral view, Bobby's brashness, criticized by many, launched him into the role as a prominent critic of LBJ's Vietnam policy.

Thus, Bobby, not Ted, took to opposing the war. After a Christmas halt on bombing North Vietnam, on January 31, 1966, Johnson resumed the bombing. Rising on the Senate floor on January 31, 1966, Robert Kennedy sharply condemned the renewed air war:

> If we regard bombing as the answer in Vietnam, we are headed straight for disaster. In the past, bombing has not proved a decisive weapon against a rural economy—or against a guerrilla army. And the temptation will now be to argue that if limited bombing does not produce a solution, that further bombing, more extended military action, is the answer. The danger is that the decision to resume may become the first in a series of steps on a road

from which there is no turning back—a road which leads to catastrophe for all mankind.[13]

At the same time in early 1966, Ted Kennedy announced a decidedly different stance on the bombing of North Vietnam than his brother Bobby. Ted Kennedy said that if bombing "served to convince Hanoi and Peking of our determination to stay in Vietnam and defend the people there, this in itself could bring about the changed attitude on the other side."[14]

Focusing on early 1966, the stated positions of brothers Bobby and Ted differed with respect to the utility of increased bombing on North Vietnam and on the United States' policy on Vietnam in general. In this regard, Robert Kennedy's disdain for LBJ and brashness as a junior senator catapulted him into an early lead critic of the Vietnam War.

Ted Kennedy, two years Bobby's senior in the Senate, had a decidedly alternative approach. Viewing the positions in hindsight, Bobby comes across as the visionary. But taking a long-term view, Ted Kennedy's continued deferential position, longing to support the president as much as possible, seems the more defensible stance. Where Bobby jumped early to seek out a role for himself, Ted Kennedy worked with the president.

As the Vietnam War continued to divide the country, Ted Kennedy would espouse in a more restrained fashion a view toward changing the dynamic of America's involvement in the Vietnam War. But again, Ted deftly cajoled his Senate elders and kept an open dialogue with President Lyndon Baines Johnson.

But, Robert Kennedy "was more volatile than the rest ... he blasted the administration's policy of allowing no sanctuary in China or elsewhere for any planes; the practice of sending American fighters over North Vietnam, inviting attack."[15] Having achieved national prominence as JFK's Attorney General, Robert Kennedy viewed his role as a national leader. No doubt, many Americans agreed. As the older of the remaining Kennedy brothers, if anyone would ascend to national prominence, Bobby would do so before Ted. This, despite the fact that Ted Kennedy had more seniority in the Senate, and frankly held high regard with senators on both sides of the aisle. To many senators, Bobby, they thought, came in with an attitude as JFK's handpicked Attorney General and held contempt for the long-honored traditions of the Senate.

But much more explains the divergent approaches of Bobby and

Ted than just the position in the family. Ted revered the Senate protocol and abided by the long honored rules and regulations. Recognizing in 1966 that, at 34 years old, he had still only served 4 years in the Senate, Ted Kennedy displayed caution in his acts. This appears especially ironic now, given the Republican right's continued accusations of Ted Kennedy, even after his death, as an out-of-control liberal.

In 1966, Ted Kennedy felt he had time to make a mark on the nation. Bobby felt a sense of urgency, and that ambition propelled Robert Kennedy to a position to challenge incumbent Lyndon Baines Johnson on an antiwar platform in his brief but compelling 82-day presidential campaign.[16]

Ted Kennedy, on the other hand, in 1966 attacked the Vietnam War in more subtle ways. Instead of opposing the war strategy in its entirety, Senator Kennedy expressed concern on two issues: the refugee situation and the draft.

With respect to refugees, Ted Kennedy's disenchantment regarding South Vietnam's action became public. On January 25, 1966, Kennedy chided Saigon and Washington for not fighting the civilian problem "with the same ferocity" as they fought the war.[17] Kennedy expressed discouragement to hear from American officials "again and again that in Vietnam the problem of refugees is just that—a problem and a burden."[18] Summarizing his disgust with South Vietnamese apathy, Kennedy proclaimed,

> While in Vietnam, I saw for myself the indifference of the Saigon government to the plight of their own. Government officials assured me that the refugee situation was well in hand—yet I inspected one camp of over six hundred people without a toilet. Construction was started on seven refugee camps in anticipation of my visit. Work stopped when my plans were temporarily altered. It began again when it was finally possible for me to go.[19]

Kennedy also increasingly spoke out about the unfairness of the structure of the draft. Appearing on the ABC television program "Issues and Answers," Kennedy complained on June 12, 1966, "Those who have the economic resources to go to college are given a deferment."[20] Kennedy favored a lottery, a system that would eventually operate. In retrospect, Kennedy's position on the draft would make today's Republicans salivate. Kennedy abhorred a system that allowed deferments to the rich and powerful. These days, Republicans attack many Democrats for avoiding the war and for Vietnam protests. Under Kennedy's view everyone should serve, regardless of class.

Kennedy biographer Adam Clymer also cites isolated commentary by Ted Kennedy in 1966 on the benefits of negotiations with North Vietnam. However, Ted Kennedy's stance in 1966 on Vietnam did not constitute a frontal assault on the war.[21] In a Senate speech reiterated on TV on Huntley-Brinkley and Cronkite, Kennedy accused Johnson of unwisely escalating the Vietnam War.

Curiously, though, Robert Kennedy retreated in 1966 from his Vietnam attacks. Ted Kennedy followed suit. The height of antiwar attacks would wait until 1968. In fact, in 1966 and 1967, the press took a far more active role in criticizing the war than leaders in Congress. Robert Kennedy's lull from full-out opposition appears to have stemmed from his indecision on dealing with the Johnson presidency and upcoming campaign in 1968. With Bobby yielding for the time being, Ted Kennedy focused on other issues, mostly domestic. The press, however, led by Walter Cronkite, helped "intensify public doubts that had been rising primarily because of discouraging causality figures in 1966 and 1967."[22] A speech at Harvard Medical School in October 1967 began to signal a shift in Ted Kennedy's views on the Vietnam War.

> I believe it is time to redefine our position in Vietnam, to question whether these people can be one in a land secured by guns alone. I believe we must rethink our total approach and ask ourselves whether the losses we have suffered and the resources we have extended have resulted in any real gains in affecting the political inclinations of the South Vietnamese.[23]

However, it took an event, the Tet offensive on January 30, 1968, to fortify antiwar opposition: "The initial thrusts of the Tet offensive, especially the breach of the embassy wall, convinced already skeptical Americans that Johnson, [General] Westmoreland and other administration officials had been lying all along."[24] The Tet offensive led to renewed discussion regarding Robert Kennedy running for president. Previously, antiwar activists had sought RFK as their standard bearer, but when he declined to throw his hat in the ring such activists looked to Eugene McCarthy.

One of Ted Kennedy's biographers, Adam Clymer, views Ted's efforts central to RFK's decision to enter the 1968 campaign.

> Any questions about Robert's running inevitably involved Ted. Since they started serving in the Senate, Ted and Robert had grown very close. They walked together from the Senate to their office buildings several times a day after votes.[25]

To the contrary, Thurston Clarke, in his recent book regarding Robert Kennedy's 82-day campaign, scarcely mentions Ted Kennedy at all and attributes RFK's decision to his belief in his call to inject "mutual leadership." RFK's speech announcing his candidacy on March 16, 2008, declared,

> I am today announcing my candidacy for the presidency of the United States.... I do not lightly discuss the dangers and the difficulties of challenging an incumbent President. But these are not ordinary times or an ordinary election. At stake is not simply the leadership or our party, and even our county. It is our right to the moral leadership of this planet.[26]

Neither Clymer nor Clarke accurately portray the role (or lack thereof) of Ted Kennedy's participation in RKF's decision to run for the presidency. Clymer overemphasizes Ted Kennedy's influence. Yes, Robert and Ted had grown closer in the Senate, but RFK had a wide array of advisors, many from JFK's presidency. Clarke, on the other hand, virtually worships RFK in *The Last Campaign*. Surely, RFK's candidacy had its moral features, but political calculation figured prominently in the decision.[27]

RFK relied on many advisors, among them Adam Walinsky, Joe Dolan, and Frank Mankiewicz. Those three, among others, strongly urged RFK to run as early as 1967.[28] Ted Sorenson, Pierre Salinger and Ted Kennedy favored a run in 1972 or beyond.[29] Ted's viewpoint bore its roots from his understanding of the role of a freshman senator in respecting the party and, of course, to an incumbent president. Wary of the shakeup in the party a Robert Kennedy campaign would arouse, Ted assuredly warned Bobby that his time would come. With a split in advisors, Bobby waffled on whether to throw his hat in the ring for the 1968 presidential candidacy.

In the end, the Tet offensive and McCarthy's stunning showing in the New Hampshire primary stirred RFK to announce his candidacy. Bobby did not make the decision on his own, nor did Ted Kennedy in the end play an important part in the decision.[30] To put it simply, Bobby did not enjoy the back seat a freshman senator needed to take. He could not sit in the background. He had a vision for the country and a strong vision at that. In a bold turn, in divisive America in 1968, Bobby Kennedy decided to take on incumbent Lyndon Baines Johnson without concern of further fracturing his own party.

And fracture the party it did. Just two weeks later on March 31, 1968, President Johnson addressed the nation on television about Vietnam. The president announced a sharp reduction in the bombing of North Vietnam and appealed for negotiations. He finished his speech with a now-famous bombshell:

> With American's sons and the field far away, with American's future under challenge right at home, with our hopes and the world's hopes for peace and balance every day, I do not believe that I should devote an hour a day of my time to partisan political causes…. Accordingly, I shall not seek and I will not accept the nomination of my party for another term as your President.[31]

LBJ's shocking announcement fueled RFK's barely two-week-old candidacy. With a path to the president now clear, Ted became a hardworking solider in the campaign, casting aside his visions in the Senate for the time being.

Thus, once RFK announced his candidacy and LBJ made his speech not to run, Ted Kennedy "threw himself and his staff into the campaign."[32] Although conspicuously absent from Clarke's recent account of the campaign, Ted Kennedy helped organize the critical May 7, 1968, Indiana primary run. He recruited Gerald Doherty, who brought dozens of Massachusetts supporters to organize the primary run. Ted Kennedy indeed traveled to Indiana and actively campaigned. Curiously, Clarke in *The Last Campaign* makes no mention of Ted Kennedy's efforts. But, unquestionably, Bobby looked to Ted Kennedy as both an organizer and inspirational speaker in his 1968 presidential Campaign. With his increasing influence in the Senate, Ted stood to get backing of leaders in the borderline states that could catapult Bobby to the presidency. Bobby had already burned many bridges in the Senate during his brief stint, and he stood to gain from the many relationships Ted Kennedy had forged.

Following Indiana, RFK lost to McCarthy in Oregon. The California primary loomed large. On the eve of RFK's California primary victory, Ted stayed in San Francisco, where he had campaigned hard to win the support of powerful Speaker of the California State Assembly, Jesse Unruh. Then came the tragic news of RFK's assassination. RFK won the California Democratic primary convincingly. With the presidential nomination now all but a foregone conclusion, RFK and his team went to the Ambassador Hotel in Los Angeles for the triumphant victory speech. After giving the speech, Bobby headed out of the crowd toward the kitchen. Then, a young Palestinian, Sirhan Sirhan, reached out from the crowd and pointed a revolver at Kennedy's head. Roosevelt "Rosie"

Greer, a former football player, wrestled Sirhan down. RFK did not survive the shots.[33]

A frenzied nation, just five years from the assassination of John F. Kennedy and two months from the assassination of the Reverend Martin Luther King, Jr., stood in disbelief as the news came from the West Coast. Glued as reports confirmed RFK's death, many Americans wondered if Ted Kennedy would step in to finish the unfinished campaign of Bobby Kennedy.

Once again, though, Ted Kennedy first had to bury a slain older brother. The burden, of course, is beyond description. Just 36 at the time, the pressures on Ted Kennedy to keep the Kennedy tradition must have tormented him. While Ted kept a strong public persona, having two brothers assassinated within five years must have had devastating personal effects. And soon enough, Ted Kennedy would have a personal tragedy that would forever tarnish his reputation.

After dispatching rumors of a presidential run and then a vice presidential nomination by now front runner Hubert Humphrey, Ted Kennedy for the first time made the Vietnam War his own cause. He demanded that "we now resolve to bring an end to this war ... as quickly as is physically possible."[34] He turned to a cause, rather than seeking public emotion and the moment to seize a potential presidential nomination and certain vice presidential nomination that may have vaulted him to the presidency in 1972 or 1976.

Ted Kennedy, picking up his slain brother's cause, became and remained until the end a vocal critic of the Vietnam War. Relinquishing his cautious role in the Senate, Ted Kennedy condemned on the Senate floor Nixon's assault on Hamburger Hill.[35] In a rally in Washington, D.C., in front of about 250,000 demonstrators, Kennedy stated, "I do believe this nation is in danger of committing itself to goals and personalities that guarantee the war's continuance."[36] Kennedy called for the withdrawal of combat troops by October 1970 and all forces by the end of 1972.

By no means did Ted Kennedy bring about an end to the war. His moral efforts, however, led to his reputation as an antiwar activist. The death of RFK dramatically changed Ted Kennedy's vision of himself and his actions in the Senate. Vietnam provides only one example. Focusing on domestic legislation, Ted Kennedy would strive to make a difference, only to face a personal disaster raising real questions about Kennedy's character that would forever change the course of his political career.

Following the assassination of Robert F. Kennedy, Ted Kennedy retreated from the national scene. Aides and friends encouraged Kennedy to take time to recover. Therefore, Kennedy "took a small role in the Senate for the rest of 1968."[37]

While courted by the Humphrey/Muskie presidential ticket to campaign vigorously, Kennedy did nothing of the sort. Some view this decision as disdain for Humphrey's failure to depart from Johnson's Vietnam stance. Others, rightfully so, attribute Kennedy's tepid response to the campaign as a natural period of retrenchment following an unspeakable tragedy.

Regardless of the reason, Kennedy had to face the music when Republican Richard M. Nixon secured the presidency by a popular vote of 43.4 percent to 42.7 percent over Humphrey.[38] Kennedy thus found himself in the new position of serving in a Senate Democratic majority with a Republican president.

Following Nixon's election, Kennedy turned his attention to claiming a leadership role in the Senate. Therefore, he decided to run for majority whip, or deputy majority leader. "When the 91st Congress convened as 1968 opened, Ted Kennedy ... decided to wrest the post of Democratic whip or assistant majority leader from Sen. Russell B. Long of Louisiana."[39] As Kennedy says in his memoir "on New Year's Eve 1968, three weeks before the inauguration of Richard Nixon as the thirty-seventh president, I announced to Mike Mansfield that I would challenge Russell Long for his position as assistant majority leader."[40]

Several theories have emerged as to why Kennedy sought the whip post. A very detail-oriented and thankless job, the whip needed to spend hours scheduling votes and handling parliamentary duties. One view credits the decision to a desire to "confront the new Nixon administration and its expected threats to Democratic programs."[41] Another theory "is that Kennedy's decision to seek the whip's job, with its routine, always menial requirements, was based on a desire to slip into anonymity."[42] Yet another argument advanced: "As whip he could do more about putting across his own notions, and Bobby's for that matter."[43]

Kennedy's own contemporaneous stated views appear most convincing. Far from slipping into anonymity or seeking to push RFK's agenda, the decision to run for majority whip seems a natural outgrowth of the cautious steps, to date, Kennedy had taken to advance in the Senate. While not a glamorous job, the majority whip gained invaluable experience in the day-to-day running of the Senate. Kennedy "cited the backing of Muskie and Humphrey and argued that Congressional Democrats had greater responsibilities now that Republicans were in the White House."[44] Also contributing to the decision, Theo Lippman, Jr., recites a 1974 conversation with Kennedy in which Kennedy stated, "I just thought it an opportunity to learn more about the range of issues that was coming up, to become more of a generalist than a specialist."[45]

Kennedy's opponent for majority whip, Russell B. Long of Louisiana, had "lined up enough votes to beat Muskie."[46] However, Kennedy's unexpected decision to seek the whip post caught Long by surprise. He announced his decision on December 31, 1968, and on January 3, 1969, secured the position by a vote of 31 to 26.[47] "He was the youngest majority whip in the history of the Senate."[48]

Having obtained the majority whip position, the question remained what exactly Kennedy had won. The majority whip, historically, held little power and hardly qualified as a leadership position. Perhaps Kennedy took his cue from Lyndon Baines Johnson. Johnson, closely tethered to Senate protocol, took the step of becoming majority whip at a time when the position held absolutely no clout. However, Johnson took the position seriously, which catapulted him to become majority leader, thereby fortifying his role in the Senate.[49] From the Senate leadership role, of course, Johnson improbably became JFK's vice presidential nominee to secure the all-important electoral college votes in Texas in 1960, and became president in 1963 following JFK's assassination.

Some attribute Kennedy's decision to run for and win the majority whip position as similar to Johnson's ultimate quest for the presidency. Lester David writes,

> Thus in an amazing one week offensive, Teddy had propelled himself from the Senate's back bench to its front-rank leadership. With one swift stroke he had catapulted into a position of national leadership within the party. Even more notably, his blitz had drawn a sharp line between himself and two other potential party leaders, Muskie and McCarthy. He had thus taken a giant step toward the party's presidential nomination in 1972.[50]

David's soaring rhetoric bears no resemblance to the truth. To begin, Kennedy since 1962 had hardly sat in the "back bench" of the Senate. While sporting only modest Legislative accomplishments, Kennedy had forged ahead with the Immigration Bill in 1965, become increasingly outspoken in his criticisms of the Vietnam War and gained respect of Senate colleagues with his cautious and restrained approach.

David also resorts to unsupportable hyperbole in describing Kennedy's January 3, 1969, victory in the majority whip race as placing him in a position of "national leadership." Far from it, frankly. The majority whip does the behind-the-scenes dirty work, and surely Kennedy would have chosen a different path if he simply sought a road to the 1972 presidential nomination.

In fact, Kennedy brushed off speculation of a presidential run. Rather, it seems, holding the majority whip position served a means to gain influence as a senator. For while Kennedy during six years in the Senate had hardly slumbered, his record demonstrated modest achievements.

> After six years, he enjoyed the ways of the Senate and had an easy rapport with Senators twice his age. He had been comfortable in the supporting role that junior Senators get more often than star parts. His legislative record was short. With Howard Baker he had blocked the redistricting bill, fighting off the Senate leaders. Otherwise the poll tax had been an admirable defeat and the immigration bill a sure thing. Community health centers and the teacher corps had been accomplishments, but modest ones achieved without battles.[51]

The Senate majority whip post positioned Kennedy to achieve modest but more significant Legislative accomplishments. According to Lippman, "Kennedy began the job as whip with customary enthusiasm and imagination."[52] But not surprisingly, Kennedy achieved little in the first six months in his new post. His role, as with other Democratic senators, had radically changed. No longer working with a president of his party, Kennedy and others needed to turn their efforts to opposing Nixon policies and initiatives. Fearing Soviet rancor, Kennedy opposed Nixon's intent to press forward with antiballistic missiles.[53]

Nixon, characteristically, viewed Kennedy as an enemy and his inevitable opponent in the 1972 presidential race. While nobody can know whether Kennedy would have run in 1972, a number of factors militate against such an argument. First, Kennedy continued to take the traditional and cautious role in the Senate. He actively avoided confrontations with Nixon. Second, the history of Kennedy's Senate activity from 1962 to 1969 suggests that Kennedy sought to solidify his position in the Senate. Indeed, with two slain brothers, Kennedy logically may well have sought to avoid such an immediate presidential run.

In any event, while Kennedy forged positions against Nixon policies, he cannot claim any Legislative successes in the first six months of 1969. Of course, the events of July 18, 1969, in Chappaquiddick changed everything. Accounts of Chappaquiddick abound. Ted Kennedy, driving with 28-year-old Mary Jo Kopechne following a party, toppled from Dyke Bridge into Poucha Pond. He swam to safety but Kopechne tragically died. Even worse, Kennedy did not report the matter to authorities until nearly ten hours after the incident. If not a Kennedy, no doubt having aides call on favors in unrevealed behind-the-scenes efforts, the police would have arrested him for a felony hit-and-run and likely charged him with manslaughter. Any lay person would have stood trial or entered a plea with jail time. Most senators, faced with less or comparable scandals, would have resigned in disgrace rather than face ethics charges.

Without question, an event such as Chappaquiddick would have ended the careers of most senators. Ted Kennedy, whether through favoritism or means we shall never know, managed to survive his disgraceful conduct that night and remain a senator. His decision to have Chappaquiddick aired publicly and not resign the Senate may have shown arrogance and a disregard for the law, as some argue. To others, it seems, his actions demonstrated a commitment to public service and a resolve to make a difference. Regardless, the Chappaquiddick incident revealed likely criminal conduct, and a concerted campaign to avoid jail time.

Despite the indefensible nature of the incident, Kennedy apologists strain to defend his conduct. One of Kennedy's biographers declares, "Kennedy suffered a moderate brain concussion in the accident, an injury which causes confusion and memory failure. That undoubtedly affected his actions and his subsequent accounts of them."[54] Others attempt to portray Kennedy's actions as heroic.[55] In truth, "even by his own account ... [Kennedy's] response to the situation came close to criminal irresponsibility."[56] As Kennedy stated: "I regard as indefensible the fact that I did not report the accident to the police immediately."[57]

Though cleared by authorities of criminal negligence,[58] what impact did the Chappaquiddick scandal have on Kennedy's performance as a senator? Without question, Kennedy's "political influence in Washington was ... diluted."[59] In the shorter term ... Kennedy's influence had plainly diminished."[60] Chappaquiddick had kept Kennedy "away from the Senate for long intervals and put a damper on his customary desire to make speeches and take a leading role in making Senate policy."[61]

More importantly, the Chappaquiddick incident bolstered blistering attacks on Ted Kennedy and his family's influence. To begin, Ted cheated at Harvard only to eventually receive reinstatement and graduate. Surely, some believed anyone not with the Kennedy name could not have returned to Harvard. Then, Kennedy's legendary debauchery came back into prominent question. Few believe that intoxication and infidelity did not play a role in the Chappaquiddick tragedy. Finally, many believe, and properly so, that Kennedy received favorable treatment from local police. Any normal citizen, many say, would have served jail time, at a minimum, for fleeing the scene of an accident.

Yet, while Kennedy plainly suffered in Senate prominence as a result of Chappaquiddick, his refugee subcommittee weighed in on the disaster in Biafra. In pressing for greater relief efforts, Kennedy coordinated with President Nixon as well as his national security advisor, Henry Kissinger.[62] Kennedy also embraced health care legislation designed to adopt a system of national health care insurance. Backed by United Auto Workers President Walter Reuther, Kennedy introduced a far-reaching health care bill for Senate consideration.[63]

Kennedy also sat on the Judiciary Committee during path-breaking rejections of two Nixon nominees for the United States Supreme Court, Clement Haynsworth and G. Harrold Carswell. Both arch conservatives and deeply opposed to civil rights legislation, the Judiciary Committee's scrutiny of these two nominees marked the first time since 1930 that *any* presidential appointment for the United States Supreme Court met Senate rejection.[64] Nixon's first nominee, Haynsworth, a conservative from South Carolina and Chief Justice of the Fourth Circuit Court of Appeal, consistently opposed school desegregation efforts. Labor and civil rights groups opposed confirmation. On November 21, 1969, the Senate rejected Haynsworth's nomination 55–45.[65]

Next Nixon nominated Carswell, a member of the Fifth Circuit Court of Appeals. In 1948, Carswell gave a speech asserting that "segregating of the races is proper and the only practical and correct way of life in our states. I have always so believed and I shall always so act."[66] Kennedy, while hardly playing a central role, opposed the Carswell nomination in Judiciary Committee Hearings.

> Can we accept the proposition that the appointment of Supreme Court justices in the President's own make, unfettered by Senate review? The Constitution says no; logic says no; history says no; past senators have repeatedly said no; and I believe this Senate will say no.[67]

Without question, other senators played a far more prominent role in Carswell's defeat. By vote of 51–45, however, Carswell lost his bid for a seat on the highest court of the land.

Despite Kennedy's outward activities on Biafra, health care legislation, and Judiciary Committee denunciation of Nixon's Southern strategy,
such efforts masked Senate discontent with Kennedy's Chappaquiddick
debacle. Having worked hard since 1962 to gain the trust of senior senators by observing Senate rules and protocol, the Chappaquiddick incident and its aftermath spoiled Kennedy's relationship with many of his
own counterparts. Previously, Kennedy had avoided any criticism of
riding on JFK's coattails by cautiously earning the trust of his Senate
elders. Following Chappaquiddick, however, many viewed Kennedy's
survival as a function of the spin put on by Kennedy family loyalists and
aides. This alienated many of Kennedy's colleagues.[68]

Thus, as surprising as Kennedy's appointment as majority whip in
early 1969, Kennedy suffered a political setback when Robert Byrd of
West Virginia mounted a successful campaign to wrest the whip position
from Kennedy.[69] A *Washington Evening Star* editorial described Byrd's
triumph as a "humiliation for Kennedy and a setback for any future
national political plans he may have."[70] No doubt, Kennedy's Chappaquiddick debacle played a huge role in his unsuspected loss of the unim-
portant majority whip position. This signaled a decided view by the
Democratic party to distance itself from Ted Kennedy's transgressions
and to dissuade him from a 1972 presidential run he possibly wished to
avoid in the first instance.

Senator Kennedy lost a strategic position to Senator Byrd in 1971.
However, the loss turned Kennedy back to legislative tasks. In a new era
with a slim Democratic majority in the Senate, and Republican President
Richard M. Nixon at the helm, Kennedy had legislative initiatives to
test. And in the era before Watergate, Kennedy moved forward on such
efforts.

According to the *Boston Globe* and the *Seattle Times*, "Kennedy and
Representative Paul G. Rogers of Florida passed legislation establishing
a federal cancer research program in 1971 that quadrupled the amount
spent fighting cancer."[71] Hailed by these two newspapers as a highlight
of Senator Kennedy's legislative accomplishments, a review of the text
of the National Cancer Act of 1971 and Senate debates shed light on
Kennedy's true role.

America's efforts in fighting cancer reveals a checkered history:

> The controversies over smoking during the 1960s and 1970s reproduced in
> microcosm broad differences in American attitudes toward cancer. On the
> one hand, manifestations of cancer phobia mounted in the United States....

On the other hand, the well established alliance against cancer was more helpful than ever.... The result, the landmark in the American experience of the disease, was the "war on cancer," started by the National Cancer Act of 1971.[72]

Other than newspaper headlines, few have chronicled Kennedy's role in the passage of the National Cancer Act of 1971, or analyzed the actual bill itself.

Kennedy biographer Adam Clymer reveals the most about his congressional efforts. For several years, Mary Lasker, a New York philanthropist, "had been promoting the idea of a government war on cancer."[73] President Nixon, seeking to take charge of the initiative, planned an increase of a million dollars for the National Cancer Institute (NCI).[74] Realizing Nixon's symbolic efforts failed to make a dent into the cancer health problem, Kennedy and Jacob Javits introduced Senate Bill 34, which called for four times the money as Nixon had proposed, over 1.2 billion dollars over three years.[75]

The "national war on cancer," however, had a difficult path due to infighting among cancer advocates. "Defenders of federal efforts replied also that the NCI was making a good-faith effort to promote cancer control."[76] Critics "questioned the priorities of the NCI in spending its research money."[77] While James Shannon favored basic biological research, Lasker lobbied hard for more applied research. "This controversy flared openly in the early 1970s during acrimonious debates over the National Cancer Act."[78]

Discerning Kennedy's role, at first blush, has its difficulties because of political machinations in effect before passage of the National Cancer Act. In early March 1971, "Kennedy ran two days of hearings which focused less on money than on creating a separate agency outside the National Institute of Health."[79] Nixon, though, by mid–April 1971, worried that Kennedy, viewed by him as a potential rival in the 1972 presidential election, would gain credit for passage of the bill.[80] Accordingly, Nixon entered the fray.

Others who joined the war resurrected the idea that beating cancer was like smashing the atom. President Nixon, who converted to the cancer war in 1971, took this approach. Nixon's reasons were mainly political: he was anxious to outflank Senator Ted Kennedy, a potential presidential candidate who was then leading the Lasker forces.[81]

Kennedy's willingness to remove his name from the bill so that Nixon could take credit for the National Cancer Act led to its passage.

On June 16, 1971, the Kennedy-Javitz bill, but under Bill Number S.1828 sponsored as an administration measure by Republican Peter Dominick of Colorado, receive the full approval of the Senate health subcommittee.[82] The day before the "Dominick bill" passed the entire Senate by a 79–1 vote, Kennedy spoke on its behalf on the Senate floor:

> The conquest of cancer is a special problem of such an enormous concern to all Americans. We can quote statistics, but I think everyone of us in this body, and most families across the country, have been touched by this disease one way or another.[83]

The Committee on Labor and Public Welfare stated its lofty goals in its report released on June 28, 1971:

> There is broad agreement that cancer research has advanced to the stage where a substantial increase in resources and effort could be very productive. There seems to be a consensus among cancer researchers that they are within striking distance of achieving the basic understanding of cancer cells which has eluded the most brilliant medical minds in the world. While it is true that breakthroughs in science are often serendipitous, and cannot be forced, the committee feels that a substantial increase in resources, along with increased organization efficiency will shorten the time necessary to achieve them.[84]

The House took its time when it received the bill. Dubious about creating a separate agency, it excised that provision from the Senate bill. On the other hand, the House authorized more money: 1.5 billion over three years. The National Cancer Act of 1971, passed on December 23, 1971, sought to "expeditiously utilize existing research facilities and personnel of the National Institute of Health accelerating exploration of opportunities in areas of special promise."[85] The bill authorized "$20,000,000 for the fiscal year ending June 30, 1972, $30,000,000 for the fiscal year ending June 30, 1973, and $40,000,000 for the fiscal year ending June 30, 1974 for programs in the diagnosis, prevention and treatment of cancer."[86] The act also provided the Director of the National Cancer Institute with the authority to establish up to 15 new centers for clinical research with funding not to exceed $5,000,000 per year per center.[87]

In a separate section titled "Authorizations of Appropriations," the National Cancer Act of 1971 appropriated "$40,000,000 for the fiscal year ending June 30, 1972, $50,000,000 for the fiscal year ending June 30, 1973, and $60,000,000 for the fiscal year ending June 30, 1974."[88] Further the Act created grants of up to $35,000 for "cancer research and training."[89]

Summarizing the contents of the National Cancer Act of 1971, historian James T. Patterson writes,

> After hard infighting a compromise satisfied most of the contenders. The final bill stipulated that the NCI director was to be appointed directly by the president and to submit NCI financial requests to the budget office. These measures give the NCI special status among the institutes of the NIH, but it otherwise remained under the overall management of the NIH. This was an awkward arrangement, but both houses finally approved it.[90]

While Kennedy decried the lack of independence from the president, who had unfettered appointment power of the NCI directors, he did not seek to block its passage, in a nonpartisan effort to steward the very bill he initiated to conclusion.

While the National Cancer Act of 1971 receives curiously little mention by Kennedy biographers, the breadth and scope of the act plainly makes it Kennedy's most important Legislative achievement up to 1971. As Patterson observes,

> Most striking was the consensus among almost all involved—Democrats as well as Republicans, liberals as well as conservatives—that the Federal government must be the source of action against cancer, and that much more money was needed. Few people seriously questioned these premises or argued that other national needs were more deserving of support.[91]

The ultimate passage of the National Cancer Act of 1971, originally the Kennedy-Javitz bill, sheds considerable light on the effectiveness of Ted Kennedy as a senator in his first decade of service. Still reeling from the disgrace of Chappaquiddick, Kennedy began his sponsorship of the act by enlisting Jacob Javitz, a Republican (albeit liberal) to co-author the bill. Particularly in a time of strident division among the Senate and indeed mainstream Americans on the Vietnam War, this effort from the start to forge bipartisan support for the act illustrates a continuation of Kennedy's willingness to reach across the aisle.

Nor did Kennedy allow Nixon's fierce need to take credit for the act derail it. Rather than aggressively fighting the administration's insistence that the president appoint the NCI Director and potentially stalling passage of the bill, Kennedy acceded to the compromise. When Nixon chafed at backing a Kennedy-sponsored bill given his fear of a 1972 presidential battle, Kennedy stepped aside and gave his full support to Republican Peter Dominick having his name on the bill so that the full Senate could vote. A bill emerging for the vote from a Committee with a minority sponsor rarely occurs. Nonetheless, Kennedy wanted the National Cancer Act embodied into law.

The process of the bill becoming the law also bears discussion. The development of the act belies the characterization of Kennedy as a "tax and spend liberal," at least with respect to this bill. The original Kennedy-Javitz version contained *less* funds for expenditure than the final bill approved and signed by Republican Nixon. Kennedy's primary concern involved the lack of independence of the NCI Director, but that issue, too, fell from the forefront.

Therefore, as of 1971, Ted Kennedy had continued the ways that marked his entry into the Senate. Cautious in observing Senate protocol, Kennedy avoided divisive battles that would stall or block otherwise needed legislation. Despite Chappaquiddick, he continued to earn the respect of his colleagues across the aisle. Far less confrontational than Robert F. Kennedy, he refused to battle needlessly with Republicans, including Nixon, much less members of his own party.

The passage of the National Cancer Act of 1971 also shatters the myth, advanced by critics, that Kennedy ceaselessly sought national attention for political aggrandizement. Undoubtedly, the large bipartisan majorities behind both the Immigration Act of 1965 and the National Cancer Act of 1971 made it easier for Kennedy to avoid political feuds. Yet, in his first two Legislative achievements Kennedy had demonstrated an aptitude for consensus building.

The Watergate era, however, would soon test the very assumptions under which Kennedy operated in the Senate since his election in 1962.

3

The Title IX Education Amendments of 1972

Following the National Cancer Act of 1971, Kennedy disabused any notion that he would run for the presidency in 1972.[1] In the spring of 1972, however, the Watergate scandal broke. It began with President Nixon's attempts to cover up a burglary of the Democratic National Committee headquarters at the Watergate Complex in Washington. Kennedy sought to lead the charge for investigation into President Nixon, but Senate majority leader Mike Mansfield "excluded Kennedy from the Watergate investigation."[2] Mansfield viewed the continuing distraction of rumors of Kennedy running for president or accepting a vice presidential nomination as divisive. Naturally, the Chappaquiddick scandal still loomed large, and many in the Democratic leadership worried that Kennedy could not effectively marshal public support for the first impeachment proceeding on a sitting president in a century.

Indeed, Kennedy's Senate and political career appeared in serious decline in 1972. To be sure, Kennedy had rebounded following Chappaquiddick when he won the majority whip position. But he then lost the position and had some years without sponsoring any major legislation. Mansfield's decision to relegate Kennedy to the background in the Watergate investigation struck another serious blow into Kennedy's clout as he neared the conclusion of his second term in the Senate.

Kennedy's legislative efforts always stemmed from his fervent views against discrimination. His support for the Civil Rights Act of 1964 reflected Kennedy's broad support for Civil Rights. Kennedy furthered these efforts through his sponsoring the Immigration Act of 1965. However, in the next seven years, Kennedy did not sponsor, much less play a leading role, on any antidiscrimination legislation.

Kennedy did finally back antidiscrimination legislation in 1972.

Instead of throwing his hat into the presidential arena or acting in the forefront of the Watergate investigation, Kennedy, according to the *Seattle Times*, "was a key Senate backer of Title IX, a 1972 amendment requiring colleges and universities to provide equal funding for men's and women's athletics."[3] Aside from overstating Kennedy's role in the passage of the act, it also misconstrues the original language and purpose of Title IX. As discussed below, Title IX eliminated discrimination in education. However, at least as adopted in 1972, no evidence exists that Ted Kennedy intended Title IX to provide equal funding for men's and women's athletics, much less the sponsors of the act.

None of Kennedy's biographers discuss the legislation at any length—if at all. Nor does Kennedy address Title IX in his memoir. Instead, in this time period, Kennedy biographers tend to overemphasize his role on the national scene, waxing reminiscently on Kennedy's impact during the Watergate era. These attempts to vault Kennedy into a prominent role in the Watergate scandal lack merit. Indeed, it remains odd that none of the many Kennedy biographers cited in this book examine Title IX, his first backing of antidiscrimination legislation of any magnitude for seven years since the Immigration Act of 1965. This raises two questions: (1) what role did Kennedy play in the passage of the controversial legislation; and (2) what impact, since the passage of the legislation, unintended or not, has occurred? Title IX of the Education Amendments of 1972 eventually changed the landscape of college athletics. Prior to passage of Title IX, men and women's sports at universities hardly stood on equal footing. The enactment of Title IX on June 23, 1972, and subsequent amendments and regulations changed all that.[4]

Viewing Kennedy's legislative efforts over a ten-year period since his entrance in the Senate in 1962, a common theme emerges. First supporting the Civil Rights Act of 1964, Kennedy then turned to the racist immigration system to foster equal opportunity in the passage of the Immigration Act of 1965. The core of Kennedy's legislative efforts stemmed from the belief that the eradication of discrimination was a national imperative. Even his failed efforts in 1965 in attempting to enact a voting rights act demonstrate Kennedy's true commitment to attack discrimination on a number of fronts. The Civil Rights Act of 1964 concerned discrimination in employment. Kennedy would later tackle this issue both in his active support of the Americans with Disabilities Act of 1990 but also in his prominent role in the Family Medical Leave Act of 1993. The Immigration Act dealt with broader societal discrimination in what many have fondly called America's "melting pot." And his voters rights act efforts plainly aimed to end racist voting procedures.

Title IX follows the same path of illustrating Kennedy's keen sense of attacking discrimination, this time in the field of education. According to the Legislative Summary, Title IX "prohibits sex discrimination in all aspects of Federal educational programs."[5] As enacted, the Act states:

> No person in the United States shall, on the basis of sex, be excluded from participation and be denied the benefit of, or be subjected to discrimination under any education program, or activity receiving Federal financial assistance.[6]

Simply viewing the language of the Act, the intentions seem unobjectionable. Critics of the act admit that "at issue is not the Title IX statute itself which simply outlaws discrimination in educational institutions. The problem is the way in which Title IX has been applied."[7] By virtue of Title IX, college institutions receiving federal funding could not discriminate between males and females. The wide sweep of the enactment, applying to virtually every college institution, received little attention initially. However, the unintended consequences of the legislation would rear its ugly head in years to come.

To begin, the definition of "educational institution" provides proof of the broad sweep of the legislation. Section 1681(c) makes it clear that private as well as public institutions had to comply with its dictates: "For purposes of this chapter an educational institution means any public or *private* preschool, elementary, or secondary school, or an institution of vocational, professional, or higher education."[8] The act, therefore, was not limited to public institutions. This, itself, seems fair on its face. The initial intent of the legislation stemmed from a view that any institution that received federal funding could not discriminate between males and females.

At its core, Title IX rectified blatant sexual discrimination in the provision of educational services. Females, as of 1972, simply did not have opportunities in education equal to their male counterparts. Without question, Congress needed to address this unfairness and equalize the playing field. Had the subsequent interpretation of the act stopped at this point, historians and Kennedy admirers most certainly would have written extensively about it. Instead, the most even-handed Kennedy biographer relegated discussion of the 1972 Education Act to one sentence, and highlights its improvement in education of Native Americans.[9]

Why do none of the Kennedy biographers mention Title IX? Even a recent biography by a team of the *Boston Globe* writers makes no mention of Title IX.[10] Such omission appears curious indeed, when on May 21, 2008, the *Boston Globe* summarized highlights of important Kennedy backed legislation:

> Kennedy was a key Senate backer of Title IX, a 1972 amendment to the federal education law that helped spur the growth of women's college sports by requiring colleges and universities to provide equal funding for men's and women's athletics.[11]

Title IX has a checkered legacy. On the one hand, the sweeping amendments fostered gender equality, particularly in higher education. A natural outgrowth of the Civil Rights Act of 1964, Title IX radically improved educational equality among the sexes. Just consider some of the positive effects of the act:

- In 1972, women earned 9 percent of medical degrees. In 1994, women earned 38 percent.
- In 1972, women earned 7 percent of law degrees. In 1994, women earned 43 percent.
- In 1972, women earned 25 percent of doctoral degrees. In 1994, women earned 44 percent.
- In 1971, 18 percent of women had completed four years of college, compared to 26 percent of men. In 1994, 27 percent of both men and women had earned a bachelor's degree.
- In 1972, women composed 15 percent of college student athletes. In 1995, women composed 37 percent.
- In 1972, 300,000 high school girls participated in athletics. In 1996, there were 2.4 million.[12]

In this regard, Title IX represents a continuation of Ted Kennedy's quest through major legislation of rectifying discrimination. Just as the Immigration Act of 1965 eradicated a racist quota system, Title IX prohibited sex discrimination in education. As supporters of the act observe, "the basic idea behind statutes such as Title VI and Title IX is that federal tax money should not be used to support programs that discriminate on certain bases."[13] The legislative summary further describes the purposes of the act:

> To amend the Higher Education Act of 1965, the General Education Provisions Act (creating a National Foundation for Postsecondary Education and a National Institute of Education), the Elementary and Secondary Act of 1965, Public Law 874, Eighty-first Congress, and related Acts, and for other purposes.

Comprehensive authorization for broad range of OE programs in higher education, including college libraries, junior or community colleges, student assistance, professional development, facilities construction, assistance in major disaster areas, graduate fellowships, and occupational education. Establishes an Office of Indian Education and a National Advisory Council on Indian Education.

Provides for an ethnic heritage program consumer's education and extends land grant status for college of the Virgin Islands and the University of Guam.

Provides programs for children of migratory workers and for investigation of youth camp safety. Includes section on general provisions related to assignment of transportation of students to overcome racial imbalance.[14]

Given amendments and subsequent regulations, however, Title IX had profound positive effects on women's sports. Back in 1972, few could have envisioned that a female head coach of the Tennessee women's basketball team, Pat Summitt, would have garnered national attention for her thousandth win as head coach. Nationally televised on ESPN in 2009, with legendary and controversial coach Bob Knight extolling her virtues, women's collegiate basketball reached its pinnacle in terms of public interest and acceptance as a major sport. Indeed, the continued vitality of the WNBA, the professional women's basketball league, speaks of the opportunity Title IX has provided women with the ability to truly compete in serious college sports. In the absence of truly competitive women's collegiate basketball teams, a professional league could not exist nor garner the attraction it has received, with television deals with ESPN and the like. Going a step further, the Los Angeles Sparks of the WNBA has two female owners. Nobody could have predicted any of this back in 1972 when Congress enacted Title IX and President Nixon signed it into law.

Yet, Title IX's unintended side effects have manifested themselves in the systematic dismantling of men's sports teams, particularly at the college level, to comply with the strict mandates of subsequent amendments to the act. Men's collegiate football and basketball earn millions for universities across the country. Accordingly, expenditures on these programs dwarf expenditures on women's programs, thus leading to violations of Title IX. Therefore, in the years since its passage, many institutions have needed to pare down men's sports teams, including golf, hockey, water polo, and volleyball. Critics of Title IX rightfully complain that the act has resulted in unfairness in the treatment of male athletes.[15] Very few universities, in fact, have male volleyball teams, even though high schools emphasize the sport. Still, these same universities have female volleyball teams, thus illustrating the lessened opportunities for many excellent male athletes who in high school chose an alternative sport to football, basketball or baseball.

Detractors of Title IX blame the unanticipated effect on male sports on post-legislative events. According to a recent article,

> there are, in effect two Title IX's: a law passed in 1972 by a Congress that wanted to prohibit sex discrimination in schools and a reinterpretation of the law, created by unelected bureaucrats and the Department of Education Office of Civil Rights (OCR). Unlike the vast majority of civil rights laws and regulations ... the [OCR] test was never debated in, or approved by Congress.... Worse [OCR's interpretation] functions as a strict quota law, clearly at odds with the statutory language. The OCR's reinterpretation of Title IX has resulted in the wholesale devastation of several men's sports at the collegiate level.[16]

While the Kasic and Schuld article overstates the situation, the case *Cohen v. Brown University* provides fascinating insight into the debate regarding the consequences of Title IX. In the spring of 1991, Brown University, an Ivy League school, for financial reasons announced that it planned to drop four sports from its intercollegiate varsity athletics roster: women's volleyball and gymnastics, and men's golf and water polo.[17] Brown estimated that eliminating these four varsity teams "would save $77,813 per annum, broken down as follows: women's volleyball $37,127, women's gymnastics $24,901; men's water polo $9,250 and men's golf $6,545."[18] Before the cuts, Brown athletics offered an aggregate of 328 varsity slots for male athletes. Thus, women had 36.7 percent of the athletic opportunities and men 63.3 percent.[19]

Abolishing the four varsity teams took substantially more dollars from the women's athletic budget than from the men's budget. Following announcement of the cutbacks, disappointed members of the women's volleyball and gymnastics teams brought suit under Title IX. The Plaintiffs charged that Brown's athletic arrangement violated Title IX's ban on gender-based discrimination.[20]

The case proceeded at the trial court level before Senior District Judge Pettine. In two separate Orders, the Court granted Plaintiffs' motion for class certification, meaning the case could proceed as a class action, and denied Brown's motion to dismiss.[21] The parties then presented a total of 14 days of testimony and 20 witnesses on the preliminary injunction motion seeking (1) reinstatement of the women's gymnastics and volleyball teams to full varsity status, and (2) prohibiting Brown from eliminating or reducing the status of any other Brown-funded women's intercollegiate athletic teams unless the percentage of opportunities to participate in intercollegiate athletics equaled the percentage of women enrolled in the undergraduate program.[22]

Judge Pettine granted the Plaintiffs' motion for injunctive relief. In so doing, he directed "Brown to immediately restore women's gymnastics and women's volleyball to their former status as fully funded intercollegiate varsity teams and to provide these teams with all of the incidental benefits accorded varsity teams at the university."[23] This order would only remain in effect pending a full trial on the merits.

Brown appealed, and the First Circuit stayed execution of the Order, meaning that it declined to require Brown at this initial stage to restore the women's gymnastics and volleyball teams. However, the First Circuit also heard the matter on an expedited basis.[24]

The First Circuit's decision, issued on April 16, 1993, elucidates the problems arising from the vague wording of Title IX as well as the sparse Legislative history of the act. As the First Circuit noted,

> part of the confusion about the scope of Title IX's coverage and the acceptable avenues of compliance arose from the absolute absence of secondary legislative materials. Congress included no committee report with the final bill and there were apparently only two mentions of intercollegiate athletics during the congressional debate.[25]

This observation by the First Circuit illustrates the haste in which some legislation gets enacted. The absence of a committee report and the sparse congressional debate demonstrates the lack of thought of the potential sweep of Title IX. Candidly, most thought, including Kennedy, that the legislation was a "no brainer," as it simply sought to end discrimination in college based on sex. To the contrary the absence of clear legislative directives in the enactment of Title IX led to regulative interpretation that expanded Title IX beyond its original scope. Indeed, while Title IX now is associated with collegiate sports, its initial purpose as demonstrated by the wording of the act and the lack of debate on sports during passage of the bill demonstrate that the sponsors of Title IX sought to eliminate discrimination in *education*, not sports.

Nevertheless, under congressional direction to implement Title IX, the Secretary of Health, Education and Welfare (HEW) promulgated regulations in 1975 which included provisions for college athletics. Four years later, in what the First Circuit describes as "adding another layer of regulatory exegesis,"[26] HEW's Office of Civil Rights (OCR) published a "Policy Interpretation" that offered a more detailed measure of equal athletic opportunity.[27]

In 1984, the United States Supreme Court altered the contemporary reading of Title IX and placed virtually all collegiate programs beyond its reach. This raised the question of whether the backers of Title IX in 1972 ever envisioned it to govern college athletics, or merely sought to eliminate discrimination in education. In any event, in 1987, Congress clarified its intentions by passing The Restoration Act. The floor debate leaves little doubt that the enactment aimed, in part, at creating a more level playing field for female athletes.[28]

The Department of Education issued regulations specific to the issue of college athletes. The regulations provide:

> No person shall, on the basis of sex, be excluded from participation, be denied the benefits of, be treated differently from another person or otherwise discriminated against in any interscholastic, intercollegiate, club or intramural athletics offered by a recipient, and no recipient shall provide any such athletics separately on such basis.[29]

Analyzing these regulations and the history of the act, the First Circuit held that with regard to effective accommodation of students' interests, "an institution that offers women a smaller number of athletics opportunities than the statute requires may not rectify that violation by lavishing more resources on those women or achieving equivalence in other respects."[30] The First Circuit therefore upheld the injunction. The Court wrote:

> We summarize succinctly, beginning with the probability of Plaintiffs' success. In an era where the practices of higher education must adjust to stunted revenues, careening costs, and challenging demographics, colleges might well be obliged to curb spending on programs, like athletics, that do not lie on the epicenter of their institutional mission. Title IX does not purport to override financial necessity. Yet, the pruning of athletic budgets cannot take place solely in comptroller's offices, isolated from the legislative and regulatory imperatives that Title IX imposes.[31]

Concluding its opinion, the First Circuit held that "requiring Brown to maintain the women's volleyball and gymnastics teams in varsity status for the time being is a remedial choice within the district court's discretion."[32] Hearkening back to the initial language of the 1972 act, the First Circuit stated that "the beacon by which we must steer is Congress' unmistakably clear mandate that educational institutions not use federal monies to perpetuate gender-based discrimination."[33]

Critics of the First Circuit opinion abound. In a 1996 amicus brief to the United States Supreme Court, former secretary of defense Caspar Weinberger argued that the proportionality test would prevent schools from choosing to provide opportunities in response to actual student interest. Instead, Weinberger argued, the First Circuit decision forced schools to allocate opportunities so as to equalize the rates of participation by men and women. The Supreme Court rejected this argument, and the proportionality test stood as legal guidance for other courts in Title IX compliance.[34]

A law review article also criticized the expanded scope of Title IX:

> The Policy Interpretation has taken on a life of its own, becoming the most controversial guidepost in the Title IX regulatory morass. It has expanded the scope of Title IX to the point of subverting the statute's original purpose of prohibiting educational discrimination against either sex. The fact remains Congress never reviewed, debated or approved—either by an affirmative vote or a failure to act—what would become the most powerful and controversial component of its antidiscrimination law.[35]

While expressing disagreement with subsequent interpretation of the act and the *Cohen* decision, the quoted language in the article simply ignores Congress's express amendment embodied in The Restoration Act of 1987, which specifically addressed the inequality in collegiate athletics between men's and women's sports. Unfortunately, Kennedy appears to have taken no role, much less a position, in the subsequent amendments. To be sure, he voted in favor of the Restoration Act of 1987. But his silence remains troubling. By 1987, Kennedy found himself consumed by other issues, such as the Bork nomination, and it seems clear that he paid little attention to the path Title IX had taken. Very little, if anything, illuminates the feelings of Ted Kennedy about Title IX and its subsequently enacted amendments. He has never written on the subject, much less spoken about Title IX's turn either in Congressional debates or other forums. Thus, it remains a mystery as to whether Kennedy supported the broad expansion of Title IX into the area of collegiate sports, or if he supported subsequent court opinions interpreting the Act and its regulations. Moreover, even after his death, controversy still abounds with respect to Title IX.

In fact, a recent case further illuminates the continuing debate over Title IX. In *Mansourian v. Regents of the University of California*, 594 F.3d 1095 (9th Cir. 2010), the Ninth Circuit addressed whether aggrieved women suing for damages must first provide the university notice of their disadvantageous treatment and an opportunity to correct it. The Ninth Circuit resoundingly held no and reversed the District Court's decision.[36]

In *Mansourian*, the plaintiffs, wrestlers, chose to attend University of California, Davis (UCD) so that they could participate in the University's acclaimed wrestling program, which long provided opportunities to women. During the 2000–2001 academic year, UCD eliminated all women from the wrestling team. Following student protest, UCD again allowed women to participate in wrestling but conditioned participation on their ability to defeat the best male wrestlers in their weight class. As a result, the female wrestlers could not compete and lost their varsity status, including scholarships and academic credit.[37] In considering the merits of the students' damages claims, the Ninth Circuit began by setting the statutory and regulatory framework governing Title IX athletics cases. In citing the statutory language, the Ninth Circuit noted, "As applied to intercollegiate athletics, the Department of Education's regulations interpret the statute as requiring funding recipients to 'provide equal athletic opportunity for members of both sexes.'" 34 C.F.R. §106.41(c).'"[38]

The Ninth Circuit continued by observing that the regulations establish two components of Title IX's equal athletic opportunity requirement: "effective accommodation" and "equal treatment." "Effective accommodation" requirements derive from the Title IX regulation at 34 C.F.R. §106.41(c)(1), which bases Title IX compliance in part on whether "the selection of sports and levels of competition effectively accommodate the interests and abilities of members of both sexes."[39] The "equal treatment" Title IX standard, in contrast, derives from 34 C.F.R. §106.41(c)(2)(10), which has been interpreted by OCR to require "equivalence in the availability, quality and kinds of other athletic benefits and opportunity provided male and female athletes."[40] Effective accommodation claims thus concern the opportunity to participate in athletics, while equal treatment claims allege sex-based differences in the schedules, equipment, coaching, and other factors affecting participants in athletics.

Turning to the intent of Congress, the Ninth Circuit held that a three-part test gives universities three options for demonstrating compliance with Title IX: (1) showing substantial proportionality (the number of women in intercollegiate athletics is proportionate to their enrollment); (2) proving that the institution has a "history and continuing practice of program expansion" for the underrepresented sex (in this case women); or (3) where the university cannot satisfy either of the two options, establishing that it nonetheless "fully and effectively accommodates" the interests of women. 44 Fed. Reg. 71, 4108.[41]

The District Court determined that the plaintiffs could not recover any money damages unless they had given notice of and an opportunity to rectify the specific violation alleged by them. Finding that the plaintiffs had failed to provide such notice, the District court granted summary judgment to UCD and dismissed the case.

The Ninth Circuit rejected this notice argument, particularly the analogy to Title IX sexual harassment cases. The Ninth Circuit held that

> judicially imposed notice requirement would be superfluous in light of universities' ongoing obligations to certify compliance with Title IX's athletics requirements and to track athletics gender equity data. OCR regulations require funding recipients to evaluate policies and certify, as a condition for receiving funds, that they are taking whatever remedial action is necessary to eliminate discrimination. UCD and other funding recipients therefore have an affirmative obligation to ensure compliance of at least one prong of the three part effective accommodation test.[42]

The Ninth Circuit also rejected the argument that UCD had demonstrated "a history and continuing practice of program expansion" for women that satisfied Option No. 2 of the three-part test. While recognizing that UCD took a significant step towards Title IX compliance by adding three women's teams in 1996, the Ninth Circuit concluded that Option No. 2 requires more than a single step:

> It requires having continuous progress towards the mandate of gender equality that Title IX imposed on funding recipients for the past 30 years. The record does not contain undisputed facts showing a history and continuing practice of program expansion that is responsive to women's interest.[43]

Accordingly, the Ninth Circuit reversed the District Court's dismissal of the case.

> The statute known as Title IX, 20 USC §1681, is widely recognized as a source of vast expansion of athletic opportunities for women in the nation's schools and universities.... Despite that renown, the district court in this case held that a university that receives federal funds cannot be held liable in damages for failing effectively to accommodate the athletic interest of both men and women unless the "aggrieved women first provide the appropriate university officials with notice of their disadvantageous treatment and an opportunity to cure it." We disagree.[44]

The *Mansourian* case plainly illustrates the continuing tension involving Title IX implementation and compliance. Indeed, Title IX plainly has both its supporters and detractors. In the decades since the enactment of Title IX, the most intolerable barriers to women's advancement in education have fallen. Some issues, however, remain at the forefront of public attention. One controversial issue concerns Title IX's funding of men's and women's sports, particularly at the collegiate level. Title IX detractors claim the OCR's interpretation of Title IX policy has forced the elimination of some men's sports by requiring schools to spend proportionate amounts on both women's and men's sports. Title IX advocates argue that proportionality in spending is only one indicator of compliance, with other factors not based on numbers. They claim that by offering men extremely costly programs, such as football, colleges and universities have created the need to cut lesser sports.

Both sides have their points. However, regardless of the initial intention of the act, the amendments and subsequent regulations have opened up opportunities to female athletes never dreamed of before. The meteoric increase in female participation in college athletics no doubt has its genesis in the act. So, too, a rippling effect has occurred with the vast increase in girls playing high school and club sports. With the real possibility now of college scholarships, many teen girls, unlike before, now do not give up on their athletic endeavors, because true opportunity exists in college.

And one cannot divorce opportunity from actual expenditures. The more money available for women's athletic programs in college the greater the participation. In this regard, the cynical view of Kasic and Schuld that Title IX provides "few or no new opportunities for women" lacks merit. Just go to any field on any weekend in any locale and the burgeoning participation by women in sports becomes readily apparent. Club teams, unheard of even a decade ago, now abound for female athletes as young as nine or ten years old. Called "travel teams," these clubs have heightened practice schedules, involve significant travel, and play against stiff competition. The goal—to ready young females for high school and college sports—certainly owes much to Title IX and its subsequent implementation.

Moreover, Brown's elimination of women's gymnastics illustrates another benefit of subsequent interpretation of Title IX. Since Brown took that action in 1971, women's gymnastics has spiraled in both American excellence and public interest. Without question, women's gymnastics has one of the highest viewer ratings in the Summer Olympics every four years. Unavailability of college women's gymnastics programs would severely hamper these great strides. In fact, gymnastic clubs in larger cities appear in multiple sites. Trainers vie for the opportunity to train girls as young as five.

Finally, proportionality in expenditures may well foster increased participation opportunities for professional women's sports. Increased popularity of these sports also has other beneficial effects. For example, as noted, the women's basketball professional team, the L.A. Sparks, now has female ownership. Only through excellent and well-funded college programs can these professional teams survive.

A recent series of articles in *Sports Illustrated* titled "The Legacy of Title IX: Forty Years of Seismic Change in Women's Sports in America" provides nine different human interest stories as examples of some of the act's successes.[45] According to the lead into the set of articles, "Title IX radically altered the sport's landscape. Because of its impact, the players on the Cross Creek High Girl's Team in Augusta, Georgia, can dream of playing college and pro ball."[46] Subtitled "The Power of Play," *Sports Illustrated* took the position that "Title IX has reached well beyond the playing field, forever changing the role of women in society. As the fortieth anniversary of the law approaches, SI examines nine stories that reflect the spirit of IX."[47]

The first article, written by Kelli Anderson, discusses Tara Van-Derveer and the three Indiana basketball teammates that she roomed with during the winter of 1974. As they sat around a dinner table they asked, "What if? What if they could have gotten scholarships? What if they traveled by air instead of vans? Competing in sold out arenas, were seen by far friends and relatives and friends? Imagine getting paid to play! A pro draft!"[48] According to VanDerveer, now with 27 years of tenure as the women's basketball coach at Stanford, "At the time it was all fantasy."[49]

According to the article, prior to the enactment of Title IX, underfunded and under-appreciated female athletes were confined to sandlots and backyard hoops, banned from major leagues and varsities. Ascribing the legislation as first proposed by Oregon Representative Edith Green and the brain child of educator Bernice Sandler (remember Kennedy was not a named sponsor of the bill), the statute known as Title IX had been drafted and introduced by Hawaii representative Patsy Mink, championed by Indiana Senator Birch Bayh and signed into law by

President Nixon on June 23, 1972. The 37 words that formed the basis of the legislation, a part of the education amendments of 1972, read: "No person in the United States shall, on the basis of sex, be excluded from participation in, be denied the benefits, or be subjected to discrimination under any educational program or activity receiving federal assistance."[50]

Anderson's article continues to argue that while the effect on opportunities in education has been profound—"the number of medical and law degrees going to women has jumped from 7 percent and 9 percent, respectively, in 1972 to 47 percent and 48 percent in 2010—the athletic gains have been seismic. According to a report provided by the Women's Foundation, 294,015 girls competed in high schools four decades ago. By 2011 the number had ballooned to 3,173,549.[51]

Graced with a picture of softball player Joelle Arrante of Rising Sun High in Northeast Maryland in 2002, Anderson's article claimed, "Title IX's effects extended into the classroom and beyond. Research suggests that the legislation has contributed to the rise in the number of women who work full time and who have moved into formerly male occupations."[52]

Anderson recognized in her article, however, that work still needed to be done. She noted that while opportunities in high school have increased for both girls and boys, girls have 1.3 million fewer chances to play. Anderson wrote that inequities in resources and resistance in equal access to women persists. However, Anderson concluded,

> The benefits of Title IX, to women and society, are almost incalculable. Girls who compete in sports get better grades, graduate at a higher rates and have more confidence. The vast majority avoid unplanned pregnancies, drugs, obesity, depression and suicide. Two generations of female athletes—who once could not venture closer than the sideline—have felt the adrenaline rush of competition, learned the value of teamwork, pushed themselves to their physical limits, then coped with the consequences of defeat. They have earned recognition, received scholarships, inspired celebration—even, yes, been drafted and made a living out of their talent.[53]

In the second article written by Anderson, titled "Olympic Movement," the journey of the women's Olympic championship basketball team in the 1996 games in Atlanta are chronicled. Noting that following the enactment of Title IX the NBA provided 3 million dollars in financial and marketing support, Anderson observes that Olympic success led to success in other sports, though monetizing the successes proved difficult.[54] As examples, Anderson describes that the women's soccer team rode the momentum in home-soil victory in the 1999 World Cup; the final game against China in the Rose Bowl remains the most attended women's sporting event in history (90,186). Moreover, of all the leagues that started for women, including the Women's United Soccer Association and the Women's Pro Fast Pitch, both of which shut down, the Women's Basketball National Association (WBNA) has defied the odds and remains a viable sport.[55] Anderson's example of the shining Olympic moment in Atlanta in 1996 demonstrates some of the good achieved by the enactment of Title IX.

The series of articles in *Sports Illustrated* also included one by Michael Bamberger, describing the actions of 19 female Yale rowers in 1976. The rowers were fed up with waiting on a bus every day after practice, sweating and stinking and cold, while their male counterparts took warm showers. And they resented that even after placing second and third in the national championships, they rowed in dingy boats while the men's were state of the art. Chris Ernst and 18 of her teammates, on a cold March day in 1976, marched into the office of Joni Barnett, the Director of Women's Sports. They made a bold political statement that would resonate around the country. They entered Barnett's office accompanied by a stringer for the *New York Times* and a photographer who both knew what was coming. When Barnett stood up to see what was going on, all 19 women removed their bulky blue sweatpants and sweatshirts and stood naked in front of her. On their chest and backs in bold letters were a single word and a roman number "Title IX." The message was clear: Yale, which first admitted women in 1969, needed to comply with federal law.[56]

That summer in Montreal, Ernst and Yale teammate Anne Warner were on the U.S. team at the first Olympics to include women rowing. Years later, Ernst still visits the new complex at Yale for women's rowing, called Guilder Boathouse, named for Richard Guilder, who contributed a million dollars for construction. Guilder's daughter Jayne had marched into Barnett's office with Ernst in 1976.

Melissa Segura, in the next article, provides a stirring example of the benefits of Title IX on women's sports. Maria Pepe tried out as an eleven-year-old for the boys' little league team in Hoboken, New Jersey, before the passage of Title IX in the spring of 1972. Amid doubts that she could play, Maria dominated the tryouts. But opposing coaches and parents protested Maria's participation, citing a little league bylaw that allowed boys only ages 8–12 to play. Her third game coach, Jimmy Farina, received a call from little league headquarters in Williamsport, Pennsylvania, stating that Maria needed to be dropped from the roster or the league would lose its charter. Farina refused, but Maria did not want to jeopardize her friends chance to play. So she handed over her gray jersey.[57]

The National Organization for Women (NOW) told Maria that she should be allowed to keep her roster spot. NOW filed a lawsuit on her behalf against the little league in New Jersey's Division on Civil Rights. On November 7, 1973, Civil Rights Examiner Sylvia Pressler rejected arguments made by lawyers for little league, among them that girls may suffer breast cancer if girls were to get hit in the chest with a ball. In the wake of the passage of Title IX, similar lawsuits against little league were being filed around the country, and in 1974, the organization amended its charter to include female players because "of the change in social climate." Since then, roughly 10 million girls have donned little league uniforms.[58]

The next article, "Spirits of '72," chronicles three Olympians born in 1972, the year of the enactment of Title IX. Lisa Leslie (basketball), Mia Hamm (soccer) and Summer Sanders (swimming) all came into the world in 1972. They were born at the perfect time to take advantage of opportunities the law helped to create. Each one holds national championships or individual titles and used their athletic success and popularity to earn lucrative endorsement deals. In retirement they have helped both boys and girls to find the power of sports.[59] The author of the article, Phil Taylor, describes that even with the existence of Title IX, Leslie remembers inequities, like the men's basketball players at USC staying in hotels the night before home games and having much better meals. She realizes that although conditions have improved, the legislation has not solved everything.[60]

Alexander Wolff, in an article titled "Winning at Political Football," describes Republican attempts to dismantle Title IX's impact just two years after its enactment. Republican Senator John Tower and Texas football coach and director Darrell Royal backed the Tower Amendment, which would exempt football and men's basketball from Title IX's compliance determinations. Senator Birch Bayh (Democrat from Indiana) and other friends of Title IX defeated the Tower Amendment and instead helped pass a rider offered by Senator Jacob Javis (Republican from New York) that directed the Health, Education and Welfare Committee to issue regulations that made "reasonable provisions considering the nature of particular sports."[61] Gender-equity advocate Donna Lopiano said that every few years after 1975, some party mounted a challenge to Title IX and every few years that party was turned away. According to Lopiano the message is clear: "Sue their school—her employer—on Title IX grounds."[62]

In an article by L. Jon Wertheim titled "When Billy Met Bobby," he reminisces about the 1973 battle of the sexes match between then women's champion Billy Jean King and Bobby Riggs, a 55 year old hustler. King crushed Riggs, and she has continued to be a tireless champion for equality in sports and other Title IX issues. She and Riggs grew close, and King spoke to him shortly before he died of prostate cancer in 1985. King states that Riggs said to her, "We made a difference. We really did. Didn't we."[63]

George Dohrmann, in "Chance to Be a Champion," describes the active role that the NCAA took in fighting the passage of Title IX, even taking the action of filing a lawsuit in 1976 in an attempt to have the legislation overturned. Then led by Executive Director Walter Byers, the organization had no interest in sharing the money designated for men's sports. The NCAA thought of women's sports as extracurricular activities, like taking a physical education class.[64]

In the meantime, an alternative model to the NCAA, the Association for Intercollegiate Athletics for Women (AIAW) was formed. The AIAW embraced many progressive policies. Athletes were free to transfer without having to sit out a year. Prospective athletes had to spend their own money for official visits, to help schools with bigger budgets from having a recruiting advantage. There was a code of ethics that guided scheduling appropriate practices and providing safe transfer for athletes.[65] By 1980, the NCAA realized Title IX was not going away and voted to begin offering championships for women sports. The article provides significant recognition of the efforts of the AIAW, an association scarcely known by many Americans.

Alexander Wolff, in "Father Figures," describes Herb Dempsey in 1992 watching cheerleaders in gowns escort members of Bethel High's football team to the front row of the homecoming gala, while his daughter Jan's volleyball team was only fleetingly recognized. Dempsey has since filed nearly 1,000 Title IX discrimination complaints; making a random check in 2007, he found he had been involved in more than 62.5 percent of the actions brought before the Office for Civil Rights in the state of Washington in the last ten years.[66]

The 1970s featured unlikely Title IX champions. In Illinois, Paul Bucha, a retired army colonel who had worked with Eisenhower to plan the Normandy invasion, sued to help enable his daughter Sandra to become a champion swimmer. In Delaware, a former big league pitcher and future manager Dallas Green lent the name of his nine-year-old daughter Kim to one of the lawsuits to help end the little league boys only policy. More recently, battles focused on girls' softball have been led by Ron Randolph, a firefighter in Oklahoma; Pat Egan, a contractor in Kentucky; and Russell Johnson, a pipe fitter in Alabama.[67]

Dempsey, now a grandfather, remains active in the cause. According to Dempsey, "It is hard to believe how bad it still is because people want to celebrate how good it has become."[68] As will be discussed in summarizing the effects of Title IX, Dempsey's comments prove prescient.

The last article in *Sports Illustrated*, written by Nancey Ramsey and titled "Testing the Waters," describes the efforts of Miami's Vice President of Student Affairs, William Butler, in persuading the Board of Trustees of Miami to approve 15 scholarships for women in golf, swimming and tennis. Sharon Berg of Miami won AIAW titles in the 200 and 400 freestyle as a freshman, and in her sophomore and junior years, the Hurricanes won two national championships. The squad was first-rate, but Berg and her teammates did not exactly travel in style. Older teammates drove the swimmers to swim meets in their own station wagons. Berg, now 56, teaches swimming to Stanford alumni and staff. She states, "I felt a responsibility to do really well because this was something new ... it was the feeling of being a pioneer. You do it right."[69]

The series of *Sports Illustrated* articles provides a one-sided glowing assessment of the achievements of Title IX. The articles ignore many unintended consequences of the act and the rash of litigation discussed earlier in this chapter.

Senator Kennedy has not commented in his writings on Title IX and its subsequent interpretations, nor has his biographers addressed the issue in any comprehensive fashion. Despite the glowing series of articles in *Sports Illustrated*, it is debatable that Title IX, then, given its problems that have surfaced over the years, stands as a "highlight" of Ted Kennedy's time in the Senate, as the *Boston Globe* has termed it.[70] Rather it reflects an emerging theme regarding Kennedy-backed legislation. While one can scarcely criticize Ted Kennedy for pressing the Immigration Act of 1965, the National Cancer Act of 1971 or Title IX of the Education Amendments of 1972, efforts marshaling the aftereffects of these well intentioned enactments fail in many respects.

Title IX and its subsequent regulatory interpretations, amendments and Court decisions construing it also shed light on the limitations of a senator's role. Conceiving of an idea and even sponsoring a bill only begins the process. As this and subsequent chapters show, originators of legislation frequently accede to compromise to major revisions and, in fact, often cannot claim credit for authoring the legislation finally signed by the president. Even then, agencies issue interpretations of such laws, and of course the courts ultimately have the final say on the reach and effect of the legislation. By this time, years have passed and a senator may well have moved on to other issues.

Title IX exemplifies this reality. First, the United States Supreme Court held the act did not apply to athletics. Next, Congress amended Title IX and made clear that it did apply to college sports. Next, a series of cases, most prominently *Cohen* and *Mansourian,* applied the amended law in light of all of the subsequent history.

Certainly a perfect senator should retain involvement through all such developments. Realistically, however, politics does not work in this fashion. To be sure, this provides no excuse. And as the first three chapters of this book demonstrate, Ted Kennedy did little if any follow up with respect to his first three critical pieces of legislation: The Immigration Act of 1965, The National Cancer Act of 1971, and Title IX of 1972.

This fact, not before revealed by Kennedy biographers, sheds considerable light on his legacy. A consummate Legislator cannot support initial legislation and then hide when subsequent regulations and enactments change the course of the original intent of the act. Surely, Ted Kennedy and virtually all senators fall into this trap. Nonetheless, in assessing the historical effectiveness of a Legislator, this has to factor in. On Title IX, Kennedy earns points on the original intent of eradicating sex discrimination in education. As a whole, though, his absence in any meaningful debate on the effects of regulations and further legislation stain his original accomplishments. Follow through, of course, means everything.

One point of view, deserving of attention, claims that a senator cannot be blamed for the unintended consequences of the enactment of initial legislation. These believers, they say, ascribe fault to subsequent events beyond the particular legislator's control.

A contrary position, espoused by many, view the role of a senator as a continuing obligation. Particularly if the initial proponent of legislation remains in Congress, constant monitoring of the course of the legislation, including attacking contrary regulations, seems appropriate.

Here, Kennedy had every opportunity to comment publicly on the very unusual course Title IX took over the years. In judging his role historically, Kennedy must have known of the expansive interpretation of Title IX, and one must conclude he supported the path since no historical evidence exists that he voiced objection.

With this in mind, though, Title IX enacted in 1972 does represent a continuation of Kennedy's focus on antidiscrimination efforts. Far ahead of his time, it would be wrong to judge Kennedy too harshly for the course Title IX eventually took.

Indeed, the controversy over Title IX persists today. In California, the Irvine University school district recently was sued by the National Women's Law Center, along with 11 other school districts in the United States, for allegedly failing to comply with Title IX requirements to offer equal sports opportunities to women.[71] Cassie Parham, an assistant superintendent for the Irvine schools and once a three-sport athlete, expressed surprise that her school district had allegedly violated Title IX:

> We pride ourselves in terms of multiple offerings.... I know I always felt that I had the chance to do everything sports-wise kids wanted. Kids at our school are very involved in many things. I just don't see any basis for this complaint.[72]

Data from 2004 to 2006 showed a growing gap of 10 percent between the number of men and women who play sports at the high school level in Irvine. Yet Ian Hanigan, public information officer for the Irvine District, said the data failed to show opportunities offered: "The analysis is somewhat flawed in that it looks only at participation rates."[73]

Since 2006, Irvine schools added women's lacrosse and offered eight sports for boys and girls. Eric Pearson, chairman of the College Sports Council, advocates changes in Title IX: "It's not like at the college level, where you have recruiting. It's far more difficult to achieve proportionality at the high school level."[74] Thus, nearly 30 years since its passage, the debate between allowing equal participation as the impetus for the law versus strict proportionality remains unanswered.

Notably, the three acts described in this book so far represent only

10 years of Ted Kennedy's 47 years in the Senate. Still a young senator at the time of passage of Title IX, 42-year-old Kennedy undoubtedly still had much to learn. His conduct in the Senate, therefore, cannot be judged by these first three Legislative enactments. The Watergate Era, Reagan presidency, and Clinton administration would all provide challenges for Ted Kennedy to establish his role in the Senate.

4

The Watergate Scandal and the Campaign Finance Reform Act of 1974

Given Ted Kennedy's high-profile involvement in Bobby Kennedy's campaign against Nixon in 1968, the Democratic leadership quickly and firmly asked Kennedy to take a low-key role in the Watergate hearings. "Although Kennedy's prominence kept him out of a direct role in the Watergate investigation, he remained involved at the edges."[1]

Watergate began in the aftermath of the United States Supreme Court decision ordering release of the Pentagon Papers. Nixon wished to plug any leaks and turned to John Ehrlichman to organize a staff in the Executive Office Building, called Plumbers. Nixon aide G. Gordon Liddy helped the Plumbers as did former CIA agent E. Howard Hunt. Within a month of the organization of the Plumbers, Ehrlichman authorized them to break into the psychiatric office of Lewis Fielding. Daniel Ellsberg, Fielding's patient, had leaked the Pentagon Papers to the *New York Times*. Whether Nixon originally knew about the break-in remains unclear. On Labor Day weekend, Hunt, Liddy, and others staged the break-in, only to find nothing of interest.[2] By itself, the break-in seemed petty, but the subsequent attempted cover up by Nixon doomed his presidency. Nixon's attempts to cover Watergate up "were crude, cynical and illegal acts to obstruct justice."[3]

The Watergate incident grew out of Nixon's irrational fear of the George McGovern campaign in 1972. McGovern, a senator from South Dakota, faced a formidable challenge in the primary from Edmund Muskie. Kennedy, like most analysts, thought Muskie would win the Democratic nomination. Kennedy plainly miscalculated in this regard. While Muskie won the New Hampshire primary on March 7, 1972, McGovern scared

Muskie with his strong showing. Then on April 4, 1972, McGovern beat Muskie in Wisconsin. By this time, Nixon thought that Ted Kennedy would emerge as a consensus candidate in a fractured primary. He assumed that Democratic leaders would not let McGovern prevail.

Some Democratic leaders thought so too, and at least Kennedy gave some consideration to the prospect of a deadlocked convention that might ask him to run. When Muskie dropped out of the primary race in April, Mayor Daley invited Kennedy to speak at his annual dinner party in Chicago and began word of a draft for a Kennedy nomination. The AFL-CIO's head, George Meany, who had no use at all for McGovern, asked Kennedy to consider accepting a draft, and initially thought he might not reject the idea.

In truth, Nixon's fears of a Kennedy opposition and optimistic views by others proved wrong. Kennedy could not shake the toll of Chappaquiddick nor adequately explain his actions that evening and after. Nixon also saw his reelection chances bolstered by another tragedy. On May 15, 1972, a deranged young man, Arthur Brenner, shot and severely wounded George Wallace. Wallace had run strongly in Democratic primaries, winning Florida, Tennessee and North Carolina, and finishing second in northern states such as Wisconsin, Indiana and Pennsylvania. Although Wallace stood no chance of winning the Democratic nomination, it seemed likely he would bolt the Democrats and run for president as an independent. If so, he stood to siphon millions of votes away from Nixon, given his right wing stances and background. This could, Nixon feared, lead to a Democratic victory in the national election in a divided vote by a divided American populace.

Nixon had won the 1968 campaign, following Bobby's death, largely on the hopes by Americans that he truly had a "secret plan" to get out of Vietnam. By 1972, no such plan emerged, and Nixon felt vulnerable. Wallace's injuries sparked Nixon's campaign chances. For while Wallace won the Maryland primary, where he had been shot, and Michigan the next day, the bullet had penetrated his spinal column and paralyzed him from the waist down. In chronic pain and a wheelchair, Wallace withdrew from the campaign.

As the primaries unfolded, Ted Kennedy embraced McGovern. Interestingly, even in the wake of continuing talks of a Kennedy convention draft, Bobby's children began campaigning for McGovern. And Ted Kennedy told columnist Anthony Lewis of the *New York Times*, a friend of JFK, that he favored McGovern and would endorse him.

By June 1992, McGovern seemed to have a safe margin in delegates. But he feared a late challenge by Hubert Humphrey, who had lost to Nixon in the 1968 campaign. Humphrey campaigned vigorously in the decisive California primary. Humphrey depicted McGovern as a radical, attempting to reach the moderates of the Democratic party in California. McGovern staggered to a narrow victory in California, but Humphrey's attacks on McGovern surely helped Nixon. Nixon relished the thought of repeating Humphrey's attacks in the national campaign ahead.

McGovern also blundered in his choice for a vice president running mate. McGovern first sought Ted Kennedy as his running mate, and in fact called him the night he received the official nomination. McGovern said that campaign polls showed that a Kennedy run for vice president would help him put Chappaquiddick behind him. Kennedy, though, declined. Kennedy's decision in this respect remains enigmatic. On the one hand, even if a McGovern/Kennedy ticket would have lost, the demons of Chappaquiddick would have aired and led to the possibility of a subsequent presidential campaign. On the other hand, Kennedy knew McGovern faced an uphill battle no matter who his running mate was. Kennedy, in the end, declined the vice presidential nomination, thus placing McGovern in a decided bind.

With polls showing McGovern far behind of Nixon, he scrambled to find a vice presidential nominee. Muskie and Humphrey had no interest, so McGovern finally settled on Senator Thomas Eagleton of Missouri. Nixon then got one more unexpected bit of good luck. Ten days after the end of the Democratic convention, Eagleton admitted that he had earlier in his life undergone electroshock therapy for depression. McGovern at first stood behind his running mate. But controversy over Eagleton's mental health intensified. Such revelations about depression today would likely have little repercussions. Millions of Americans take antidepressants and engage in various forms of talk psychotherapy. McGovern and Eagleton may well have seized the disclosure as an opportunity to raise to the forefront mental health issues, and the need for health care reform. Indeed, Kennedy had attempted to advance national health insurance in Congress, but to no avail. However, in 1972 depression remained a stark secret reviled by many. Average Americans, McGovern thought, would not embrace a candidacy who some might view as "crazy." Yet, McGovern truly could have rallied behind Eagleton and educated Americans on the subject. No doubt he would have garnered support from psychiatrists, and the American Medical Association (AMA), a strong lobby group.

Nonetheless, McGovern backed down and dispatched Eagleton, thereby displaying inconsistency and indecisiveness. McGovern settled on Sergeant Shriver, but by then his already uphill battle became even more implausible given his public foibles. Viewed as a bumbling left-of-center liberal, McGovern soon saw support even in his own party diminish. The AFL-CIO executive council refused to endorse him for the presidency. So did leaders of individual unions, especially in the building trades. These union groups, the backbone of Democratic regimes, virtually assured a resounding McGovern defeat. In addition, many working class Democrats, traditionally the heart of the party, also felt disaffected. Some regarded McGovern as a leftist who spoke for middle class liberals and intellectuals, but not the working man. In truth, McGovern stood as the most left-of-center presidential candidate for the presidency in history. Moreover, McGovern's campaign, ineffectual at best, had no central plan. As the election neared, McGovern had seemingly given up. With an anti–Vietnam platform but no defined, defensible plan, Nixon portrayed him as a political gadfly. In the face of this, in the 1972 election millions of one-time Democratic individuals voted for Nixon or refused to vote at all.

Nixon won a resounding victory in November 1972. He received 47.1 million votes, 60.7 percent of the total cast, to McGovern's 29.1 million. Nixon carried every state except Massachusetts and the District of Columbia. McGovern received 2 million fewer votes than Humphrey got four years before. Yet despite this lopsided victory, Nixon had demons in his closet. Whether or not he ordered the Watergate break-in during the summer of 1972 or not, Nixon's paranoia certainly contributed to the botched attempt.

Liddy and Hunt, the Plumbers, landed in Judge John Sirica's courtroom and a jury found them guilty in January 1973. A select Senate investigating committee, led by Sam Ervin of North Carolina, began to probe into the affair. By late August 1973, Nixon's counsel John Dean quit. Ervin's committee opened televised hearing.

Many have overemphasized Kennedy's role in the Watergate hearings, and the banishment of the president. Without question, Kennedy added his two cents regarding Nixon's deplorable conduct. Quoted in the *Boston Globe*, Kennedy decried Nixon's firing of Special Prosecutor Archibald Cox (actually carried out by then Solicitor General Robert

Bork) as "a reckless act of desperation by a president who is afraid of the Supreme Court, who has no respect for law and no regard for men of conscience."[4]

But other accounts border on hyperbole. In a recent biography of Ted Kennedy, Edward Klein asserts,

> Ted had his sights set on 1976. And Ted was under no illusions; he understood Nixon would stop at nothing to discredit him. That left Ted with little choice if he wanted to keep his 1976 hopes alive, he had to take on Richard Nixon.[5]

According to Klein, Kennedy set up a secret plan against Nixon, despite a senator he respected, Mike Mansfield, asking him to stay out of the fray:

> Ted had an unusually able man to assist him in the largely sub-rosa campaign that he waged against Richard Nixon. The man's name was Jim Flug and he was the Chief Counsel on Ted's Administrative Practices and Procedures Subcommittee of the Judiciary Committee. Working closely with Ted Kennedy, Jim Flug gathered a mountain of incriminating information against the Nixon administration, which was later used in the Watergate investigation.[6]

One can only characterize this description as fanciful. What information did Kennedy unearth that added to the pending investigation of Nixon and the Watergate hearings? Precisely what "incriminating information" did any of the main players in the Watergate hearings use from Kennedy's "sub-rosa campaign." Klein, recklessly, makes these assertions without any support. Indeed, Kennedy, who had created the Ad-Hoc subcommittee, writes, "I had indeed hesitated to advance my subcommittee, believing that an investigation would be more credible with the public if led by a chairman more conservative than myself."[7]

No doubt the main players in Watergate and Nixon's demise did not include Ted Kennedy. Sam Ervin, Judge Sirica and the United States Supreme Court all played a critical role. Historical evidence does not support the view of a main influence of Kennedy in Watergate. Ironically, despite the longstanding Kennedy/Nixon feud stemming from the 1960 presidential election, Ted Kennedy had, at best, a behind-the-scenes role during the Watergate era.

The lack of Kennedy's involvement in Watergate and the eventual resignation of Nixon as president cuts both ways. On the one hand, it points to Kennedy's diminished role as a senator following the Chappaquiddick scandal. First, Kennedy lost the majority whip position.

Next, Mansfield asked Kennedy to stay out of the mainstream attack on Nixon in the Watergate scandals. Had Chappaquiddick not occurred, Ted Kennedy undoubtedly would have run against Nixon in 1972, and may well have won. Relegated to a minor role in the party, Kennedy did not hold a position of national prominence in 1972 and through Nixon's ultimate resignation in 1974.

Nonetheless, according to some accounts, Ted Kennedy's role as senator soared post Watergate. The *Boston Globe* reported glowingly of a bipartisan effort with Republican Senate leader Hugh Scott, claiming he spearheaded the first campaign finance reform bill. As the *Boston Globe* reports,

> joining with Senator Hugh Scott Republican of Pennsylvania, Kennedy sponsored the sweeping overhaul of ethics rules after Watergate that imposed limits on contributions to political candidates and set up the public financing system for presidential candidates in 1974.[8]

The idea of campaign finance reform had deep roots. As far back as 1907, Theodore Roosevelt had proposed reform to avoid corruption in the expenditure of public funds in election campaigns. That year Congress passed the Tillman Act, which prohibited corporations and national banks from contributing money to federal campaigns. In 1910, federal campaign legislation affected House elections only. Amendments in 1911 covered Senate elections as well and set spending limits for all Congressional candidates.[9]

The Federal Corrupt Practices Act of 1925, which affected general election activity only, strengthened disclosure requirements and increased expenditure limits. The Hatch Act of 1939 and its amendments in 1940 enabled Congress to regulate primary elections and included provisions limiting the contributions and expenditures in Congressional elections. The Taft-Hartley Act of 1947 barred both labor unions and corporations from making expenditures and contributions in Federal elections.[10]

These campaign finance provisions failed to provide an institutional framework to administer their provisions effectively. The evasion of disclosure provisions led Congress to consolidate its earlier reform efforts in the Federal Election Campaign Act (FECA) of 1971. FECA instituted more stringent disclosure requirements for federal candidates, political parties and political action committees (PACs). Still, without a central administrative authority, enforcement of campaign finance reform remained difficult.[11]

Nonetheless, FECA achieved a degree of success. In 1968, House and Senate candidates reported spending only $8.5 million. In 1972, after the passage of FECA, spending reported by Congressional candidates jumped to $88.9 million.[12]

Prior to Watergate, though, campaign finance reform never garnered significant attention. Lax enforcement, the absence of an efficient administrative body and penalties for violations rendered FECA ineffective.

Thus, Kennedy biographer Adam Clymer states, "Watergate led Kennedy into major legislative efforts on election law reform, using the fundraising scandals unearthed by the Watergate investigations as an argument for using government (or taxpayers') money to pay for federal election campaigns."[13] In 1974, Congress did enact comprehensive amendments to FECA in the wake of Watergate.

But Clymer inaccurately describes Kennedy's role in the Campaign Finance Reform legislation. Kennedy did seek and obtain the backing of Republican leader Hugh Scott in a bill titled the "Congressional Election Financing Act,"[14] S. 4196, introduced on November 26, 1974. However, the bill never made it out of committee. The bill that passed, Senate Bill 3044, known as the "Federal Campaign Act Amendments of 1974," did not have Kennedy as a sponsor and passed *before* the Kennedy/Scott bill.[15]

Tracing the various bills regarding Campaign Finance Reform in 1974 sheds light on Kennedy's role. Starting with the Kennedy/Scott bill, S. 4196, a synopsis of the bill appears in the *Digest of Public General Bills and Resolutions*, 93rd Congress, on pages A-194 and A-195. The bill, introduced on November 26, 1974, requires a candidate for Federal office

> (1) to obtain and to furnish to the Commission all evidence it may request about his campaign expenditures and contributions; (2) to keep and to furnish to the Commission information it may request; (3) to permit an audit and examination for the Commission and to pay any amounts required; and (4) to furnish statements of campaign expenditures.[16]

Thus, for the first time the Kennedy/Scott bill would have created an independent regulatory agency, the Federal Election Commission, to administer and enforce campaign finance law.

Following each congressional election, the Kennedy/Scott proposal would have required "the commission [to] conduct a thorough examination and audit of the campaign expenditures of a candidate who received payments under this title."[17] Further, the proposed bill directed the Commission "to make available for public inspection summaries of all such statements."[18] Finally, the bill would have imposed a fine of $50,000 and/or up to five years imprisonment for violation of the proposed act.[19] But the Kennedy/Scott bill, curiously, came before the Finance Committee after passage of the Federal Campaign Act Amendment of 1974. S. 3044, sponsored by Howard W. Cannon and introduced on February 21, 1974, had as its co-sponsor Senator Howard Metzenbaum of Ohio.[20] The bill and its enactments predate the Kennedy/Scott bill, as disclosed by the following summary of major actions:

2/21/74 Introduced to Senate
2/21/74 Reported to Senate from the Committee on Rules and Administrations, S. Report 93–689
4/11/1974 Passed/Agreed to in Senate, amended roll call #146 (53–32)
8/8/1974 Committee House Administration discharged in House
8/8/1974 Passed/Agreed to in House: Measure passed in House, in lieu of H.R. 16090
10/7/1974 Conference report filed in House, H. Rept. 93–1438
10/7/1974 Conference report filed in Senate, S. Rept. 93–1237
10/8/1974 Conference report agreed to in Senate: Senate agreed to conference report, roll call # 466 (60–16)
10/10/1974 Conference report agreed to in House: House agreed to conference report roll call # 5–97 (365–24)
10/15/1974 Measure presented to President
10/15/1974 Signed by President
10/15/1974 Public law 93–443[21]

The corruption and abuses "of the electoral process uncovered during the Watergate investigations promoted the 1974 amendments to the Federal Election Campaign Act (FEC) which regulates financing of federal election campaigns."[22] The Campaign Reform bill that passed established the Federal Election Commission and imposed limitations on campaign contributions, an aggregate of $25,000 in case of an individual and $20,000,000 in the case of a candidate for the office of president.[23] The bill also imposed limitations on campaign expenditures. Finally, it also imposed criminal penalties for (1) excess campaign expenses; (2) unlawful use of payments; (3) false statements or information; and (4) kickbacks or illegal payments in violation of the provisions of the act.[24]

On October 15, 1974, President Gerald Ford signed into law the

Federal Election Campaign Act Amendments of 1974, Public Law No. 93–443. In a statement released regarding the act, President Ford said,

> Today I am signing into law the Federal [Election] Campaign Act Amendments of 1974.
>
> By removing whatever influence big money and special interests may have on our Federal electoral process, this bill should stand as a landmark of campaign reform legislation. In brief the bill provides for reforms in five areas:
>
> • It limits the amounts that can be contributed to any candidate in any Federal election, and it limits the amounts that those candidates can expend in their campaigns.
> • It provides for matching funds for presidential primaries and public financing for presidential nominating conventions and presidential elections through use of the $1 voluntary tax checkoff.
> • It tightens the rules on any use of cash, it limits the amount of speaking honorariums, and it outlaws campaign dirty tricks.
> • It establishes a bipartisan six member Federal Election Commission to see that the provisions of the act are followed.
>
> Although I support the aims of this legislation, I still have some reservations about it—especially about the use of Federal funds to finance elections. I am pleased that the money used for Federal financing will come from the $1 check off, however, thus allowing each taxpayer to make his own decision as to whether he wants his money spent this way. I maintain my strong hope that the voluntary contribution will not become mandatory and that it will not in the future be extended to Congressional races. And although I do have reservations about the first amendment implications inherent in the limitations on individual contributions and candidate expenditures, I am sure that such issues can be resolved in the courts.
>
> I am pleased with the bipartisan spirit that has led to this legislation. Both the Republican National Committee and the Democratic National Committee have expressed their pleasure with this bill, noting that it allows them to compete fairly. The times demand this legislation.
>
> There are certain periods in our Nation's history when it becomes necessary to face up to certain unpleasant truths. We have passed through one of those periods....
>
> This bill will help to right that wrong.
>
> I commend the extensive work done by my colleagues in both houses of Congress on this bill, and I am pleased to sign it today.[25]

By lending support to the bill, Ted Kennedy pursued a cautious and well-thought-out approach in the aftermath of Watergate. Watergate created a national fissure, indeed a Constitutional crisis so deep as to threaten United States democracy in a manner not seen since the Civil War. Many Democrats, seeking impeachment and criminal prosecution, wanted Nixon's head on a platter. To his credit, Jerry Ford, despite humiliating *Saturday Night Live* episodes about his mishaps and bumbling, gathered a torn nation and crafted a campaign reform bill in the aftermath of Watergate.

Technically a series of amendments to the Federal Election Campaign Act (FECA) of 1971, the 1974 bill provides private campaign contribution limitations as well as limitations on Public Action Committee (PAC) contributions.[26] Under the amendments, no private individual could contribute more than $1,000 to an electoral campaign and no PAC $5,000.[27]

Defenders of the amendments hail the limits as a method to deter "buying" electoral candidates with the concomitant result of the politician owing his financial backers. As Ted Kennedy said at the time, "At a single stroke, by enacting a program of public financing of federal elections, we can shut off the underground rivers of private money that pollute politics at every level of the federal government."[28] The idea, limiting private contributions, held wide appeal in the aftermath of the Watergate scandal. Kennedy, vocal in the aftermath of the bill's passage, once again avoided the limelight and sat back as a compromise legislative packet reached President Ford's desk. No doubt, though, Kennedy remained an ardent supporter of campaign finance reform even though his Kennedy/Scott bill did not become the law.

Opponents to campaign finance reform point out that the limitations favor incumbents by keeping new candidates from raising necessary funds to effectively compete in elections. Such critics point out that in 1974, following passage of the campaign finance reform amendments, 87.7 percent of House members who sought reelections won reelection.[29] According to the Heritage Foundation, a conservative group, by 1988 those members seeking reelection won 98.5 percent of the time.[30] Andrew J. Corwin points out that "(1) Congressmen already receive public financing exceeding 1.5 million per election cycle in the form of franked mail, staff support and other resources that increase their reelection prospects; and (2) campaign spending limits diminish electoral competition even more by limiting challengers' ability to spend the funds necessary to achieve name recognition with voters."[31]

Tracking such statistics to the 1974 reforms oversimplifies the incumbent advantage. Historically incumbents always have experienced significant advantages and won reelection by large margins. These critics ignore the statistics pre–1974. Nonetheless, the private spending limitations no doubt have favored incumbents, who have built-in use of federal funds while in office.

Of course, the argument that more competitive elections will occur with an increase in private political donations favors conservatives in many respects. Usually tied to high-income backers and big business, such challengers would benefit from loosening of private donation rules. In fact, while campaign finance reform still remains prominent today, the strident results of the 1974 and 2010 midterm elections demonstrate that, when conditions dictate, the power of incumbency loses its clout. Yet, in such other periods, name recognition and the tremendous financial resources available to incumbents leads to predictable results in "safe" districts.

The incumbency issue—plainly a valid concern—does not simply reflect flaws in the 1974 reforms. Rather, combating the problem requires further reforms, not an elimination of reforms in place. Challengers would benefit from required debates, thereby preventing powerful incumbents from hiding behind their office. So, too, resurrection of the Fairness Doctrine, allowing equal access to television and radio media, would foster increased competitiveness. Redistricting, meaning a hard look at how Congressional districts are set up to favor incumbents, also needs to be addressed in a bipartisan fashion. The problem, though, consists of the fact that partisanship currently reigns at such a heightened level as to preclude a reasoned current approach on this issue.

The 1974 reforms to FECA, however, just as President Ford predicted, soon faced judicial challenges. A lawsuit filed by James C. Buckley (Republican senator of New York) and Eugene McCarthy (former Democratic senator from Minnesota), attacked key features of the 1974 amendments to FECA as unconstitutional.[32] The United States Supreme Court upheld limitations on campaign contributions due to the actuality and appearance of corruption. The Court held, however, that the restrictions in campaign expenditures could not withstand constitutional scrutiny.

In *Buckley*, the Court struck down as violating the First Amendment those portions of the FECA Amendments of 1974 that imposed a ceiling on (1) independent expenditures on behalf of a specifically designated candidate; (2) a $25,000 ceiling on expenditures by a candidate from his or her personal or family funds; and (3) a limit on aggregate campaign expenditures by any one candidate.[33] The Court equated political expenditures with political speech and subjected the direct limitations to the strictest scrutiny.[34]

On the other hand, the Court upheld contributions limitations, including (1) a $1,000 limit on contributions by individuals or groups to any candidate for federal office; (2) a $25,000 limit on the aggregate contributions that an individual may make annually to all political campaigns; and (3) a $5,000 limit on contributions by political committees.[35] According to the Court, the state interest in limiting contributions as a hedge against campaign corruption sufficiently outweighed the contributors' free speech interests.[36]

Notably, the *Buckley* decision also found that the method for appointing FEC Commissioners violated the constitutional principles of separation of powers. Under the 1974 amendments, the president, the Speaker of the House and the president pro tempore of the Senate each appointed two of the six voting commissioners. As a result of the *Buckley* decision, the president appointed the six commissioners, subject to confirmation by the Senate.

Subsequent amendments and litigation refined the act further. But campaign finance reform still remained a hot topic after the 1974 amendments. Indeed, amendments in 1988 have received significant criticism as well. According to Cowin, in August 1988 Congress "voted to force taxpayers to help fund incumbent reelections while making it difficult for the challenger to become as well known as the incumbent."[37] Cowin recommends certain reforms, worthy of thought:

> Challengers in House races should be allowed to raise up to $400,000 in contributions of any size. Although this does not approach the $11.5 million in perks that a congressman can spend over a two year term, it at least allows a challenger to raise enough money to begin a discussion of the issues and the incumbent's record.[38]

In addition to this proposal, Cowin offers a scathing assessment of the campaign reform legislation:

> The measures passed by Congress do little to alter the system of influence-peddling that now dominates Washington.... Another Congress passed reform that fails to address the underlying causes of congressional influence-peddling is that limiting political action committee (PAC) contributions.... If the goal of campaign finance reform is to reduce influence-peddling, *full public reporting of all campaign contributions is the only applicable reform.*[39]

As with many bills, further amendments to refine well-intentioned ideas plainly need to occur. So too with the Campaign reforms of 1974. And the United States Supreme Court recently added a wrinkle, voting five to four that the First Amendment prohibited limitations on corporate donations to candidate campaigns.[40] In the *Citizens United* case, Justice Kennedy, writing for a bare 5–4 majority, expressly overruled prior Supreme Court precedent, including a case decided just seven years earlier and a prior case.[41] In a brazen opinion, Justice Kennedy dispatched in one sentence the long-honored tradition of the Supreme Court following its own precedents, called *stare decisis*. Kennedy and the conservative majority, Chief Justice Roberts, Samuel Alito, Clarence Thomas and Antonin Scalia, held simply that "*stare decisis* does not compel the continued acceptance of *Austin*."[42] In a lengthy decision, espousing corporate "free speech," the *Citizens United* Court concluded that corporations had no restrictions on federal campaign expenditures.

In dissent, Justice John Paul Stevens, writing with the concurrence of Justices Ginsburg, Breyer, and Sotomayor, took issue with the Court's majority rewriting the law relating to campaign expenditures for profit corporations and unions, as well as the non-profit corporation at issue in the case. Justice Stevens noted that limitations on corporate spending existed since the passage of the Tillman Act in 1907. Justice Stevens lamented the Court rejecting the long-standing consensus on the need to limit corporate spending.

The decision, in essence, eviscerates campaign finance reform efforts long championed by Ted Kennedy. Of course, back in 1974, in the wake of the Watergate scandal and a Supreme Court that actively facilitated the truth, could Kennedy ever envision a decision that basically abolished the campaign finance reform he cherished and supported? Nor, or course can Kennedy bear blame for this unforeseen development. *Citizens United*, issued after Kennedy's death by an all-too-familiar 5–4 conservative majority of the United States Supreme Court, ironically rebukes the very limitations the conservative Cowin of the Heritage Foundation has advocated. And as far as Kennedy's legacy, one can only envision him taking the Senate floor excoriating the decision, had he lived. Certainly, Kennedy's devotion to campaign finance reform cannot be judged by this decision.

Indeed, in a scathing rebuke of the Supreme Court, its members sitting right in front of him, President Obama in his State of the Union speech on January 22, 2010, urged Congress to enact legislation to overturn the decision. Of course, President Obama had every right to voice his view and urge Congress to enact legislation with roots of almost 40 years. In a rare instance of judicial intemperance, Associate Justice Samuel Alito audibly mouthed the words "you are wrong" to President Obama. Surely, then, the debate on campaign finance reform will continue in full force in the years to come.

5

From Carter to Reagan and the Comprehensive Anti-Apartheid Act of 1986

According to the *Boston Globe*, in 1986 after "Reagan vetoed economic sanctions against the apartheid government of South Africa in 1986, Kennedy spearheaded the bipartisan effort in both Houses to override the veto. The law banned the purchase of gold, coal, iron, and other goods from South Africa."[1] A Ted Kennedy biographer, Adam Clymer, states:

> Just as he had stepped forward to fill a gap in civil rights ... as 1984 drew to a close Kennedy began to make South Africa an issue. Countries around the world were growing more and more impatient with the apartheid regime, under which Africans could not vote, own land, or move about the country freely. But while American universities, unions and some cities pushed to unload stocks in companies that did business there and hundreds were demonstrating and being arrested at the South African embassies in Washington, the Reagan administration was singularly supportive of the government.[2]

What precisely was Ted Kennedy's role in anti-apartheid legislation?

To answer this question requires an overview of Ted Kennedy's actions in the decade preceding the apartheid controversy. Concurrent with campaign reform and the Watergate scandal, America witnessed a Constitutional crisis live and televised. As Watergate unfolded through the trials of the conspirators before Judge Sirica, Nixon turned over tapes ordered by Sirica. One of the tapes contained the famous 18 1/2-minute gap—purportedly erased by accident by Nixon secretary Rosemary Woods. Woods volunteered that the erased portion involved a key discussion between Nixon and Haldeman. The erasure aroused a further storm of suspicion.

The Nixon presidency soon began to crumble precipitously. In late 1973, Vice President Spiro Agnew, who himself had presidential aspirations, the media disclosed, had accepted kickbacks from contractors while governor of Maryland and even while vice president. Agnew, long a controversial vice presidential choice, stood no chance of surviving. With the media strongly against him, Agnew made little effort to secure his position. On October 10, 1973, Agnew resigned as vice president in disgrace, pleading no contest to all charges of tax evasion. Nixon tapped House GOP leader Gerald R. Ford as Agnew's replacement.

Ford, a well-respected Congressional leader, soon would have fate hand him the daunting task of healing a nation. On March 1, 1974, the Grand Jury indicted seven members of the White House staff, including Haldeman, Ehrlichman and Mitchell, of obstruction of justice and impeding the Watergate investigation. The Grand Jury named Nixon as an unindicted co-conspirator. Both Sirica and the House Committee subpoenaed the many tapes Nixon still had in his possession. Nixon continued to resist, and provided Judge Sirica heavily edited tapes. Sirica insisted that Nixon turn over the entire tapes, but Nixon refused, citing executive privilege. Nixon took the case to the United States Supreme Court. On July 24, 1974, the Court decided unanimously that the executive privilege did not apply in the Watergate case, a criminal matter, and ordered Nixon to surrender all the tapes to Judge Sirica. The House of Representatives then began nationally televised hearings on articles of impeachment. The House, on July 30, voted to impeach Nixon for obstruction of justice concerning the Watergate investigation.

While the House committee voted for impeachment proceedings, Nixon's lawyers listened to the tapes. They heard Nixon order the CIA to stop the FBI from investigating just six days after the break-in. This served as the "smoking gun" that cinched, for many, the case against the president. Republican leaders began urging Nixon to resign from the presidency. These included Henry Kissinger, General Alexander Haig, Senator Barry Goldwater, and Republican national chairman George Bush. Rather than prolong the inevitable, on August 8, 1974, Nixon gave a rambling speech resigning from the presidency. Sweating profusely, Nixon walked up to fly away from the White House, pitifully signaling his peace sign. Gerald Ford was sworn in as president the next day.

Today, a museum in Whittier California, Nixon's birthplace, presents a decidedly different picture of perhaps our most enigmatic president. Extolling his foreign policy virtues, the museum in its initial movie presentation and throughout makes short shrift of Watergate. Instead, it focuses on the many perceived enemies of Nixon. Nonetheless, both Nixon and his wife are buried there, and the scene is moving. Visiting the museum sheds considerable light on certain perceptions of Nixon.

Ford, though, wasted no time in attempting to heal the nation. On September 8, 1974, Ford pardoned Nixon. While Kennedy decried the pardon in a stump speech, by all accounts Kennedy held respect for President Ford. Even though initial reports signaled a possible Kennedy campaign against Ford, Kennedy soon disabused the nation of that concept. In fact, within the very first few months of Ford's presidency, Kennedy collaborated with him and Congressional leaders in putting the final stamp on campaign finance reform.

Ford took his lumps for pardoning Nixon. Following the pardon, Ford's public approval rating plummeted in the polls. As measured by the Gallop Poll, Ford had a 76 percent approval rating in August, only to see it plummet to 56 percent after the pardon, and 50 percent by the end of September. Yet, Ford steered the nation through an unprecedented Constitutional crisis.

Nonetheless, many politicians viewed Ford as a ponderous public speaker and an unimaginative party regular. Journalists reveled in dissecting Ford's speeches, and popularized a growing sentiment of Ford as inept. With the show *Saturday Night Live* at its most popular, comedian Chevy Chase made a living out of mocking Ford. So, too, Ford's golf mishaps, including stray shots hitting observers in the audience, garnered attention.

This view of Ford as a bumbling president truly underestimates his accomplishments in his short presidency. To be sure, Ford took on the role as a "caretaker" trying to salvage a divisive nation from a Constitutional crisis. In retrospect, most Americans now understand better than in the throes of the times that Ford acted in the nation's best interest in pardoning Nixon and ending the long national debate on Watergate. Consider the other choice. If Nixon had gone through an arduous public trial, the nation would have remained deeply divided. By putting the debate on Nixon to an end, Ford attempted to return America to normalcy.

In addition, far from a party regular, Ford's scant legislative record reveals a great degree of moderate efforts. Despite two attempts on his life, he traveled widely and held 39 press conferences in his 875 days in office. Despite his accessibility, Ford stood an almost insurmountable task trying to win reelection in the wake of Watergate. With domestic and foreign relations problems putting Ford on the defensive, he had to fight off an unexpected challenge from right wing candidate Ronald Reagan. Ford fought hard, using presidential patronage to his advantage. Ford won the GOP ballot by a narrow margin, and then named Kansas Senator Robert Dole as his vice presidential running mate.

Ford knew, though, that his pardon of Nixon left him wide open for a frontal assault by Democratic foes. But Ford, to his credit, made a swift decision upon ascendency to the presidency that he would risk his political future in favor of ridding the nation from the disgrace of Watergate. While the pardon decision may well have doomed his 1976 presidency campaign, in retrospect Ford's pardon decision not only seems defensible, but assuredly helped America move forward.

As in 1972, Ted Kennedy chose not to run for president in 1976. He told the country:

> There is absolutely no circumstance or event that will alter the decision. I will not accept the nomination. I will not accept a draft. I will oppose any effort to place my name in nomination in any state or at the national convention, and I will oppose any effort to promote my candidacy in any other way.[3]

Despite not running for the presidency in 1976, Kennedy always had a distant relationship with the eventual nominee, Jimmy Carter.[4] Carter, a true outsider and hardly known before the primaries, used his lack of political experience as governor of a small southern state, Georgia, to his advantage. Vowing to not succumb to the political lobbyists who influenced so-called insiders, Carter's theme attracted many Americans still stunned by Watergate. Carter thus kept his distance from the Democratic party leadership. Kennedy, though, did stump for Carter in Massachusetts, hardly a battle state, and focused on health care: "[W]e can have a decent health care program, so that no mother that hears her sick child call in the night has to make a decision whether the child is $30 or $40 sick because that is what it costs to go to the hospital."[5]

Carter remains one of the most enigmatic figures in history. Most people who knew Carter in these times considered him a decent, gracious, and compassionate man. Yet Carter, despite Ted Kennedy's definitive pronouncements—promises kept—that he would not run in 1976, always viewed Kennedy with distrust. In 1977, when Carter entered the White House, it seemed that he had qualities that would bring him success as president. In those early days Carter reiterated his pledge that he would bring fresh approaches to government and keep his distance from Washington insiders.[6] This led, however, to Carter shunning insights from such political veterans as Ted Kennedy, who surely could have helped him in his presidency.

While coming in as an outsider, in reality Carter needed Senate and Congressional approval to foster his goals and fortify his reputation with the voting populace. Kennedy biographer Adam Clymer calls Kennedy, at least initially, "a consistent ally of Carter in 1977."[7] Kennedy voted with Carter more than three-fourths of the time. Kennedy fought, unsuccessfully, for Carter's tax reforms and supported Carter's energy plan.

Yet, by midsummer 1977, Carter's glow had dimmed and many, including Ted Kennedy, grew increasingly disenchanted. James Fallows, a presidential speechwriter, wrote a decidedly uncomplimentary two-part essay concerning Carter's presidency. Carter, he wrote, had proven complacent, arrogant and lacking in sophistication. Like his overconfident Georgia aides, Carter had entered the White House with a "blissful ignorance" about how to work with Congress. Carter, indeed, surrounded himself with local political cronies who had no experience at the national level. He persistently refused efforts at collaboration with experienced legislators. Alienating potential allies such as Kennedy did not serve Carter well. Fallows complained, especially, of the passionless nature of the Carter administration.[8] Indeed, he exuded negativity rather than a positive plan or outlook for the United States.

As his term progressed, Carter continued to make mistakes, thereby alienating the very Washington insiders he needed for his agenda. Early in 1977, Carter rejected help offered by House Speaker Tip O'Neil to develop productive relations with his colleagues on Capitol Hill. Carter, a loner, workaholic and micromanager, by late 1977 had ruffled enough feathers that many rumors began to persist of a Democratic primary challenge by Ted Kennedy.

Indeed, Kennedy achieved little during the checkered Carter presidency. However, Kennedy persisted with a theme consistent with his past legislation. Just as the Immigration Act of 1965, Title IX Amendments to the Education Act of 1972 and Campaign Finance Reform efforts in 1974 sought to end discrimination and assist the poor, Kennedy echoed his overarching aim in 1978, when he warned of "the great unmentioned problem of America today. The growth, rapid and insidious of a group in our midst, perhaps most dangerous, more bereft of hope, more difficult to confront, than any for which our history has prepared us. It is a group that threatens to become what America has never known—a permanent underclass in our society."[9]

Having won barely 50 percent of the popular vote of a fractured American populace stung by Watergate, Carter never understood that he lacked a strong popular mandate. Many liberals began to chafe at Carter's deregulation efforts. Further, Carter's second State of the Union address, deplored by many of his supporters, stated that "government cannot resolve our problems…. I cannot eliminate poverty or, provide a bountiful economy, or reduce inflation, or save our cities, or cure illiteracy, or provide energy."[10] Carter then effectively had disengaged his support. Carter's election stemmed from a desire for positive government change, not throwing up his hands and proclaiming no ability to do anything. This disaffected many prior Democrat supporters who wondered if Carter had a clue where to steer the nation.

By 1979, Kennedy began to criticize Carter on health care and energy policy. Kennedy attributes Carter's lack of priority in pressing health care reform as souring their already tenuous relationship:

> And so Jimmy Carter and I did find common cause in certain areas, after a fashion. The overreaching political cause for me, however, was health insurance, and that is where the comity really broke down between us. In fact, health care and health insurance were the issues that damaged our relations beyond repair.[11]

On June 11, 1979, with polls showing Democrats preferring Kennedy to Carter by margins over two to one, Carter told several Congressmen over dinner that if Kennedy ran, he would "whip his ass."[12] Increasingly, "many influential liberals, led by Ted Kennedy who had set his sights on running for president in 1980, considered Carter to be a hick from Plains who had been lucky to reach the highest office in the land."[13]

Although only Kennedy himself knows when he decided to run, Kennedy biographer Adam Clymer attributes Carter's July 11, 1979, "malaise" speech as the turning point. "The malaise speech was probably the last outside influence on Kennedy's decision to run."[14] That speech, with Carter in a sweater in front of a fireplace, asked Americans already hurt by a teetering economy with double-digit inflation to sacrifice. It did not go well with the nation, nor with the Democratic party. When Kennedy announced his candidacy in the fall of 1979, "liberals having stewed since 1977 over Carter's fiscal conservatism, rallied during the campaign behind Ted Kennedy."[15]

Kennedy announced his candidacy for president on November 7, 1979. By all accounts, Kennedy's campaign, for reasons unknown, lacked coherence. Having witnessed JFK's successful campaign for the presidency in 1960 and RFK's inspired 1968 campaign, it seems hard to fathom that Ted Kennedy could not mount a considered and organized campaign against Carter. Certainly, Kennedy insiders clamored for the opportunity to mount a successful Ted Kennedy campaign. None thought much of Carter, and viewed him as a liability. Kennedy had a plethora of seasoned advisors to guide him. His brother's top advisors would have relished the opportunity to steer the campaign and provide Ted Kennedy guidance. Yet, Kennedy stumbled, repeatedly. Even a recent supportive Kennedy book pulls no punches:

> For Ted, it would start and end badly. Almost as soon as the applause ended at Faneuil Hall, Democrat loyalists and outsiders alike found themselves shocked by the sorry state of his early campaign.... The whole effort felt like a drive-by operation. He was late, low on money and organization.[16]

Over time Kennedy's campaign picked up, and he won decisive victories in California and New Jersey.

One issue Kennedy failed to seize on remains baffling. Under Carter's watch, the Iran hostage crisis unfolded. As day after day went by, including a botched rescue attempt, Carter's support diminished appreciably. Kennedy excoriated Carter over the hostage crisis but offered no real plan on solutions. Still, the crisis so hammered on an otherwise grim Carter presidency, Ted Kennedy had a great opportunity. He had many options. Kennedy could have rallied party regulars for a change and convinced voters that under his regime he would free the hostages either through more intensive diplomacy or additional military action. Here Kennedy stood a real chance to portray himself as a strong Commander-in-Chief, in contrast to Carter, who a nation now viewed as weak and ineffective. Kennedy simply failed to take advantage of this opportunity to contrast his experience with Carter's.

Kennedy came up short in the primaries, however, and unless he could change the rules that bound delegates to vote for their candidate, he stood no chance of victory at the Democratic convention, held in New York City in Madison Square Garden. Kennedy ended up getting much of what he wanted on the Democratic platform but as expected, he lost on the rule change 1930–1390. Some, but not nearly enough, Carter delegates abandoned him. "Enjoying the advantages of presidential incumbency and patronage, Carter outlasted Kennedy and won renomination on the first ballot."[17] After the rules change vote, Kennedy called Carter to congratulate him on his defeat.

With Carter having mercilessly relegated Kennedy to a non-prime-time speech, showing his continued antipathy toward Kennedy, Kennedy still triumphed. Disavowing both Carter's skepticism of government's role and Ronald Reagan's clear campaign promise to erase many of the gains of American liberals from the New Deal onward, Kennedy, while acknowledging that programs may become obsolete, still championed fairness and compassion. Kennedy told the national audience,

> Our cause has been, since the days of Thomas Jefferson, the cause of the common man—and the common woman. Our commitment has been since the days of Andrew Jackson, to all those humble members of society—the farmers, mechanics and laborers. On this foundation, we have defined our values, refined our policies, and refreshed our faith.[18]

Kennedy, of course, denounced Reagan for calling unemployment insurance a vacation plan for freeloaders. And he seized on Reagan's remarks that fascism was really the basis of the New Deal. Finishing his speech, Kennedy resorted to an emotional plea: "For all those whose cares have been our concern the work goes on, the cause endures, the hope still lives, and the dream shall never die."[19]

Perhaps the highlight of his career, the 1980 Democratic convention speech in Madison Square Garden catapulted Kennedy into a role not as a future presidential nominee, but rather an influential senator, despite Chappaquiddick, who would shape American policy over the next three decades.

By 1980, Kennedy had 18 years in the Senate and had forged modest gains through sponsored legislation. His fame—or notoriety—came from actions outside the Senate, including his support of RFK's campaign, Chappaquiddick and his run for the presidency.

But he soon faced working with a fiercely conservative president, Ronald Reagan. Ironically, Kennedy gained stature in the Senate by opposing Reagan policies. This stood in stark contrast to his uneasy role during the Carter presidency when he felt stifled to actively oppose a president in his own party who he never admired. As Kennedy writes,

> I realized at the outset that Reagan's ascendancy would require a fundamental adjustment of my role in the Senate. For the first time in my career I found myself in the minority party. More challenging still, many colleagues whom I counted as reliably liberal began to move right from the issues we had championed together over the years.[20]

The 1981–1984 era, under the Reagan presidency, proved a fresh new challenge for Kennedy. Returning to the Senate in 1981, Kennedy faced the reality that nine Democratic incumbents had lost, including strong liberal voices like Idaho's Frank Church, South Dakota's George McGovern, his close friend Birch Bayh and Iowa's John Culver. Kennedy now served in the minority, and victories came rare indeed. Ironically, though, Kennedy thrived in this most difficult situation. As Garry Wills noted, "Kennedy is at his best when he is not running."[21] Kennedy now had to deal with a president who opposed affirmative action, choice and big government. Reagan stood stubbornly and proudly on the right wing of his party.

But Reagan did not wage a war for social conservatism. Rather, he focused the beginning of his presidency on foreign affairs, gloating that the Iran hostages returned under his watch, not Carter's. Reagan, unfortunately, completely ignored the ceaseless diplomatic efforts of Warren Christopher, Deputy Secretary of State under Carter, who met the hostages in Algiers and oversaw their safe departure. But Christopher, the consummate statesman, let Reagan take the credit and remained silent as to his intensive and exhausting efforts that resulted in the freeing of the hostages.

Reagan also concentrated on increasing expenditures on the military, cutting domestic spending on social welfare and reducing federal income taxes by 30 percent. Called supply side economics, Reagan adopted the view that by cutting taxes, even while dramatically increasing military expenditures, the economy would strengthen because people would spend more of their disposable income. The trickle-down theory, as it became known, gained popularity in the early Reagan years.

Kennedy chose his fights carefully, realizing that he needed to tread carefully with a Senate now controlled by Republicans for the first time in his nearly two decades in the Senate. Not surprisingly, given the emerging theme of his time as a senator, Kennedy chose civil rights as his battleground: "Civil rights had defined him as a senator and a leader and he was determined to be the firewall against President Reagan's efforts to roll back some of the hard won victories of the previous 20 years."[22] His first big fight came quickly, starting in 1981, the year Reagan took office. The Voting Rights Act of 1965, scheduled to expire, needed another extension. Kennedy reached across the aisle to Maryland Republican Charles "Mac" Mathias, as well as Republican Bob Dole and Charles

Grassley, to forge a compromise necessary to extend the bill that Kennedy initially could not get enacted back in 1965.

Kennedy also gained his first Committee chairmanship on the Armed Service Committee. He worked with Reagan on reforming the federal criminal code.[23] He did not run for president in 1984, and "Ted played no role in the first six months of the 1984 presidential campaign. Mondale sought his endorsement after winning the Iowa caucuses and was annoyed when Kennedy held back."[24] Mondale tried to sway the nation from the Reagan tide through a number of innovative efforts, but to no avail. Most notably, hoping to stir the women's vote, Mondale tapped Geraldine Ferraro as his vice presidential nominee. Ferraro, the first female chosen as a vice presidential candidate, could not help defeat an incumbent president presiding over a then-healthy economy and viewed as a strong militarist. Reagan swept to victory to serve a second term, humiliating Mondale and the Democratic party in a decisive defeat and a clear mandate for Reagan's policies.

Considering his commitment to equality and antipathy toward discrimination, Kennedy turned his attention to South Africa and the apartheid regime. Kennedy arrived in Johannesburg on January 5, 1985. He then toured Soweto, dismayed by the conditions. Kennedy told reporters,

> This camp is one of the most distressing and despairing visits that I have made to any facility in my lifetime. Here individuals are caught between trying to provide for their families or living with their families. That's alien to every kind of tradition in the Judeo-Christian ethic and I find it appalling today.[25]

Reagan did not visit South Africa, nor did he denounce apartheid. Social equality did not rank high on the Reagan agenda.

Rather, Reagan supported a policy called "constructive engagement." Chester Crocker, Reagan's Assistant Secretary of African American Affairs, designed the strategy. First described in an article in *Foreign Affairs* in 1981 shortly before Crocker assumed his post, constructive engagement was to use quiet diplomatic means to encourage an end to apartheid in South Africa, to foster an atmosphere conducive to resolving regional conflicts in southern Africa, and to secure independence of Namibia.[26]

Yet, as countries around the world grew more and more impatient with the apartheid regime in South Africa, under which Africans could not vote, own land or move about the country freely, the Reagan administration continued to support the government: "Reagan lifted embargoes imposed by Jimmy Carter and the State Department ... [and] argued that economic and diplomatic ties encouraged South Africa to reform its policies."[27] In truth South Africa had no intention of changing its racist policies, and Reagan's "constructive engagement" policy has proven to be one of the most serious blights on his presidency.

Soon after he returned from South Africa, Kennedy began discussing legislation to address apartheid in a manner far different than "constructive engagement":

> The measure the senators agreed on had four provisions. It prohibited new loans by U.S. banks to the government of South Africa, new investment in South Africa by U.S. companies, the sale of computers to the South Africa government, and the importation of Kruggerrands, a gold coin prized by collectors and people who wanted to possess precious metal, which U.S. law forbade private ownership of except as jewelry or coins.[28]

On March 7, 1985, Kennedy and Republican Senator Lowell Weicker introduced the Anti-Apartheid Act of 1985 in the Committee on Banking, Housing and Urban Affairs.[29] Kennedy told the press, "We cannot continue policies that actually encourage Americans to invest in racism or profit from apartheid.... There will be stronger steps to come if South Africa continues its oppressive ways."[30]

The Kennedy-Weicker bill did not require businesses to leave South Africa, but sought immediate sanctions. Reagan opposed sanctions and instead continued his policy of "constructive engagement."[31] On April 3, 1985, though, Kennedy got the Senate to pass a resolution condemning apartheid, which passed 89–4. On the question of apartheid, Kennedy told the Senate, "The United States should speak in one voice."[32]

Although teaming up with Republican Lowell Weicker, Kennedy found crossing Reagan difficult. On June 4, 1985, the Foreign Relations Committee defeated the Kennedy-Weicker bill by a 9–7 party line margin. But Christopher Dodd cited a Republican-backed bill and pushed through two sanctions sought by Kennedy: the ban on bank loans to the government and the ban on computer sales.[33]

The bill stalled, however, as divisiveness in the Senate and Reagan's lack of support for the act led to a series of conflicts. Not until October 1986 did Congress pass the Comprehensive Anti-Apartheid Act. Reagan originally vetoed "economic sanctions against South Africa's apartheid regime in 1986, [but] he conceded defeat only after Congress overruled his veto."[34]

The Comprehensive Anti-Apartheid Act of 1986, while a watered down version of the original Kennedy-Weicker bill, represented a significant victory for Kennedy in his role as a minority party senator. According to one writer,

> the passage of the 1986 Comprehensive Anti-Apartheid Act marked one of the great legislative failures of the Reagan presidency. Although President Ronald Reagan suffered other defeats on foreign policy questions before Congress, the Anti-Apartheid Act was the most direct. He refused to compromise. Thus, his party deserted him and helped override his veto. While factors in both the international and domestic environment may have made any other outcome impossible, nimble footwork and a better legislative strategy may have prevented such a defeat.[35]

The legislation included a series of sanctions vehemently opposed by Reagan, including "barring import of South Africa coal, iron, steel, Krugerrands, and agricultural products; ending landing rights in the Unites States for the government-owned South Africa airways, banning new corporate investment in South Africa and any new loans to government agencies; prohibiting U.S. banks from accepting deposits from any South Africa government (SAG) agency and loans to South Africa government agencies; banning exports of computers to SAG agencies enforcing apartheid; prohibiting petroleum or crude oil exports; banning exports of Munitions List items; and providing for further sanctions if the SAG failed to take further actions to end apartheid."[36]

However, Reagan's tepid response to the sanctions limited its reach. According to a contemporaneous report by the Congressional Research Service,

> while the Administration generally followed the Act's requirements, it continued to espouse a policy of constructive engagement. Some might question the Administration's intentions because it still expresses disapproval of the use of sanctions and has not yet called for formal, public negotiations to coordinate multinational sanctions as directed by the Act.[37]

Indeed, the CRS reports states: "The Administration supports the policy objective and the policy measures but not the sanctions."[38]

As it turned out, "the impact of international economic sanctions played a crucial role in changing South Africa, but it took three more years before Nelson Mandela was freed and serious talks began."[39] On February 11, 1989, after spending 27 years in prison, Nelson Mandela became a free man. Kennedy invited him to Boston, and Mandela arrived June 23. At a luncheon at the Kennedy library, the senator said, "We will not give up, we will not give in, until apartheid has been wiped off the face of the earth." Then, he introduced Mandela as the statesman of our time: "He represents what courage and commitment is all about…. Nelson Mandela is today the true father of a new South Africa."[40]

Even so, Reagan's persistent recalcitrance on the apartheid issue stalled its demise. Under the Clinton administration, "South Africa finally ended apartheid in early 1994."[41] Viewing the issue of apartheid more than 20 years after the landmark legislation, we take for granted that apartheid's end seemed preordained. Decidedly not. But for the actions of Kennedy and his colleagues, Reagan would not have placed one sanction on this racist regime.

Assessing Kennedy's role in the anti-apartheid legislation in 1985 through the historical visit of Mandela in 1989 yields the conclusion that, of all his legislative efforts to date, this was the most far reaching. Keeping within his theme of equality among all individuals, Kennedy's attack on apartheid led to real reform. At the time he took up the cause, nobody could have envisioned the day Nelson Mandela would walk out of prison a free man. In this respect, one cannot understate the achievement, felt nationwide and internationally, of the anti-apartheid efforts.

Even more telling, Kennedy did not give up when his initial bill with Lowell Weicker stalled. Accepting compromise so that a bill with real sanctions could eventually override a popular president's veto, Kennedy achieved a true legislative victory.

While other efforts toward expanding antidiscrimination laws soon occupied Ted Kennedy's attention, the Anti-Apartheid legislation and emancipation of Mandela stand as a historical achievement, remarkably the one least understood or written about by Kennedy biographers or historians generally.

What escapes many, it seems, involves the difficulties of a minority senator having true impact on national policy. The comprehensive Anti-Apartheid act illustrates a profound shift in assessing Kennedy's role as a senator. No doubt many liberals clamored for Kennedy to run for president as early as 1968 when his brother Robert Kennedy tragically died at the Ambassador hotel at the hands of Sirhan Sirhan. The events of Chappaquiddick, just a year later in 1969, no matter what the spin or political efforts, doomed a successful national run for the presidency. However, Ted Kennedy gamely trudged on, to the dismay of many who heartily felt he deserved jail time over Chappaquiddick and that the Kennedy family bought itself out of a career-ending plight.

Still, Kennedy persevered, after learning all too well that Chappaquiddick would never cease as a central attacking ground. Kennedy stepped back after the unsuccessful 1980 presidential run and reassessed his role. Never again, even though a young man, would Kennedy consider a presidential run. Instead, finding himself in the confining position of the minority, Kennedy pulled out the Anti-Apartheid legislation—a true definition of his commitment to combat discrimination.

Two issues loomed ahead. Having experienced his own personal tragedies—his son lost a leg to cancer and his own sister was committed after shock therapy, robbing her of any meaningful life—Ted Kennedy turned to the plight of the disabled with the Americans with Disabilities Act. He also used that empathy to forge ahead with the Family Medical Leave Act, which addressed the plight of workers who need to care for ill family members or who have suffered serious illnesses themselves. These two bills, enacted in the 1990s, would define Ted Kennedy's role as the lead senator combating discrimination.

6

From the Bork Hearing to the Americans with Disabilities Act of 1990

Following the passage of the 1986 Comprehensive Anti-Apartheid Act, Kennedy continued to increase his stature as a senior senator in a minority role. Collaborating with Republican Orrin Hatch of Utah, Kennedy joined Hatch in efforts to increase oversight of mine workers under the preexisting Mine Safety and Health Administration (MSHA).[1]

This continued effort at bipartisan reform and his development of relationships across the aisle paid dividends when after the retirement of Supreme Court Justice Lewis F. Powell, a member of the majority in *Roe v. Wade*, Reagan nominated arch conservative Robert H. Bork of the United States Court of Appeals for the District of Columbia Circuit, the most important appellate court (except perhaps the Ninth Circuit) below the United States Supreme Court.

Nobody could challenge Bork's intellect. For years "he engaged in spirited academic debates…. He believed in a jurisprudence of original intent—meaning that the various provisions in the Constitution should be interpreted in the way the framers did in their own era. Liberal jurists felt otherwise, claiming the Constitution was a living document, open to evolving interpretation as the times changed."[2]

Now with a strict constructionist majority on the Supreme Court, Bork's position may seem trivial, but back in 1987 his viewpoints stood far out of the mainstream. With a Court comprised of such moderate to liberal justices as Harry Blackmun, Sandra Day O'Conner, John Paul Stevens, William Brennan and Thurgood Marshall, Kennedy viewed the nomination of Bork as a frontal attack against all that he stood for. Indeed, Kennedy's opposition to Bork stemmed from Reagan's nomination of Justice Rehnquist as Chief Justice of the Supreme Court in 1986 upon the retirement of Chief Justice Warren Burger.

At this time, Rehnquist had forged plainly the most conservative position on the Court. Kennedy led the effort to block his nomination to Chief Justice. Kennedy opposed Rehnquist's conservative judicial philosophy, but many senators did not feel ideology stood as a reason to deny confirmation. Kennedy felt differently and advocated a broad role for the Senate in vetting Supreme Court nominees:

> The Framers of the Constitution envisioned a major role for the Senate in the appointment of judges. It is historical nonsense to suggest that all the Senate has to do is check the nominee's IQ, make sure he has a law degree and no arrests and rubberstamp the President's choice.[3]

Kennedy portrayed Rehnquist as an extremist, often the lone dissenter on well established issues.

Indeed, Kennedy pointed out that Rehnquist had worked in Republican efforts to challenge black voters in polling places in Phoenix in the fifties and sixties. Kennedy also pressed on a memorandum Rehnquist wrote in 1952 as a clerk to Supreme Court Justice Robert H. Jackson arguing that the desegregation efforts of the ultimately unanimous Warren Court in *Brown v. Board* lacked merit. Rehnquist's memorandum insisted that the concept of "separate but equal" schools, meaning separation of blacks and whites, was correct. In the Senate hearings, Rehnquist attributed these views to the justice he clerked for, Robert Jackson, not to him. This claim, though, did not then and does not now pass muster. Numerous works detail the considerable influence of United States Supreme Court Justices' clerks, and Rehnquist held formidable influence. Even more importantly, in the many years following *Brown v. Board*, Rehnquist never disavowed the views espoused in his memorandum.

While Rehnquist was disingenuous, Kennedy could not muster opposition to election of Rehnquist during the conservative Reagan era. Although he led a five-day filibuster, the Senate confirmed Rehnquist as the new Chief Justice of the United States Supreme Court by a vote of 65–33. Although it stood as small solace this amounted to the closest vote against a Chief Justice in history. The United States Supreme Court now had a fervent conservative as its Chief Justice. This situation still stands today, since upon Rehnquist's death, George W. Bush appointed former Rehnquist law clerk John Roberts as Chief Justice. In doing so, Bush ignored sitting members of the Court, a highly controversial decision.

In any event, although not the Chairman of the Senate Judiciary Committee, Kennedy then took the lead in attacking Bork's nomination on the heels of his failure to stop Rehnquist's ascension. Even ardent supporters of Kennedy have launched criticism of his role in the Bork nomination. One supportive Kennedy biographer stated that when "Reagan nominated Judge Robert H. Bork to the U.S. Supreme Court, Ted unleashed a torrent of invectives. For those with a short memory, Ted reminded them that it had been Bork, as solicitor general, who had done Richard Nixon's dirty work and fired Archibald Cox as the special Watergate prosecutor."[4]

Less than an hour after Reagan announced Bork's nomination, "Ted stood in the well of the Senate and delivered a blistering attack against the nominee."[5] According to Kennedy biographer Adam Clymer, Kennedy gave one of the most important and controversial floor speeches of his career.[6]

"Robert Bork's America," Kennedy said, "is a land in which women would be forced into back alley abortions, blacks would sit at segregated lunch counters, rogue police could break down citizen's doors in midnight raids, school children could not be taught about evolution, writers and artists could be censored at the whim of government, and the doors of the federal courts would be shut on the fingers of millions of citizens for whom the judiciary is—and often only is—protector of the individual rights that are at the heart of our democracy."[7]

While certainly hyperbole, Kennedy surely hit on some salient points. First, Bork stood firmly against abortion, even in the face of *Roe v. Wade*, a precedent declaring abortion as constitutionally protected under some circumstances. *Roe v. Wade* had recognized a Constitutional right of privacy in a women's freedom of choice. Usually conservative justices adhere to the doctrine of *stare decisis*, meaning that they follow precedent. Bork made it clear, however, that he would vote to overrule *Roe v. Wade*. Second, Kennedy pointed to Bork's persistent renouncement of antidiscrimination laws. While plainly over the top in his rhetoric, Kennedy raised true concerns over cutbacks on long-ago fought antidiscrimination laws. Finally, Kennedy raised serious issues regarding criminal justice matters, particularly the potential overruling of *Miranda* and its rights afforded to those criminally accused.

Even so, Kennedy biographer Klein concludes that Ted came in for some well deserved criticism for painting Bork as a wild-eyed fascist, which was potentially unfair to the judge.[8] Indeed, the Kennedy charge against Bork has received condemnation for transforming the United States Supreme Court appointment process from examining the nominee's qualifications to the nominee's political and social views:

> In an extended, vicious battle in late 1987, they [minority group leaders] coalesced with other liberals to bring about the defeat (58–42) in the Senate with other liberals to the Supreme Court. Bork, a federal judge who had earlier been a law professor at Yale, was an outspoken conservative who had served as Nixon's compliant solicitor general. He had also opposed the Civil Right Act of 1964, affirmative action, and *Roe v. Wade*. This extraordinary bitter confirmation struggle, which centered on Bork's political and social views, not his qualifications—those were solid—featured mudslinging from both sides. It indicated that appointments to the Court, which was then deeply divided, were becoming highly partisan.[9]

Critics of Kennedy's demeanor in the Bork hearings certainly have a defensible viewpoint. Without question Kennedy's over-the-top rhetoric had an unnecessarily divisive effect. Kennedy, though, defended his conduct. No doubt hearkening back to the rubber stamp approval of Byron White when Kennedy, as a new senator, witnessed a United Stated Supreme Court nominee approved without real inquiry, Kennedy argued that the framers of the Constitution envisioned a major role for the Senate in United States Supreme Court nominations.[10] Kennedy thus correctly observed that the framers of the Constitution purposely set up a system of checks and balances on the three branches of government. Senate oversight of the Supreme Court nomination process by partisan presidents surely stands as a critical check and balance. The challenge posed by Kennedy to Bork's nomination properly sparked a legal debate which to this date resonates through many Supreme Court appointments.

In fact, Kennedy properly recognized that Bork had an inflexible view on constitutional interpretation: "Ted charged that Bork interpreted the Constitution in a radically different way than it had been read for fifty years, which put him outside the mainstream of judicial thinking."[11] And Kennedy was right. Bork fell far outside mainstream thinking at the time. Now, with Antonin Scalia, Chief Justice John Roberts and Samuel Alito on the Court, Bork's strict constructionism has its adherents. However, in 1987, his way of thinking simply did not comport with mainstream constitutional scholarship.   In addition, Bork's far-fetched views, such as opposing the Civil Rights Act of 1964, had absolutely nothing to do with constitutional interpretation or legal scholarship. In fact, Bork's espoused opposition to legislation, hypocritical at best, demonstrated that *he* interjected his own political and social viewpoints in the debate, hardly Kennedy's fault. Indeed, a supposed conservative Supreme Court Justice should defer to the legislature, not express opposition to proper legislative policymaking. In truth, the Bork hearings exposed a hypocrite. While supposedly a constitutional scholar, he made it clear he opposed properly enacted legislation and could care less about the time-honored doctrine of *stare decisis*, meaning that judges do not overrule prior court decisions based on their political views. Bork's nomination, no matter what his qualifications, rightly met defeat in the Senate.

In fact, reviewing the recent history of judicial nominations prior to the Bork hearings serves a useful purpose. As previously noted Kennedy just missed participating in the appointment of Byron "Whizzer" White in the spring of 1962. A lack of scrutiny of presidential Supreme Court nominees ruled the day in those years. Yet, a decade later when President Nixon tried to appoint Clement F. Haynsworth and Harrold G. Carswell, the Senate did indeed consider their prior racist history, and their nominations failed. True, both received ratings of unqualified by the Judicial Committee, but had served as federal judges just as Bork. Bork's express opposition to the Civil Rights Act of 1964 provided ample cause for the Senate to defeat his nomination, for the same reason as Haynsworth and Carswell did not become Supreme Court justices.

The insidious, unintended effect of the Bork nomination process is that candidates no longer are forthcoming on their views. To Bork's credit, he did say he would overrule *Roe v. Wade*. Now, getting an honest answer is like pulling teeth. For such an important, lifetime appointed position, with presidents now purposely appointing nominees in their mid–40s and early 50s so they can serve for 30 years or more, our nation deserves to know their true views, so that senators representing us can vote in an informed fashion.

Unfortunately, then, an unintended side effect of the Bork nomination process has been the cloak of secrecy surrounding subsequent Supreme Court nominees. Following Bork's rejection by the Senate, nominees now state they have no predetermined views on the validity of *Roe v. Wade*. Indeed, Chief Justice Roberts deftly avoided similar ideological questions even though, as a former clerk of Chief Justice William Rehnquist, his views and rulings since assuming his role on the Court come as no surprise. Roberts has recently waged a war with President

Obama, publicly rebuking the president's agenda. (Although Roberts' recent majority decision declaring "Obamacare" Constitutional raises interesting questions as to the legacy Roberts intends for himself.) Frankly, although the Bork defeat led by Kennedy demonstrated unnecessary vitriol, the failure to properly get recent nominees to explain their positions shares similar problems. A nominee for Chief Justice, such as Roberts, who may serve well over 30 years, should answer hard questions truthfully. Senators voting on his nomination and the American populace deserved to know his strong, preconceived ideology.

So, too, a thorough vetting of Justice Samuel Alito should have occurred. A reactionary Alito has systematically dismantled longstanding precedent and ignored the doctrine of *stare decisis*. While not unexpected, true conservative senators should have felt wary of approving such a nominee. Certainly, such senators will have to look to the past to justify not approving liberal activists, since they wholeheartedly embraced conservative activists. To date, President Obama has appointed moderate, well-qualified individuals to the United States Supreme Court. Both Justice Sotomayor and Justice Kagan received little firm opposition in the Senate. Certainly, though, with Obama winning a second term, he may nominate more activist liberal justices should the opportunity arise.

In any event, following the Bork nomination hearings, a new presidential election dawned. With Reagan serving his two terms, his vice president, previously a moderate, George Herbert Walker Bush, ran as the Republican nominee. This time, Bush embraced the Reagan conservative movement. Previously, when he ran in the Republican primary against Reagan in 1980, Bush referred to Reagan as supporting "voodoo economics."

Bush, piggybacking on the Reagan conservatism that brought over to the Republican party many workplace Democrats, decided not to stray from that theme in his campaign. Several Democrats vied for the nomination. Gary Hart, an energetic Democrat with promise, soon had to withdraw from the primary after he mocked the press and urged them to unearth his infidelities. With Hart caught on a boat with a companion, not his wife, he withdrew from consideration.

So too Joe Biden, now vice president to Obama, had considerable momentum. Yet, a plagiarism scandal dismantled his primary run. Interestingly, 20 years later, when Obama nominated him for vice president, the plagiarism issue never surfaced.

This left Ted Kennedy's Massachusetts colleague Mike Dukakis as the Democratic nominee. Dukakis, wooden in his speeches, hardly inspired a nation to depart from the Reagan/Bush platform. Even worse, Dukakis humiliated himself when he dressed up in military gear and was photographed on a tank. The Bush campaign mocked Dukakis, and he had no answer. Bush ran an effective campaign, resulting in negative ads depicting Dukakis as pardoning the murderer Willie Horton. Dukakis did not have the fight in him and refused to engage in similar negative campaigning. In some senses, he effectively conceded the election. Bush won convincingly and Ted Kennedy stood again with the daunting task of shepherding legislation through a president of a different party.

With the ensuing election of George Herbert Walker Bush as president, Kennedy turned his attention to yet another measure of equality—this time the Americans with Disabilities Act (ADA). Kennedy's support of the Americans with Disabilities Act formally started in 1986 with Republican colleague Lowell Weicker, who had a son with Down's syndrome. But of course Ted Kennedy's empathy for individuals with disabilities has far deeper roots. Ted's sister Rosemary had a mental disability not understood at the time. In 1941, without telling the family, father Joe Kennedy, who feared Rosemary had mild retardation (the word in those days), had her lobotomized.

> The procedure was supposed to fix her mood swings and calm her down, and Joe believed he was doing the right thing. But the operation left her severely brain damaged, and at the age of 23 Rosemary was confined to an institutional setting. She would spend most of her life at the St. Coletta School for Exceptional Children in Jefferson, Wisconsin, until her death in 2005.[12]

The lobotomy, a barbaric procedure that consists of cutting the connections to and from the prefrontal cortex of the brain, reduced Ted Kennedy's sister Rosemary into a life of despair. Kennedy, just nine at the time, never knew, until much later, the reason for Rosemary's mysterious disappearance from the household.

No doubt the early experience with his sister Rosemary left a scar that fueled Ted Kennedy's passion for the plight of the disabled. Another event, however, involving his son, had a dramatic impact. His son Teddy, in 1973, developed cancer in his leg. Teddy, an athletic seventh grader at St. Albany's school in Washington went home sick on Tuesday, November 6. All thought a reddish bump below his knee resulted from a football injury. Nonetheless, following thorough doctor's examinations, they diagnosed cancer. Even worse, the cancer had spread, and Ted Kennedy's son needed to have his leg amputated.[13]

These events, the butchered treatment of his disabled sister Rosemary, and the tragedy of his son losing a leg, surely shaped Ted Kennedy's views on the disabled. But Kennedy had also forged a history in the Senate of supporting and proposing antidiscrimination legislation. Starting initially with the Immigration Act of 1965, Kennedy sought to rectify a racist quota system with respect to immigrants. The Title IX Amendments to the Education Act aimed to equalize educational opportunities in males and females. The Anti-Apartheid Act provided for heavy sanctions on South Africa's racist apartheid system. The ADA, then, stands as an expected outgrowth of Kennedy's prior antidiscrimination legislation efforts.

Turning to attempts to enact the ADA, the Kennedy/Weicker proposal met resistance by the Reagan administration and faltered by 1988. However, Republican presidential nominee George H.W. Bush pledged to support the bill. Weicker met defeat in 1988, and Kennedy now worked with Senator Harkin as the bill's co-sponsor.

A series of debates ensued, with both Republicans and Democrats supporting various versions of the ADA. Republicans feared excessive litigation from enactment of the legislation. Senator Bob Dole, himself disabled in the Vietnam War, testified in favor of the bill but worried about too much litigation. The "opening up the floodgates" mantra, all too familiar, resonated with some. Surely, as discussed below, some abuses of the ADA have occurred. However, its benefits in providing disabled workers and individuals new rights surely outweigh its detriments.

Thus, on July 28, Senators Harkin, Kennedy, Hatch, David Durenberger (a Minnesota Republican) and Dole met in Dole's office in the Capitol with John Sununu, Richard Thornburgh (Attorney General), Roger Porter of the White House staff and Bobby Silverstein, Harkin's chief aide, among others, to pitch the bill. Sununu complained that the bill would bankrupt small businesses. After a number of compromises, the Labor Committee of the Senate voted 16–0 in favor of the bill. President Bush also formally endorsed the legislation. Kennedy spoke on the Senate floor, touting the bill as "one of the great civil rights laws of our generation." He said,

Disabled citizens deserve the opportunity to work for a living, ride a bus, have access to public and commercial buildings, and do all the other things that the rest of us take for granted. Mindless physical barriers and outdated social attitudes have made them second class citizens for too long. This legislation is a bill of rights for the disabled, and Americans will be a better and fairer nation because of it.[14]

The ADA, as enacted in 1990, prohibited employment discrimination by employers against disabled persons.[15] As originally enacted, the ADA applied to employers with 15 or more persons.[16] The ADA defined a "qualified individual with a disability" as an individual, with or without reasonable accommodation, who can perform the essential function of his or her position that such individual holds or desires. Reasonable accommodation, in the employment setting, included job restructuring and modified or part-time work duties. An employer had a defense under the ADA if the accommodation caused an undue hardship, thus placating Sununu's concern that the act would cause employers to go bankrupt. According to the act, its purpose was to "provide a clear and comprehensive national mandate for the elimination of discrimination against individuals with disabilities."[17]

The Americans with Disabilities Act of 1990, which prohibits disability discrimination in employment, expressly incorporates the powers, remedies, and procedures set forth in Title VII's enforcement provisions. Therefore, individuals who suffer disability discrimination due to violations of the ADA have the same right to file civil actions as they do under Title VII, after they exhaust certain specified administrative requirements, including filing an administrative claim with the EEOC.[18] This has caused problems with timely enforcement of rights for the disabled. The EEOC rarely conducts a timely investigation and only in unusual circumstances in a high profile case will it act decisively and sue. Still one cannot fault Kennedy and the ADA's supporters for backing the same system that applied, federally, to other discrimination matters in employment.

With respect to what standards apply to alleged ADA violations, courts apply the general theories of liability used under most other equal employment opportunity laws—i.e., "disparate treatment" and "disparate impact." In fact, the ADA expressly prohibits practices that have a disparate impact on disabled persons, unless justified by business necessity. Business necessity requires a showing of undue hardship, meaning that the employer must open up its financial books if claiming a hardship in accommodating an employee with a disability. Many employers make serious mistakes in attempting to claim "undue hardship." Even in this economy such a defense proves virtually impossible to prove. Juries hold sympathy for the displaced worker, wondering why an employer could not accommodate a disability.

The remedies available for unlawful discrimination under the ADA include equitable relief, back pay, and front pay, as under Title VII. The prevailing plaintiff also, absent unusual circumstances, receives attorney's fees expended in the litigation. A prevailing defendant (employer) can only receive attorney's fees by showing frivolousness, a nearly impossible standard.

In addition, pursuant to the Civil Rights Act of 1991, in an action brought by a complaining party under the ADA against an employer that engaged in unlawful intentional discrimination (i.e., not an employment practice that is unlawful because of its disparate impact), the complaining party may recover economic, emotional distress and punitive damages as discussed below, in addition to any relief authorized by Title VII. The "complaining party" for this purpose means the Equal Employment Opportunity Commission, the Attorney General, or a person who may bring an action or proceeding under the ADA.

A complaining party (or plaintiff in a civil suit) may recover punitive damages in an ADA civil action against an employer (other than a government, government agency, or political subdivision) if the plaintiff demonstrates that the employer engaged in a discriminatory practice or practices with malice or with reckless indifference to the federally protected rights of a disabled worker. However, punitive damage recovery, while often widely publicized, occurs rarely, in less than 2 percent of discrimination cases. In addition, the now conservative United States Supreme Court has issued decisions greatly circumscribing the amount of recoverable punitive damages. This greatly hampers low-wage earners from obtaining legal counsel, as the amount of punitive damages, the U.S. Supreme Court has decided, must bear a relationship to damages for lost wages and compensatory damages.

"Compensatory damages" for purposes of the Civil Rights Act of 1991 includes amounts awarded for future economic losses, emotional pain, suffering, inconvenience, mental anguish, loss of enjoyment of life, and other non-wage-based losses. The sum of the amount of such damages and the amount of punitive damages awarded may not exceed the following amounts for each complaining party:

1. in the case of an employer who has more than 14 and fewer than 101 employees in each of 20 or more calendar weeks in the current or preceeding calendar year, $50,000;

2. in the case of an employer who has more than 100 and fewer than 201 employees in each of 20 or more calendar weeks in the current or preceding calendar year, $100,000;

3. in the case of an employer who has more than 200 and fewer than 501 employees in each of 20 or more calendar weeks in the current or preceding calendar year, $200,000; and

4. in the case of an employer who has more than 500 employees in each of 20 or more calendar weeks in the current or preceding calendar year, $300,000.[19]

In cases in which a discriminatory practice involves the failure to provide reasonable accommodation pursuant to the ADA or implementing regulations, an employer may avoid liability under the Civil Rights Act of 1991 if it demonstrates good-faith efforts, in consultation with the employee with the disability who has informed the employer of a needed accommodation. This process, called the "interactive process," places an affirmative duty on the employer to identify and make reasonable accommodations that would provide an employee the opportunity to work and would not cause an undue hardship in the operation of the business. In addition, an employer must advise an employee with a disability of any vacant position for which the employee may be qualified to perform. While the employee must advise of needed accommodations, an employer cannot shirk its responsibilities by not offering "light duty" or leaves of absence that do not create an undue hardship.

The ADA sets forth various affirmative defenses to a disability discrimination claim, including business necessity/job-relatedness, danger to the health and safety of other employees, a "religious entity" exemption, and specified infectious and communicable diseases transmitted through the handling of food. In addition, the United States Supreme Court has decided three related cases which have significantly affected the determination of whether the plaintiff meets the threshold test of a "qualified individual with a disability." This involves a factual determination on a case-by-case basis.

Broad in its intended scope, the act over the years has received a relatively narrow judicial interpretation. By way of example, the act defines disability as an impairment that "substantially" limits a major life activity. Other state antidiscrimination laws, such as FEHA in California, only require a "limitation," not a "substantial limitation," of a major life activity. This distinction in wording has led to marked differences in the coverage of the ADA such that experienced employment lawyers in California will virtually always sue under FEHA.

The first hurdle under the ADA, showing a "qualifying disability," soon met with rigid interpretations by the Court. For example, courts began dismissing cases by finding that the claimed disability did not limit a major life activity.[20]

The United States Supreme Court in *Sutton v. United Airlines*, 527 U.S. 471 (1979) seized on the word "substantial" to greatly limit the type of disability that received protection under the act. In a rare act rebuking the ADA Amendments Act of 2008, effective January 1, 2009, the United States Supreme Court expressly imposed the *Sutton* limitation and disregarded the clear legislative intent to eliminate discrimination based on disability and to provide broad coverage.[21]

According to the ADA Amendments Act of 2008, the term "substantially limits" in the definition of disability need not limit other life activities, only one. An impairment in remission or episodic impairment constitutes a disability if it would substantially limit a major life activity when active.[22] This broad sweep of ADA amendments, however, soon found disfavor by the United States Supreme Court.

Such retrenchment from the act, especially given the intent of its sponsors, is shameful indeed. Senators from both sides of the aisle felt passionate about the passage of the ADA in 1990. Senator Harken used sign language to speak to his deaf brother. Then he explained in the Senate, "I just wanted to say to my brother Frank that today was my proudest day in 16 years of Congress, that today Congress opens the doors to all Americans, and that we say no prejudice."[23]

Republican Orrin Hatch spoke of his brother in law, Raymond Hanson, who earned two engineering degrees, despite contracting two types of polio. He worked until the day he died, going into an iron lung each day to survive. Hatch called him "the greatest inspiration of a dogged determination to do what was right and to make his life worthwhile of anybody I knew of in my life."[24]

Ted Kennedy's support of the ADA resonates to this day, even after his death. Speaking on the Senate floor, following passage of the final Act, Kennedy summarized his passion for the Act:

Many of us have been touched by others with disabilities. My sister Rosemary is retarded; my son lost a leg to cancer. And others who support the legislation believe in it for similar special reasons. I cannot be unmindful of the extraordinary contributions of those who have been lucky enough to have members of their families or children who are facing the same challenges and know what the legislation means.[25]

In the wake of these sentiments by both Republicans and Democratic senators, it defies imagination that in June 2009, just two months before Ted Kennedy's passing, the United States Supreme Court in a majority opinion authored by former EEOC head Clarence Thomas could write a decision concerning the Age Discrimination in Employment Act (ADEA) that potentially may limit the ADA, despite clear Legislative intent, due to a hypertechnical reading of the wording of the law. But ignoring legislative history, Associate Justice Clarence Thomas did just that with the ADEA, in what will go down as one of the most controversial Supreme Court decisions of all time.

In a case under the Age Discrimination in Employment Act (ADEA), separate from Title VII just as the ADA, Justice Thomas, writing for a bare 5–4 majority, ruled that Congress intended to differentiate the burden of proof required in an age discrimination case as opposed to discrimination cases brought under Title VII of the Civil Rights Act of 1964 for race, sex and national origin discrimination. While not directly applicable to the later passed ADA, the decision presages an ominous future for disabled employees seeking redress from the courts.

In *Gross v. FBL Financial Services, Inc.*, 129 S. Ct. 2343 (2009), the United States Supreme Court ruled that Congress, enacting legislation in 1967 under Lyndon Baines Johnson's signature, meant to provide older workers a tougher chance to win in court than under Title VII enacted just three years earlier in 1964. Imagine the turn the current court may take regarding the ADA, enacted during Republican George H.W. Bush's presidency in 1990.

In *Gross*, the Supreme Court reversed (meaning threw out) a $46,945 verdict in favor of the older worker. In so doing, the United States Supreme Court decided that the standard of proving that a termination had a "motivating factor" of age discrimination was wrong. This not only repudiated all prior law, but cynically differentiated age discrimination from race, sex and national origin discrimination. What, conceivably, could have led the Legislature to think, particularly in this economy, that older workers deserve less protection than others covered by antidiscrimination laws?

In layman's terms, the United States Supreme Court changed the rules. In every case, including sponsored Judicial Council jury instructions approved by California Justices, the standard applied amounts to whether a "substantial motivating reason" for the termination was discriminatory. It does not have to be the only reason. Simply put, if a jury concludes that an employer, motivated by a discriminatory reason even if it had other legitimate reasons, violates the law.

In *Gross v. FBL Financial Services, Inc.*, the United States Supreme Court decided in an age discrimination case that an employee must meet a heightened burden in order to prevail. Under Title VII of the Civil Rights Act of 1964, employees suing for race, national origin or sex discrimination must prove by a preponderance of the evidence that a prohibited reason played a "motivating factor" in the termination. Therefore, even if the employer shows that other legitimate reasons factored into the termination decision, the employee wins.

In *Gross*, Justice Thomas in a 5–4 decision concluded otherwise for age discrimination cases under the ADEA. Rationalizing that the ADEA had the words "because of" in it, the Thomas majority concluded that an employee must demonstrate that "but for" the illegal reason, the employee would not have been terminated.[26] In other words, a plaintiff must now show that age was a "but for" cause of the adverse employment decision. The majority reached this decision without any evidence that Congress intended to make it harder for an employee to win an age discrimination case that those suing for race, national origin or sex discrimination.

Perhaps even more alarming, and plainly applicable to the ADA, the majority suggested that it would not apply the "motivating factor" test in future cases under Title VII. In an ominous statement, Justice Thomas wrote for the majority: "In any event, it is far from clear that the Court would have the same approach were it to consider the question today in the first instance."[27] Thus, the 5–4 conservative majority strongly hinted that it stands ready to make it more difficult for individuals suing under Title VII or the ADA to win discrimination cases.

In a stinging dissent, Justice Stevens accused the majority of making a "decision to engage in unnecessary lawmaking."[28] Stevens also pointed out a disturbing feature of the decision itself. When the United States Supreme Court decides to take a case, it grants certiorari on a specific question or questions. In *Gross*, the Court did not grant certiorari on the issue it ultimately decided—whether a mixed motive analysis applies to the ADA. In fact, the question the Supreme Court stated it would decide was whether in a mixed motive case a plaintiff must present direct evidence of discriminatory intent—nothing else.

Thus, the conservative majority in *Gross* engaged in unbridled judicial activism, not the judicial restraint Chief Justice Roberts promised during his Senate confirmation hearing. Ted Kennedy voted against confirming Roberts, but surely he could not have imagined the torrent unleashed against the antidiscrimination laws he championed during his time in the Senate. Sadly, the *Gross* decision, decided just weeks before Ted Kennedy's death, stands as a shroud to his main cause during his Senate career.

To be sure, the *Gross* decision stems partly from abuses of the antidiscrimination laws. One of the unintended consequences of the ADA has involved the number of cases spawned by "disabilities" the sponsors of the act never envisioned in 1990. While the act was plainly aimed at serious disabilities, over the years virtually any medical condition now qualifies under the ADA and thus has coverage under the act. This means that many employers have to offer reasonable accommodations to a whole host of employees Congress assuredly never envisioned.

This has created a burden on small employers. Particularly in this economy, many small employers cannot shoulder the burden of providing sometimes indefinite leaves of absences to employees with conditions varying from carpal tunnel syndrome, sore backs and anxiety. Many of these types of maladies, it seems, are far more suited for treatment under the worker's compensation system if caused by work.

Proponents of the broad definition provided under the ADA and even broader state antidiscrimination laws such as the Fair Employment and Housing Act (FEHA) in California argue that with the hard economy and aging work population, even small employers need to have flexibility in dealing with their workers. Cost effective, reasonable accommodations such as ergonomic work stations cost little in the long run and can provide a solution to workers' medical issues for years.

Both sides of the debate have their points. In the nearly two decades since passage of the ADA the act has witnessed significant abuse. Many workers, unfortunately, can find a doctor to place them on leave while on the cusp of receiving severe disciplinary action up to and including termination. Such doctor's notes, often vague in describing the medical condition and extending leaves time and again, cause employers significant uncertainty.

On the other hand, the fact that there is some abuse of the system does not mean that the courts should limit Congress's intent in enacting the ADA. Designed to provide disabled persons a real chance in the workplace against harsh odds, employers should have to abide by the act's requirement of providing reasonable accommodations to workers' disabilities so that they can productively work. The "interactive process" contemplated by the act, a fancy legal term for requiring employers to speak with their employees about their needs to accommodate a disability, frequently does not occur. Many employers, large and small, remain remarkably ill informed about their legal obligations in this respect. Many employers, in fact, provide rigid limitations to the length of a disability leave, a plain violation of the ADA. Absent business necessity or undue hardship, how can a cancer victim enduring chemotherapy and radiation be denied a necessary lengthy leave of absence and not have a vacant job waiting upon their return to health? The law prohibits such ever-present employment policies.

Another important aspect of the ADA involved Title II, access to public accommodations. In this arena, a serious debate involves whether litigants have abused the system or whether the act has made inroads to eradicating barriers to the disabled.

A recent case, *Antoninetti v. Chipotle Mexican Grill*, 643 F.3d 1165 (9th Cir. 2010), exemplifies the debate on the unintended consequences of the ADA. While Title I of the ADA governs discrimination based on disability in employment, Title II of the ADA has sweeping language regarding accessibility in public accommodations for the disabled. Prior to the enactment of the ADA in 1990, the disabled faced many obstacles in public daily life. Try to enter a public library in a wheelchair with no ramp and only steps. Rails and subways lacked suitable access. Many restaurants did not have suitable accommodations for the disabled. Back in 1971, one could scarcely find parking spaces reserved for the handicapped.

Title II of the ADA changed all that. Title II of the ADA requires that "public accommodations" built after January 26, 1993, be "readily accessible to and usable by individuals with disabilities."[29] To satisfy this standard, new construction and alterations needed to comply with standards for accessible design promulgated by the Attorney General of the United States. Since that time the Attorney General has promulgated detailed, architectural standards, known as the Guidelines, which govern the applicability of the act to a variety of public accommodations. Failure to comply with the act constitutes prohibited discrimination. The enforcement provisions of Title II of the ADA allows any person subjected to discrimination in public accommodations to file a civil action for preventive relief, including an injunction. Injunctive relief may include a court order to alter them to make facilities accessible and usable to disabled employees.

On the one hand, Title II of the ADA has led to meaningful changes that have helped individuals with disabilities in their daily lives. On the other hand, the act has spawned serial litigants solicited by lawyers who bring dozens of accessibility lawsuits. These professional plaintiffs, many say, have sullied the intent of the act.

In *Antonitetti*, the litigant suing Chipotle's restaurant had sued over 20 business entities in accessibility litigation. The lower court used this litigation history as a basis to deny injunctive relief. The Ninth Circuit, on the twentieth anniversary of enactment of the ADA, ruled otherwise. According to the Court, for the ADA to yield its promises of equal access for the disabled it may, indeed, require committed individuals to act as serial litigants. The Ninth Circuit went on to hold that Chipotle's high wall deprived the disabled of the "Chipotle experience" and thus violated the ADA. The Court thus required the restaurant to redesign its facilities.

While the ruling in the *Chipotle* case appears legally correct, nonetheless it reflects an uneasy strain between well-intended remedial efforts and excessive litigation. Indeed, some ADA litigants have been deemed "vexatious litigants," meaning that the courts have precluded them from suing again. Some lawyers soliciting such litigants and bringing suit after suit have been disbarred.

Enacted with altruistic motives, Ted Kennedy backed the ADA with visions of helping disabled individuals such as his sister Rosemary and son Teddy. This act, following Kennedy's strong support of Title VII, elimination of racist immigration quotas and leadership role in the Comprehensive Anti-Apartheid Act, represents a continuation of Kennedy's history of attempting to eradicate discrimination. And just three years after the ADA, Kennedy would play a key role in enactment of yet another form of antidiscrimination via the Family Medical Leave Act of 1993. Nonetheless, unintended consequences of the act continue to spark debate about its efficacy.

7

The Family Medical Leave
Act of 1993 and Its Aftermath

Following the passage of the ADA in 1990, the country faced an unprecedented crisis as Iraq launched scud missiles towards Israel and military intervention seemed inevitable. President Bush cautiously built a coalition against Iraq and its president, Saddam Hussein, whose army had invaded the Kingdom of Kuwait on August 2, 1990. Bush sent troops bordering Saudi Arabia and vowed the invasion would not stand. He won United States Security Council support for a ban on all trade with oil-rich Iraq.

Ted Kennedy supported Bush's dispatch of troops to Saudi Arabia. However, he criticized the open-ended means as to the use of the troops. The Foreign Relations Committee prepared a resolution supporting Bush's actions and authorized continued action by the president in accordance with decisions of the United Nations Security Council. This authorization included broad-based support of funds by Congress to deter aggression and to protect American lives in the region. Kennedy opposed the resolution, likening it to a "Tonkin Gulf resolution for the Persian Gulf."[1] For Kennedy to liken the Persian Gulf incursion to the Tonkin Gulf surely signaled a change in direction. Back when the Gulf of Tonkin fiasco occurred in 1965, Kennedy stood silent and supported LBJ's efforts. Now, he used the Gulf of Tonkin as a symbol to oppose the Bush resolution. Kennedy lamented that if the president intended to go to war, the Constitution required him to do so with the approval of Congress, in advance, with specific terms. While technically right, Kennedy stood deeply in the minority, and the resolution passed 95–3.

On November 8, 1990, two days after the midterm elections, President Bush ordered almost a doubling of the troops in the Gulf, to develop an adequate offensive military option. Kennedy feared Bush had called for a headlong course to war without giving sanctions a fair chance to work. When Congress debated the issue, Kennedy urged patience, again stating his conviction that war stood as the last option, and that President Bush had not exhausted all diplomatic objectives.

On Saturday January 12, 1991, the Senate voted 52–47 to authorize Bush to go to war. Kennedy, along with 44 Democrats, voted no. The vote stands as an enigma. Long a supporter of Israel, Kennedy surely knew that Saddam Hussein time and again deceived United Nations inspectors and boldly attacked Israel. Sanctions had not worked. Yet, Kennedy would have allowed more time and more scud missiles to launch, killing Israelis in their homeland. Kennedy offers no principled explanation for not supporting the limited war against Iraq, which, ironically, helped lead to Bush's defeat to Clinton insofar as many Americans thought he should have gone further and taken out Saddam Hussein. (The poor economy surely also played a major role in Bush's defeat.)

The war began on January 16, when bombs and missiles hit Baghdad that night. For the next five weeks, a captivated nation watched CNN nightly for visual images of the bombings. Indeed, the Gulf War catapulted CNN into national prominence. CNN offered mesmerizing coverage from Baghdad of striking missiles and vibrant explosions. Iraqi scud missiles zoomed off to targets in Israel and Saudi Arabia and American patriot missiles shot up to intercept them.[2]

Operation Desert Storm, spearheaded by American General Norman Schwarzkopf, put into place the Powell doctrine. Secretary of Defense Colin Powell called for the dispatch of overwhelmingly superior power. Bush took a slightly different approach. With massive air bombings, Bush displayed Americans' awesome power. He declined, though, to send ground troops to Baghdad to capture Saddam Hussein. Despite a groundswell of national support for such action, Bush knew it would mean the loss of many American troops. He stuck with the nightly air attacks.

The Gulf War, as seen live on CNN, fortified many Americans' support of Israel. An eloquent speaker emerged. Schooled in the United States, Benjamin Netanyahu appeared almost nightly on CNN on Ted Koppel's popular show "Nightline" at 11:30 p.m. on ABC TV. Netanyahu portrayed an image of Israel-as-victim few had seen before. While decidedly militaristic, Netanyahu captivated an American populace who previously had heard Israeli leaders speaking in halting English and with yarmulkes (the Jewish religious head cap) prominently displayed.

Netanyahu, to the contrary, appeared in neatly tailored suits and looked American. He applauded Bush's efforts to halt Iraq's aggression toward Israel. While deferring Israel's own right to invade Iraq, Netamyahu also educated Americans on Israel's defense forces, which repeatedly shut down Iraq scud missiles.

With Bush experiencing soaring approval ratings, many questioned his decision to abruptly stop the fighting. Some Americans, by this point, clearly favored an all out attack on Baghdad, with the purpose of capturing or taking out Saddam Hussein. Indeed, while a faltering economy explains much about Clinton's ultimate defeat of Bush in 1992, many think that Bush's failure to "finish business" in Iraq led to a revolt against his presidency.

To be sure, the same problems that beset George W. Bush a decade later in Iraq existed at the time. The elder Bush worried about the practicality of capturing Hussein, the American casualties and a prolonged occupation thereafter. George H. W. Bush in 1991 repeatedly reinforced his view that he sought solely to free Kuwait and to drive Hussein back to Iraq. Still, many questioned why, with such military dominance, the American forces did not simply forge ahead.

Following the Gulf War, though, Bush enjoyed a virtually unprecedented degree of popularity. But as the economy faltered, several Democrats entered the fray for the 2002 election. The array of candidates included former Governor Jerry Brown of California (now again governor); Senator Bob Kerry of Nebraska, who had won the Medal of Honor in Vietnam; Senator Tom Harken of Iowa; and L. Douglas Wilder of Virginia, who in 1989 had become the first African American since Reconstruction to win a gubernatorial race. Previously, former Senator Paul Tsongas of Massachusetts had announced first.

In October 1991, Bill Clinton, who had served two six-year terms as governor of Arkansas, joined the crowd of aspirants. Hardly known, Clinton's candidacy served as a decided longshot attempt to gain the presidency. In the meantime, though, Ted Kennedy's personal indiscretions once again came to the forefront, making national news.

When Congress took its Easter recess in 1991, Kennedy went to Palm Beach. On March 29, around midnight, everyone turned in, except Ted. He asked his son Patrick and his cousin William Kennedy Smith to join him for a couple of beers at Au Bar, a trendy club. Kennedy drank Chivas Regal and soda. When they left, they returned to the six-bedroom mansion in Palm Beach. William Kennedy Smith, then 30, returned with a 29-year-old woman, and he brought her to the beach. What transpired remains unclear—William claims they had consensual sex. The woman claimed rape and filed a police complaint the next day. Ted Kennedy soon lawyered up, and he advised Smith to do the same.

Kennedy and his staff tried to divert the Palm Beach scandal, but to no avail. Kennedy's drunken episode quickly became national news. Rumors of a cover-up just like Chappaquiddick soon surfaced.

The trial of William Kennedy Smith became a national spectacle. Ted Kennedy stood up for his cousin, who was charged with rape. Initially, rumors of obstruction-of-justice charges surfaced but never came to pass. Rather, Ted gave a deposition and would eventually testify at trial. Ted testified that he heard no screams and had seen nothing of Smith and the alleged victim, Ms. Bowman, after leaving the trendy bar. His testimony proved marginal at trial, but his misconduct in another scandal certainly did not help. Smith testified that Bowman had come on to him in the bar, that they had consensual sex on the beach, and that she turned angry afterwards. The jury deliberated only 77 minutes and acquitted Smith.[3]

Without question, the rich and famous, able to pay the best lawyers, receive a different brand of justice. A little more than a decade later, this reality came into sharp focus with the shocking acquittal of O.J. Simpson in the double murder of his wife and Ron Goldman. Still, even though William Kennedy Smith received an acquittal, once again Ted Kennedy's reputation suffered a serious blow.

Perhaps this personal turmoil explains Kennedy's virtual silence during the confirmation hearings of Clarence Thomas for the United States Supreme Court. Having played such a vocal role in the Bork proceedings, in retrospect it appears difficult to justify Kennedy's indifference. Particularly with his lifelong emphasis on antidiscrimination legislation, one would have thought Kennedy craved to assume a prominent role in attacking Thomas' reputation and credentials. Yet, knowing Thomas' abysmal record as head of the EEOC, Kennedy shirked his responsibility to challenge Thomas' record. Kennedy's seeming indifference to Thomas' hearings remains a visible stain on his legislative record. Just years before, Kennedy took on nominee Robert Bork in a full frontal attack. Now, while voting against Thomas, he witnessed a 52–48 confirmation of Thomas, the closest vote ever for a nominee to the United Supreme Court. Notably, Kennedy in his memoir fails to address adequately his inexplicable silence. While one can only speculate, perhaps

Kennedy saw too many pitfalls in vocally criticizing an African American nominee to the United States Supreme Court. Indeed, even after Anita Hill came forward with lurid details of sexual harassment by the then-head of the EEOC, the agency charged to combat discrimination and harassment, Kennedy remained at best a behind-the-scenes critic.

Following Thomas' nomination, which profoundly changed the shape of the Supreme Court to this day, Kennedy's attention turned to presidential politics. As the luster of the Gulf War receded and the recession dragged on, Kennedy saw real prospects for the return of a Democratic president after 12 years. Kennedy, however, played a minuscule role in the 1992 election. In March 1992, Kennedy endorsed fellow Massachusetts colleague Paul Tsongas over the rising "new Democrat," Bill Clinton. After some concern over Clinton's moderate platform, Kennedy on April 23, 1992, endorsed Clinton and urged Democrats to rally behind him. In a bit speech in Madison Square Garden, Kennedy likened Clinton to his brother Bobby, stating "he has sought to heal, to oppose hate, to reach across the divides and make us whole again."[4]

Clinton campaigned as a cautious progressive who championed centrist policies directed at bringing back middle-class, blue collar voters to the party. Clinton appealed to the "Reagan Democrats." A moderate as the governor of Arkansas, he distanced himself from failed prior liberal Democratic nominees like Mondale and Dukakis, both of whom lost badly in 1984 and 1988. So, too, Clinton did not seek outspoken support from Ted Kennedy, also branded as a liberal. Clinton won, and that had a huge impact on Kennedy. For the first time in his 30 years in the Senate, Kennedy would have a position of power as a senior senator, and a presidential ally on many fronts.

One of Kennedy's passions remained fair treatment of employees in the workplace. Soon after Clinton's election, Kennedy brought to the forefront legislation he previously had unsuccessfully pursued during the Bush administration.

Kennedy biographer Adam Clymer makes no mention of the Family Medical Leave Act, as sponsored by Kennedy and Senator Christopher Dodd of Connecticut in 1990. The *Boston Globe* hailed the FMLA as a major Kennedy accomplishment:

> Family leave (1990) Kennedy and Sen. Christopher Dodd, D–Conn, authored the Family and Medical Leave Act requiring businesses to provide unpaid leave for family emergencies or after childbirth of infants. It was signed by President Clinton in 1993.[5]

The *Boston Globe* article actually understates the arduous road to passage of the act. Introduced in 1990 during George H.W. Bush's first and only term, the FMLA sought *unpaid* leave for workers in companies employing 50 or more employees for up to 12 weeks in the case of grave family illness or the birth of a child. While hotly criticized by employer groups and conservatives the bill's goals were decidedly modest. Remember, it simply sough *unpaid* leave. Indeed, "of 168 countries included in a recent global study, 163 guarantee a period of *paid* leave for childbirth."[6] The bill also did not seek to saddle small employers. It only applied to employers with 50 or more employees. With a limit of only 12 weeks of leave, and a requirement that in order to qualify an employee had to work 1,250 hours in the year, the bill seemed moderate in scope indeed. Nonetheless, despite majorities in the Senate and House passing the bill, twice President Bush vetoed it: "When Congress passed a Family and Medical Leave Act that guaranteed many workers up to 12 weeks a year of unpaid leave for medical emergencies—a measure that Bush vetoed twice—he [Clinton] was quick to sign it."[7]

The fact that Bush vetoed the bill twice, in 1990 and 1992, and Kennedy had to wait for the Democratic Clinton Administration to enact it into law demonstrates the fortitude of Kennedy as well as his patience. Imagine waiting three years for passage of a bill and enduring two vetoes.

The Bush veto in September 1992 may well have helped Clinton in his campaign. "The 1992 veto message said that while leaves for family emergencies were a good idea, the federal government should not force them on business, especially small business."[8] Kennedy insisted the bill exempted small businesses and key workers. He said, "When a medical crisis hits, when a new child is born or a family member is seriously ill, workers need leave."[9] He concluded his remarks by saying, "We know that Bill Clinton would sign it if he was now in the White House and we know he will sign it if our cause fails today."[10] However, the Senate failed to override Bush's veto.

Yet, the bill as finally passed under the new Clinton Administration, Public Law 103, had modest reach. Ultimately enacted and signed into law on February 5, 1993, the FMLA

1. entitled an "eligible employee," defined as an individual who worked at least 1,250 hours of service in the past year with an "employer" up to 12 weeks of unpaid leave for the birth of a child, the placement of a child to the employee for adoption or child care, the care of an immediate

family member with a serious health condition and a serious health condition that makes the employee unable to work[11];

2. applied to employees with more than 50 employees[12]; and
3. required medical certification of the qualifying condition.[13]

Importantly, the FMLA also guaranteed an employee restoration to the position or an equivalent position upon expiration of the leave.[14] Taken as a whole, then, the FMLA provided workers with long-needed rights in the event of family or medical necessity.

As stated in its enabling provisions, the Family and Medical Leave Act has the following purposes:

1. to balance the demands of the workplace with the needs of families, to promote the stability and economic security of families, and to promote national interests in preserving family integrity;
2. to entitle employees to take reasonable leave for medical reasons, for the birth or adoption of a child, and for the care of a child, spouse, or parent who has a serious health condition;
3. to accomplish the purposes [of the act] in a manner that accommodates the legitimate interests of employers;
4. to accomplish the purposes [of the act] in a manner that, consistent with the Equal Protection Clause of the Fourteenth Amendment, minimizes the potential for employment discrimination on the basis of sex, by ensuring generally that leave is available for eligible medical reasons (including maternity-related disability and for compelling family reasons, on a gender-neutral basis); and
5. to promote the goal of equal employment opportunity for women and men.[15]

The broad reach of the FMLA applies not only to the specific employee in question but also to spouses of the employees. Spouses employed by the same employer may take a combined total of 12 workweeks for the birth or placement of a child for adoption or foster care. Leave for birth of the employee's child or because of placement of a child for adoption or foster care must conclude within 12 months from the date of birth or placement.

The FMLA also provides for leave of either 12 or 26 weeks, depending on the situation, for family members of those in the Armed Forces. This provision has taken on increasing significance in the 2000s with the wars in Iraq and Afghanistan. California also has a law precluding retaliation against individuals for taking military leaves of absence. Thus, while the FMLA also includes family and medical leave rights for the spouses, children or parents of military service members on active duty, some states, like California, have supplemented the FMLA with additional unpaid leave for military service.

The FMLA, as noted, requires certain employers to provide eligible employees with family care and medical leave under specified circumstances. However, when used in conjunction with certain state laws, such as in California, the result is an expansion of employee rights. The California statute is the Moore-Brown-Roberti Family Rights Act (CFRA), California Government Code §12965.2. The CFRA regulations provide that they incorporate by reference the FMLA regulations to the extent that they coincide with CRFA regulations, other state law, or the California Constitution. FMLA states, "[n]othing in this Act or any amendment made by this Act shall be construed to supersede any provision of any State or local law that provides greater family or medical leave rights than the rights established under this Act or any amendment made by this Act."[16] Further, FMLA regulations state that FMLA does not modify or affect any federal or state antidiscrimination law and that employers must, therefore, comply with whichever law provides the greater rights to employees.[17] Thus, the CFRA applies even with FMLA protection if it provides equal or greater family care and medical leave rights. Accordingly, when faced with a leave request for purposes governed by both CFRA and FMLA, a covered employer in California must analyze both statutes on a provision-by-provision basis to determine which one provides the greater benefit to the employee on each aspect of the request.[18]

When the provisions of both laws apply, FMLA and CFRA leaves run concurrently and may simultaneously count against the employee's entitlement under both laws. If an employee takes leave for a purpose recognized under only one of the two laws, only that law governs the leave rights and obligations, and the employer can charge the amount of leave to that law only.

The FMLA and the CFRA make it unlawful for an employer to interfere with, restrain, or deny an employee's exercise of, or attempt to exercise, any right they provide.[19] Thus, for example, an employer normally may not consider an employee's use of FMLA leave as a factor in making an adverse employment decision. However, an employer may still terminate an employee during FMLA leave if the employer would have made the same decision had the employee not taken leave.[20] The employer, not the employee, bears the responsibility to determine whether a leave request meets the requirements covered by the FMLA.

Thus, to prevail on FMLA or CFRA interference claims, an employee need not satisfy the burden-shifting paradigm applicable to Title VII claims, but need only show by a preponderance of the evidence that taking FMLA-protected leave constituted a negative factor in the adverse employment decision. The employee can prove this claim by direct or circumstantial evidence, or both. Under the FMLA, the employer's good faith or lack of knowledge that its conduct violates the act, as a general matter, pertains to only the question of damages, not to liability. Of course, FMLA does not protect an employee against disciplinary action if the employee's absence occurs for reasons other than those enumerated in the act.

An employer complies with the FMLA by meeting or exceeding the minimum requirements. But an employer may freely change its benefit program, even if the change results in a reduction in benefits.[21] Thus, the FMLA does not require an employer to keep any particular benefits package, an important feature, especially as many employers still battling a recession have revised their sick leave and vacation leave policies to provide less paid leave and, in some cases, only unpaid leave.

An employee may assert rights under FMLA, a state antidiscrimination statute, or both. Additionally, if an employee meets the requirement of a qualified individual with a disability within the meaning of the Americans with Disabilities Act (ADA), the employer must make reasonable accommodations in accordance with the ADA, while at the same time affording an employee his or her rights under FMLA and CFRA. FMLA and CFRA may also interact with state worker's compensation law if the illness or injury occurred from work.

Both CFRA and FMLA allow family leave for the birth of a child of the employee or for the adoptive or foster-care placement of a child with the employee. FMLA and CFRA also allows an expectant mother to take leave before the actual date of birth of the child for prenatal care or if the mother's condition makes her unable to work. Birth leave under FMLA and CFRA also includes time to care for the newborn child.[22] The CFRA refers to this as baby bonding.

In the case of an adoptive or foster-care placement of a child with an employee, FMLA allows the employee's leave to begin before the actual placement if necessary to allow the placement to proceed. For example, if the employee's absence from employment occurs due to attendance at counseling sessions, court proceedings, consultations with the employee's attorney or with attorneys and doctors representing the birth parent, or physical examinations, the FMLA protects such activity.

Effective January 16, 2009, the Department of Labor promulgated rules and changed the definition of "serious medical condition" under the FMLA, in part to make it easier to gain coverage under the statute. The regulations now address leave taken prior to the birth of a child or placement of a child for adoption or foster care with the employee, in sections that cover pregnancy, birth, adoption and foster care.[23]

CFRA leave for the birth of a child may be used solely for the purposes of bonding with the child. Therefore, CFRA entitlement for this purpose is distinct from pregnancy disability leave.[24]

Both CFRA and FMLA allow medical leave for an employee's own serious health condition that renders the employee unable to perform the functions of his or her position.[25] An employee meets the FMLA requirement of being "unable to perform the functions of the position" if the employee's health care provider finds that the employee cannot work at all or cannot perform any of the essential functions of the employee's job within the meaning of the ADA. For example, an employee who must remain absent from work to receive medical treatment for a serious health condition satisfies the FMLA requirement of inability to perform the essential functions of the position during the absence for treatment. An employer has the option, in requiring certification from a health care provider, to provide a statement of the essential functions of the employee's position for the health care provider to review. A sufficient medical certification must specify what functions of the employee's position the employee is medically restricted from performing so that the employer can then determine whether the employee truly needs leave due to inability to perform one or more essential functions of the employee's position.[26]

The FMLA also allows leave for an employee to care for his or her parent, child, or spouse who has a serious health condition. "Caring for" encompasses both physical and psychological care and involves some level of participation in the ongoing treatment of a serious health condition. The term "needed to care for" also includes situations in which the employee may need to substitute for others who normally care for the family member, or to make arrangements for changes in care, such as transfer to a nursing home. For purposes of the FMLA, an employee does not meet the "caring for" requirement for her child when she moves him, not to seek medical attention, but to remove him from an unwholesome and physically violent social environment.[27] An employee's cross-country trip to retrieve the family car to reassure his pregnant wife she would soon have reliable transportation and his phone calls to her while he drove back did not provide care to a family member as required by the FMLA.[28] Similarly, when an employee took leave to help her elderly mother move from one home to another, that did not qualify as leave to care for a parent under CFRA.[29] On the other hand, a plaintiff in an action under the FMLA raised a genuine issue of material fact as to whether his activities (talking to his father about his sister's death, performing various household chores, and driving his father to counseling) necessitated care for his father's basic needs because of severe depression after his daughter's murder by her ex-husband.[30]

A "child" of an employee includes a biological, adopted, or foster child or a stepchild. However, a person age 18 or over does not qualify as a child for purposes of family leave unless he or she cannot care for him or herself because of a mental or physical disability. "Incapable of self-care because of a mental or physical disability" under the FMLA means that the child requires active assistance or supervision to provide daily self-care in three or more of the "activities of daily living" or "instrumental activities of daily living." Activities of daily living include adaptive activities such as caring appropriately for one's grooming and hygiene, bathing, dressing and eating. Instrumental activities of daily living include cooking, cleaning, shopping, taking public transportation, paying bills, maintaining a residence, using telephones and directories, using a post office, etc.[31] "Physical or mental disability" means a physical or mental impairment that substantially limits one or more of the major life activities of an individual.

Regulations issued by the Department of Labor under the FMLA now define terms related to leave to care for a child. "In loco parentis" includes day-to-day responsibilities to care for and financially support a child. The FMLA does not require a biological or legal relationship. "Adoption" means legally and permanently assuming the responsibility of raising a child as one's own; the source of an adopted child, such as whether from a licensed placement agency or otherwise does not determine eligibility for FMLA leave. "Foster care" means 24-hour care for children in substitution for and away from their parents or guardian.

The placement must occur by or with the agreement of the state as a result of a voluntary agreement between the parent or guardian that the child leave the home, or pursuant to a judicial determination of the necessity for foster care, and involves agreement between the state and foster family that the foster family will take care of the child.

For purposes of confirmation of family relationship, the employer may require the employee with the need for leave to provide reasonable documentation or a statement of certifying the family relationship. This documentation may take the form of a simple statement from the employee, or a child's birth certificate, or a court document. The employer has the entitlement to examine documentation such as a birth certificate, but the employer must return to the employee the official documentation submitted for this purpose.

A "serious health condition" under FMLA, under the law signed by President Clinton, is an illness, injury, impairment, or physical or mental condition that involves either of the following:

• Impatient care, which means an overnight stay in a hospital, hospice, or residential medical care facility. "Inpatient care" includes any period of incapacity (that is, an inability to work, attend school, or perform other regular daily activities due to the serious health condition, treatment for it, or recovery from it) and any subsequent treatment in connection with such inpatient care.

• Continuing treatment by a health care provider. For purposes of the FMLA, the term "treatment" includes (but it is not limited to) examinations to determine if a serious health condition exists and evaluations of the condition. Treatment does not include routine physical examinations, eye examinations, or dental examinations. A regimen of continuing treatment includes, for example, a course of prescription medication, such as an antibiotic, or therapy requiring special equipment to resolve or alleviate the health condition, such as oxygen. A regimen of continuing treatment that includes the taking of over-the-counter medications such as aspirin, antihistamines, or salves (or bed rest, drinking fluids, exercise, and other similar activities that can be initiated without a visit to a health care provider) is not, by itself, sufficient to constitute a regimen of continuing treatment for purposes of FMLA leave.

Cosmetic treatments, such as most treatments for acne or plastic surgery, do not qualify as "serious health conditions" unless inpatient hospital care occurs or unless complications develop. Ordinarily, unless complications arise, the following conditions do not meet the definition of "serious health condition" and do not qualify for FMLA leave:

- The common cold
- The flu
- Ear aches
- Upset stomach
- Minor ulcers
- Headaches other than migraine
- Routine dental or orthodontia problems, periodontal disease

On the other hand, restorative dental or plastic surgery after an injury or removal of cancerous growths constitute serious health conditions. Mental illness or allergies may also qualify as serious health conditions.[32]

Substance abuse may qualify as a serious health condition under the FMLA. However, FMLA leave for treatment for substance abuse requires certification by a health care provider or by a provider of health care services on referral by a health care provider. On the other hand, absence because of the employee's use of the substance, rather than for treatment, does not qualify for FMLA leave. While treatment for substance abuse does not prevent an employer from taking employment action against an employee, the employer may not take action against the employee because the employee has exercised his or her right to take FMLA leave for treatment. But if the employer has an established policy (applied in a nondiscriminatory manner) communicated to all employees that provides under certain circumstances terminations for substance abuse, an employer may terminate an employee pursuant to that policy whether or not the employee is on FMLA leave at the time. An employee also may take FMLA leave to care for a covered family member receiving treatment for substance abuse. The employer may not take action against an employee providing care for a covered family member receiving treatment for substance abuse.

A serious health condition involving continuing treatment by a health care provider includes any or more of the following:

- A period of incapacity of more than three consecutive, full calendar days, and any subsequent treatment or period of incapacity relating to the same condition, that also involves treatment two or more times, within 30 days of the first day of incapacity, unless extenuating circumstances exist, by a health care provider, by a nurse under direct supervision of a health care provider, or by a provider of health care services, e.g., a physical therapist, under orders of, or on referral by, a health care provider, or treatment by a health care provider on at least one occasion, which results in a regimen of continuing treatment under the supervision of the health care provider. This requires an in-person visit to a health care provider, and the first and only in-person treatment visit must take place within seven days of the first day of incapacity. Whether additional treatment visits or a regimen of continuing treatment is necessary within a 30-day period will be determined by the health care provider.

• Any period of incapacity due to pregnancy, or for prenatal care.

• Any period of incapacity due to a chronic serious health condition. A chronic serious health condition is one that meets each of the following conditions: Requires periodic visits, defined as at least twice a year, for treatment by a health care provider or by a nurse under direct supervisions of a health care provider; continues over an extended period of time, including recurring episodes of a single underlying condition; and may cause episodic rather than a continuing period of incapacity, such as asthma, diabetes, epilepsy, etc.

• A period of incapacity that is permanent or long term due to a condition for which treatment may not be effective. The employee or family member must be under the continuing supervision of, but need not be receiving active treatment by, a health care provider. Examples include Alzheimer's, a severe stroke, or the terminal stages of a disease.

• Any period of absence to receive multiple treatments, including any period of recovery from the treatments, by a health care provider or by a provider of health care services under orders of, or on referral by, a health care provider, for either restorative surgery after an accident or other injury or a condition that would likely result in a period of incapacity of more than three consecutive, full calendar days in the absence of medical intervention or treatment, such as cancer (chemotherapy, radiations, etc.), severe arthritis (physical therapy), or kidney disease (dialysis).[33]

Absences attributable to incapacity due to pregnancy or prenatal care or for chronic conditions qualify for FMLA leave even though the employee or the covered family member does not receive treatment from a health care provider during the absence, and even if the absence does not last more than three consecutive, full calendar days. For example, an employee with asthma may be unable to report for work due to the onset of an asthma attack or because the employee's health care provider has advised the employee to stay home when the pollen count exceeds a certain level. As a further example, an employee who is pregnant may be unable to report to work because of severe morning sickness.

Critics of the act argue that the FMLA stifles business development and places undue burden on small employers. According to these opponents of the act, employers with a business need cannot replace workers on leave for as much as three months. Such free-market advocates tie a host of social problems, including "the gender wage gap and the chronic shortage of women in corporate and political leadership,"[34] to the act. In fact, use of FMLA leave has, in the experience of many employers, been the subject of serious abuse. Many requests for use of FMLA leave, unfortunately, come on the heels of expected or actual discipline. Thus, many critics say, the FMLA serves as a convenient dodge to avoid firing. Finally, a global attack on FMLA stems from a belief that government regulation in the workplace has no place, and that the market will regulate such issues.

Advocates of the act nonetheless often criticize the modest reach of the act. Congress found that "due to the nature of the role of men and women in our society, the primary responsibilities for family caretaking often falls on women, and such responsibilities affect the working lives of women more than it affects the working lives of men."[35] Yet, proponents of the act urge for it to reach further. For example, the act narrowly defines "caregivers," and excludes many in modern society who now play an increasing role in what we used to call the "traditional family."

Critics of the FMLA focus on the burdens on employers in providing mandatory leave, even though the leave is unpaid.[36] Such critics argue that the FMLA provides an incentive to discriminate in the hiring of younger women, because the employer must "require other staff to work longer hours and/or absorb the duties of the women on leave."[37] Therefore, according to opponents of the FMLA, "freedom of contract" offers the best solution. That way, the argument goes, women who plan to never have children will be better off.[38]

As apparent from the above, the FMLA contains many complex features. Since the passage of the FMLA in 1993, the positive effects of the act far outweigh the negative predictions. To be sure, the most insidious effect of the act, fueled by doctors who will write a note for anything, has led to abuse of the taking of family leave. On the other hand, many women have benefitted greatly from the FMLA. The law recognizes that women should not forego careers simply because they have a child.

As one proponent of expansion of FMLA leave saliently notes, "abuse of public or employer leave policies is probably inevitable and impossible to prevent."[39] Even so, arguments abound for expansion of family leave, rather than retrenchment or elimination of the law. Women hold a critical role in our workplace, and recognition of their needs makes economic sense as well as promotes equality in the workforce. Businesses lose out if they train women in their jobs, only to lose them if they become pregnant or need to care for an immediate family member. The history of the FMLA since its enactment in 1993 does not bear out the fears expressed by its opponents that employers will discriminate by not hiring women in the first place. Indeed, the percentage of women in the workplace continues to increase.

Yet another piece of "equality" legislation, the FMLA stands as a major achievement in Ted Kennedy's Senate career.

8

Health Care Reform and the Health Care Act of 1996

For years, Ted Kennedy pursued health care reform. While passionate about eradicating discrimination, perhaps no issue greater defines Kennedy's legacy in the Senate as health care. Kennedy first took up the issue during the Nixon administration but did not get very far. Very outspoken on the subject, Kennedy would wait for a better political climate to champion the cause. And, of course, his son Teddy's bout with cancer also fueled his already passionate stance on the issue.

Kennedy turned to stronger efforts to enact national health care legislation during the Carter presidency. But Carter and Kennedy had different priorities: "Kennedy's prime concern was national health insurance. Carter had difficulty ranking goals, but balancing the budget, reorganizing the federal government, and dealing with energy shortage easily outranked health insurance."[1]

Kennedy thought that after the energy plan was sent to Congress, Carter would work with him as an ally to make health insurance reform the top priority on the agenda. Yet, all Carter did on the issue was to appoint Joe Califano, the Secretary of Health, Education and Welfare, to an advisory committee.

Kennedy met with Califano on May 2, 1977. Califano argued that the Administration need more time to study the costs of health insurance and to produce a sensible plan. Kennedy noted that he had worked on a plan for years, and the meeting got intense. Califano assured Kennedy at the end of the meeting that he would move as fast as he could to get Carter on board.

Two weeks later, Kennedy flew to Los Angeles and pressed the issue. He implored the Carter administration to carry out its commitment to health care reform. While Carter reaffirmed his commitment to phasing in a workable national health care insurance system, he set no timetable and vaguely stated that he aimed to submit legislation proposals sometime in 1978.

In the meantime, Kennedy suffered further personal setbacks. His wife Joan, an alcoholic, moved out, and their divorce became inevitable. Even before the tabloid era, anything involving a Kennedy assuredly resulted in significant press.

Meanwhile, Kennedy suffered a setback for his persistent desire to forge ahead with national health care reform. By 1978, Carter saw a crumbling presidency. Never before had an incumbent president received such a low approval rate. Indeed, the Gallop Poll had Kennedy leading Carter among Democrats by a 53 to 40 percent margin. While Kennedy had given no signs of a challenge to Carter in the Democratic primary, Carter dug in his heels on health care reform. Now, according to Califano, Carter considered Kennedy's plan too costly and deferred presenting any health care legislation whatsoever. Kennedy viewed this as a clear break of a promise by Carter. Eventually, in March 1978, Califano pledged to offer principles for later announced legislation.

By July, the Carter administration had announced no such principles. Kennedy by this time had abandoned his core idea of a single government plan and embraced keeping the private health insurance system alive. But Kennedy wanted a single bill with "universal coverage," which would assure insurance coverage for all Americans. Carter waffled, and would not back a single comprehensive bill. Califano, though, announced on July 29 that Carter viewed other agenda items, including inflation, as paramount. By the time of the midterm convention in December 1978, Kennedy spoke ever more of Carter's failure to provide decent health care for Americans. Hearkening back to his father's stroke, his son's cancer and his own broken back, Kennedy emphasized that these medical issues would have bankrupted any average family in the nation. Yet, Carter would not embrace Kennedy's plan. Instead, he attacked Kennedy as using health care reform for his own political advantage.

Kennedy, in the end, could not work effectively with Carter on national health insurance. As noted, even after enactment of the energy plan, Carter's top priority, the Carter administration stated that it needed more time to study the costs of health insurance and to work up a new program.

Years later, in comments made prior to the release of his book *White House Diary*, former President Jimmy Carter lashed out at Kennedy, blaming him for a three-decade political stalemate on health care reform. In an interview on *60 Minutes* aired on September 19, 2010, Carter blamed Kennedy for defeating the health care proposal made by Carter in the late 1970s. According to Carter in an interview with Leslie Stahl, "The fact is that we would have comprehensive health care now, had it not been for Ted Kennedy's deliberate blocking of the legislation I proposed. It was his fault. Ted Kennedy killed the bill."[2]

According to Carter, Kennedy derailed the bill out of personal spite. Carter said in the interview that Kennedy "did not want to see me have major success in that realm of life." Larry Horowitz, Kennedy's former chief of staff and the senator's negotiator on health care with the Carter administration, said Carter's remarks stunned him. He called the remarks "sad" and "classless" to criticize Kennedy after his death. According to the former chief of staff,

> It was so sad to see a clearly embittered former President pick a fight with Senator Kennedy a year after his death when he couldn't respond for himself. He blames Senator Kennedy for the fact that Ronald Reagan beat him, when he should be looking in the mirror.[3]

Carter's 30-years' reminiscence bears no resemblance to the facts or documented record. Kennedy favored a single-payer system, but compromised with Carter about retaining a private sector role.

Indeed, Kennedy tried to work with Joseph A. Califano, Secretary of Health, Education and Welfare for the Carter administration. Carter and Kennedy could not agree on a unified approach, a schism that helped lead to Kennedy's challenge for the presidency in 1980. In short, Carter thwarted Kennedy's continued efforts at real health care reform—reform Kennedy first sought in 1970. Carter's after-the-fact statements defy logic and the record. Everyone across the globe, from President Obama to Senator Orrin Hatch, acknowledge Kennedy's ceaseless efforts at health care reform. Carter's blistering attack no doubt stains his already tattered reputation.

During the Reagan and Bush years, any effort at reforming the health care system stalled. With Clinton's election in 1992, Kennedy's hopes for comprehensive health care legislation revived. Upon Clinton's inauguration in 1993, Kennedy found himself an ally. As Kennedy notes,

> The most single important promise Bill Clinton brought with him to the White House from my perspective at least, was that his administration would, once and for all, reform American health care…. I looked forward to working with him, not only in solving the insurance imbalance, but in

fundamentally overhauling the entire costly, inefficient and unfair system; the massive amalgam of doctors, hospitals, drug companies, insurers, health maintenance organizations, and government agencies.[4]

Clinton's initial efforts at health care reform, however, proved disastrous. Initially he envisioned a transition team with Kennedy among others. He scrapped that plan, and instead delegating health care reform to his wife, Hillary Rodham Clinton, and Ira Magaziner. Magaziner had gained prominence in the late 1960s by, as a student, reforming Brown University's educational system and creating the "new curriculum." Under the "new curriculum," Brown instituted a number of seminar-type courses, along with an option to take any class pass/fail. Magaziner, a Rhodes scholar, went to Oxford with Bill Clinton. The duo of Magaziner and Hillary Clinton, though, from the start failed to reach out to Republicans to embrace the concept of true health care reform.

Clinton plainly miscalculated by not having Kennedy as an inside member of the health care reform team. With over 20 years working on health care reform, Kennedy would have proved invaluable in calling upon political favors to forge a bipartisan consensus in a strong Democratic majority Congress. With both the House and Senate in hand, and a willing president unlike Carter, Kennedy no doubt could have ushered passage of a viable national health care plan that would have driven down insurance costs. But Clinton chose the Hillary/Magaziner team instead to spearhead reform efforts.

This proved unfortunate because Bill Clinton's major goal of 1993 involved reform of the health care system, yet he had the wrong team in place. As he emphasized in calling for reform, private expenditures for health purposes continued to skyrocket. Yet more than 35 million Americans—approximately 14 percent of the population—had no medical insurance.[5] Another 20 million lacked adequate coverage.

In selecting health care reform as his first major initiative, Bill Clinton chose a more liberal path than he seemed to steer in 1992, when he campaigned as a centrist "new Democrat." Reform of health insurance, a daunting task, had frustrated experienced senators like Ted Kennedy since as early as 1970. Still, Clinton pressed ahead with outsiders with no political clout in the House and Senate.

Unfortunately for advocates of reform, Magaziner and Hillary Clinton enshrouded their activities in secrecy. Instead of catering to Congress, they listened to a host of academics and other experts, sometimes gathering a hundred or more people who debated endlessly. When a plan finally emerged from this ill-conceived process, liberals felt disappointed that President Clinton did not recommend a single-payer plan such as in Canada. Yet, most liberals agreed that the plan, though complicated, promised to reduce economic inequality in the United States. Some large employers backed it in the hope that it would reduce the cost of health insurance for their workers.[6]

From the start, however, the Magaziner/Hillary Clinton plan ran into sharp opposition, notably from small insurers. They feared that larger companies would turn to mammoth insurers who could outbid them due to sheer volume of business. Also against the plan, small employers bristled at having to pay 80 percent of their workers' health insurance premiums. Foes such as these seriously damaged chances of reform. Clinton also refused to consider compromises that would have settled for less than universal coverage. In 1994, when Congressional committees began to consider his plans, the opposing groups mobilized. Clinton's most ambitious dream never even reached a vote on the floor of the Democratic Congress. The health care plan collapsed in August 1994. Clinton dropped the issue, leaving millions of Americans without coverage. In a resounding defeat, the Clinton plan met outright rejection and proved a national embarrassment.

This angered Kennedy, although he did not let it create a rift between him and President Clinton. The lessons from the failed health care reform efforts in 1993–1994 deserve consideration. To begin, Clinton came in as an outsider and failed to realize that he needed to capture the support of influential senators and Congressmen. His turn to an academic and his wife, instead of seasoned legislators, stands as a resounding mistake regarding Clinton's early efforts at health care reform.

To Ted Kennedy's credit, he did not publicly rebuke Bill Clinton, but rather focused on alternative measures in the light of the health care debate. Health care reform, a cornerstone of his beliefs, would never, to his death, stray as one of his core legislative efforts. Rather than sulk, Kennedy analyzed the failed Clinton efforts and assessed the best path forward. Seeking to gain backing from the Democratic party majority and ultimately his friends across the aisle, Kennedy forged ahead on a different approach.

On May 9, 1994, Kennedy introduced a bill of his own. It differed from the Clinton bill in numerous important respects:

Where the Clinton plan required all employers to insure their workers, Kennedy's exempted the smallest firms, with five or fewer employees, and allowed them to pay a 2 percent payroll tax instead. Where Clinton made participation in insurance purchasing alliances mandatory, Kennedy's only required states to set them up, allowing business and individuals to choose to buy them or through traditional agents.[7]

Kennedy also incorporated proposals by senators who opposed the Clinton approach, with the hope of finding new backers. He included Senator Bill Roth's proposal allowing individuals to join the same plan senators belonged to and choose among its options. Drawing from Senator John Chafee's bill, Kennedy offered subsidies to low-income individuals directly. He also included mental health benefits supported by Senator Pete Domenici of New Mexico.[8]

Republican senators still opposed the measure. Senator Orrin Hatch called it "nothing more than a pasteurized version of Clinton's blueprint for socialized medicine."[9] Republican Senator Nancy Kassebaum lamented that "the Kennedy bill is rather like a casserole made from the leftovers of the previous evening's meal. The ingredients are mixed up differently but they are the same ingredients."[10]

With continued opposition to his bill, Kennedy backed a bill sponsored by Senator George Mitchell that put off employer mandates and dropped price controls on insurance. Kennedy, though, praised the bill as "capable of achieving the goal of health security for all." Kennedy further spoke on the Senate floor on August 9, 1974:

> I introduced my first universal health plan in 1970 and I have been working on the issue ever since…. We must decide whether we will guarantee health insurance for every citizen, or whether we will continue to let millions of citizens suffer every year from conditions they cannot afford to treat, while millions worry about losing their insurance.[11]

On Sunday, September 18, 1994, *The New York Times* quoted Senator Packwood as having told other Republicans in August, "we've killed healthcare reform." Kennedy went back on the floor of the Senate and gave an impassioned speech in favor of health care reform.

> I will never give up the fight for health care reform until the working men and women of this country know that years of effort and hard work saving cannot be wiped out by sudden illness. The drive for comprehensive health care reform will begin again next year. We are closer than ever and I am confident we will prevail.[12]

Meanwhile, the resounding failure of Bill Clinton's health care reform efforts and the appearance of bumbling with the issue spelled trouble for Democrats in the midterm elections of 1994. Minority leader in the House Newt Gingrich advised the president and the First Lady against developing a comprehensive plan. Gingrich suggested an incremental approach that would tackle one problem at a time. But President Clinton ignored this advice and tried to push through the bill. Gingrich slammed it as "culturally alien to America" and described it as "1,300 pages of red tape."[13]

As the bill floundered, Gingrich worried that Clinton would negotiate with moderates and develop a slightly revised version of the bill. To prevent that from happening Gingrich opposed any amendments to the bill. Hillary Clinton wanted the president to go on national television and pressure Congress to pass the measure. Clinton, though, pulled the bill before it came to a vote on the floor to avoid certain defeat.

The failure of the health care reform bill played right into Gingrich's strategy for the upcoming midterm election. Gingrich sought to paint Clinton as an out-of-touch, big government liberal. Seizing on this and other issues including the Whitewater scandal and continuing rumors of Clinton's infidelities, Gingrich assailed Clinton with the aim of gaining control of Congress. Republican attacks worked because they hit a nerve with the public, tapping into doubts about Clinton's character and integrity. Thus, at the midpoint of his first term, Clinton presided over peace and prosperity but could not get above 50 percent of public approval.

The results proved disastrous. On the eve of the midterm elections, *U.S. News and World Report* discovered that many Americans viewed Clinton as ineffectual and a big spending liberal. No doubt the failed health care plan fueled this notion. Gingrich, in the meanwhile, presented his "Contract with America." The contract consisted of poll-tested ideas, many of them remnants from the Reagan years. It included various tax cuts, welfare reform, congressional term limits, capital gains cuts, increased defense spending, a balanced budget amendment, line item veto, tougher law enforcement and tort reform.

In the months leading up to the midterm election, Gingrich skillfully used alternative media, particularly talk radio. Gingrich also identified the most strong potential Republican challengers with the aim of gaining majorities in the House and Senate. Republican incumbents running in safe districts also donated money to the National Republican Congressional Committee to help support candidates in close races. Clinton pollster Dick Morris conducted a survey and suggested that Clinton stay off the campaign trail to appear presidential. Clinton disregarded that advice and as election day neared, went across the county on a nonstop seven-day journey, attacking Republicans. Many observers thought that Clinton's efforts on the campaign trail, combined with recent foreign policy successes, would help Democrats avoid disaster at the polls.

On election night, the results sent shockwaves across the nation. Republicans seized control of both houses of Congress for the first time in 40 years. In the Senate, Republicans now held a 53 to 47 majority. Gingrich, with Republicans taking the House of Representatives, became Speaker of the House. Now, Kennedy stood again in the minority, as had occurred during the Reagan years, stripped of important Committee assignments. More importantly, Kennedy found himself faced with a new crew of brash ideologues.

The new freshman ideologues, dubbed as "Gingrich's children," put a formidable obstacle in Ted Kennedy's continued health reform efforts. He soon realized that any bill would require the help of a Republican co-sponsor, and he wasted little time seeking out help from across the aisle.

Indeed, Kennedy through perseverance would get a health care reform bill passed. Much more modest in scope, Kennedy teamed with Republican Senator Nancy Kassebaum to shepherd through Congress and pass the Health Insurance Portability Act of 1996 (HIPPA).

The Kassebaum-Kennedy bill represented the culmination of Kennedy/Republican collaboration. According to the *Boston Globe*,

> Kennedy joined with Sen. Nancy Kassebaum of Kansas in 1996 to pass the Kennedy-Kassenbaum Act, which allowed employees to keep health insurance after leaving their job and prohibiting health insurance companies from refusing to renew coverage on the basis of preexisting medical conditions.[14]

According to the Legislative Summary of the act, the bill was designed "to amend the Internal Revenue Code of 1986 to improve portability and continuity of health insurance coverage in the group and individual markets, to combat waste, fraud and abuse in health insurance and health care delivery, to promote the use of medical savings accounts, to improve access to long-term care services and coverage, to simplify the administration of health insurance and for other purposes."[15]

The act scarcely accomplished all the goals in the Legislative Summary. Its key feature, however, portability through limitation on preexisting condition exclusions, marked a dramatic improvement in the delivery of health care services. Embodied in Section 701, the act prohibited the imposition of a preexisting condition exclusion unless such exclusion related to a condition within six months after diagnosis or treatment of a condition. Further, the act only allowed such an exclusion for 12 months after the enrollment date.[16]

The Health Insurance Portability and Accountability Act also contained an antidiscrimination provision against individual participants and beneficiaries based on health status. Pursuant to Section 702, a group health plan "may not establish rules for eligibility (including continued eligibility of any individual to enroll under the terms of the plan) based on any of the following health-status related factors in relation to the individual or a dependent of an individual: (A) health status; (B) medical condition (including both physical and mental illness); (C) claims experience; (D) receipt of health care; (E) medical history; (F) genetic information; (G) evidence of insurability (including conditions arising out of acts of domestic violence); and (H) disability."[17] Thus, yet another Kennedy sponsored or backed bill contained antidiscrimination provisions at the core of his beliefs and indeed the body of his legislative work.

Analyzing the act requires both an assessment of what the bill accomplished and an acknowledgment of what it did not. While one cannot minimize the strides made in the passage of the bill, plainly the act compromised the initial lofty goals of the Clinton administration and Kennedy himself. The bill does *not*

- provide universal health coverage to all Americans;
- require all employers to insure their workers;
- require employers with more than five employees to insure their workers;
- make participation in insurance-purchasing alliances mandatory; or
- require states to set up insurance programs and thereby allow businesses or individuals to buy them or purchase health insurance through traditional agents.

None of these goals, centerpieces of Clinton's plan or Kennedy's plan in 1994, became the law.

Indeed, the HIPPA Act of 1976 veered far away from the initial thrust of health care reform upon the election of Clinton. With the Hillary Clinton/Ira Magaziner plan being a bust in Congress, Kennedy and his allies needed to steer health care legislative efforts on a different path.

That path, preventing private health insurance for-profit companies from refusing coverage for individuals with preexisting medical conditions except under limited circumstances, has had profound effects. Prior to this legislation, an individual with heart disease laid off from his job could find himself uninsurable following the expiration of COBRA continuation coverage. So, too, the prohibition on discrimination against individuals based on health status and claims experience has greatly improved the availability of health care for many Americans.

Still, the supposed fraud and abuse features of the act had little if any effect. Today, we read about massive lawsuits against major insurance carriers for practices designed to have been eradicated by the act. While insurance companies have largely complied with the preexisting condition requirements, a practice just as insidious has developed. After insuring individuals and accepting premiums, some well known carriers have declined to pay for previously approved expensive medical treatment, leaving families in financial ruin. Litigation has changed these practices to some degree, but often far too late for the individuals victimized by such predatory practices.

Despite a clear record of abuse by private insurance companies since the passage of HIPPA in 1976, critics of more comprehensive health care reform brand such efforts as socialism. Thus, even though President Obama made health care reform a key aspect of his platform, significant obstacles thwarted further reform.

Fueling the fire, activist Michael Moore, a successful filmmaker beginning with *Roger and Me* about auto factories, made a documentary called *Sicko*. *Sicko* in stark terms pointed out the deficiencies in the American health care system. In his moving film, Moore poignantly depicted the plight of many Americans deprived of necessary medical treatment. He showed United Stated citizens crossing the border to Canada to receive medical treatment, at a fraction of the cost.

Moore's film, designed to provoke, unfortunately went too far. It was a necessary movie, but had Moore shown some restraint, it may have impacted the political debate on health care reform. Unfortunately, Moore went on to argue that Cuba's health system also remained a better alternative than the United States system. Such hyperbole, although good to spark controversy, led to a condemnation of health care reform by many on the right, and moderates. Moore underestimated the important role he could have played in the health care debate. While making salient points and demonstrating shortcomings in the United States system, Moore's film ultimately did not help the cause.

To be sure, though, many seniors have turned to Mexico or Canada to obtain prescription medication at a fraction of the price here. Hoarding medicines after crossing the border back to home, some have literally escaped financial ruin by driving hours to obtain necessary prescribed medicine. Such flaws in the U.S. system, even with current reform discussed below, deserve continued attention. Still, Moore's staunch advocation of public health care, such as in Canada, has to date met ardent resistance.

For example, ardent supporters of comprehensive health care reform look to the government to guarantee universal health care coverage for all residents. This position, though, ignores the financial consequences that have ruined health care delivery in many areas due to *illegal* immigration. For example, in Los Angeles, emergency rooms are inundated with patients seeking routine care, to the detriment of patients carrying health insurance with true emergencies. And emergency rooms cannot, however, turn away the uninsured in Los Angeles, even illegal immigrants. This has resulted in skyrocketing health care costs in California.

Obama's challenge involved forging a compromise between the conservative free market advocates and the liberal left wing seeking universal health care. Liberal Democrats proposed a government-backed plan to supply true competition for private insurance companies. But in the face of opposition from even his own party, Obama backed off the public option. Nonetheless, in his State of the Union Address, Obama stated his eagerness to hear Republican alternatives to health care reform. Time will tell whether Kennedy's nearly 40-year quest for major health care reform will come to fruition. Unfortunately, his death preceded his desired reform, and due to his illness he could not participate in the recent health care reform debates that led to the ultimate 2009 legislation. In fact, Kennedy's absence during the health care debate received considerable attention. As a divided Senate tangled on health care reform, a bipartisan consensus emerged on one point: Ted Kennedy could have made a big difference. Senator Tom Harkin, Democrat of Iowa and a member of the Health, Education, Labor and Pension Committee stated that "he would lend a gravitas to the issue that we're kind of missing right now."[18] Harkin's counterparts on the Republican side similarly invoked Kennedy in criticizing the health care reform process.

Colleagues routinely lamented his absence. As his health declined, Kennedy became more of an inspirational leader then a tangible one. He turned over his day-to-day committee duties to Christopher Dodd. Dodd commented that no one could better navigate the obstacles to the bill than Kennedy. Republican Senator Orrin Hatch poignantly noted, "I would like to work with him on it and have a legacy issue for him."[19]

Ultimately, though, Obama pushed through health care reform in the fall of 2009. The final bill did not include a government health care option. With scandals involving private insurance companies, it appeared an opportune time to embrace legislation containing a government option. With politics playing its role, this did not come to fruition.

Contrary to conservative opponents and some Democrats' views, a government plan would not lead to a "socialist" health care system. It would work as follows: private insurance companies still would offer their prices, reimbursement schedules and products. The government option, many think, would only appeal to low-income workers and provide minimal coverage. However, if implemented properly, a government option could well challenge private insurers to lower their outrageous rates. What harm could occur by testing this approach? Conservatives fear that any showing of a supplemental option will weaken their plank. This, decidedly, ignores a national imperative. Our health care system has spiraled out of hand. Choice of medical providers since the well-intentioned Obama law, is easily side swept by medical groups forming different alliances and thus denying supposed "insurance." Those with insurance should have continued access to their doctors of choice, many of whom have been their patients for years.

Currently, President Obama pushed through a compromise bill, to say the least, following Kennedy's death. Derisively called "Obamacare" and branded as "socialist" by critics from the right, it is scheduled to come into full force in 2014 and contained many compromises. While a symbolic victory, the bill still does not include factors designed to curb health care abuse.

First, Obama carved out the public option, perhaps the most important feature to stem private insurance abuse. The public option, so central to many, would have provided true competition to the price gouging of private insurance companies. If administered right, the public option, a nonprofit system, could have forced private insurance carriers to moderate their rates.

A prime example involves Anthem Blue Cross in California. After announcing a 28 percent increase, the then Republican insurance commissioner Steve Poizner called for an audit. Soon, the report by Anthem Blue Cross proved indefensible. Placing a hold on the premium increase, Anthem Blue Cross "corrected" its books. Eventually, the insurance commissioner approved an 18 percent increase. A governmental option, properly conceived, would have provided stiff competition to these proposed increases.

Many doctors chafe at a governmental option, claiming that the reduced rates will put them out of business. Those who counter this notion argue that a *nonprofit* government plan would result both in lower premiums to participants and higher reimbursements to doctors. With the major insurance carriers raking in record profits, one can only wonder if a well-managed nonprofit government option would serve patients and doctors better.

As things stand, the effectiveness of the latest health reform bill remains untested. Of critical concern remains spiraling premium costs, as well as diminished coverage. Aetna recently raised its premiums 19 percent. Anthem Blue Cross will beat or match that increase in the future. Prescription drugs, necessary for health, remain too expensive for many Americans, leading them to go across the border for medicine. Hospital costs defy imagination and even wealthy Americans teeter on financial ruin with one catastrophic illness.

The well-intended compromise Obama reforms do not address soaring and out-of-control health care premiums. It does make health insurance accessible to many who previously did not have insurance— a good thing. But the main ills of completely unaffordable health insurance for the masses completely remain unsolved.

Mistrust in big government and bureaucratic ineptitude, in the end, doomed the public option. Had Kennedy survived for the health care debate, many think he could have used his influence to sway more Democrats to vote for a public option. Such speculation, though, will remain unanswered. At the very least, Obama ushered in health care reform, which Kennedy fought so hard for over the years. However, the absence of a public option exemplifies the need for additional health care reform. Why not test the market? Supposed conservatives or libertarians would, if true to their beliefs, welcome all comers. Unfortunately, it remains an open question today, even as insurers continue to choose death for its insured to spare costs.

Importantly, Obama in pressing for health care reform carried to fruition, a cause dear to Kennedy's heart. Relentless in his efforts at health care reform since 1970, Obamacare could not have become the law without Kennedy's nearly 30 years of ceaseless efforts devoted to health care reform.

9

Minimum Wage
Legislation of 1996

One of Ted Kennedy's passions throughout the years has centered on minimum wage legislation. Such legislation, designed to provide a decent wage for largely unskilled workers to maintain them above the poverty level, has met with controversy throughout the years.

Ted Kennedy always associated minimum wage legislation with his brother JFK. While in the Senate, Jack pushed unsuccessfully for an increase in the minimum wage. His efforts met with defeat in 1960. But then, President JFK secured an increase in the minimum wage from $1 to $1.25 in 1961. Ted Kennedy drew from that experience and spent years learning the statistics and the history of minimum wage legislation. He also listened to arguments on both sides, attempting to create consensus on the propriety of the minimum wage and the necessity for increases to it.

As the Civil Rights Movement emerged in the 1960s, Kennedy increased his attention to poverty issues. Indeed, while Bobby and LBJ tangled on many issues, Ted Kennedy enthusiastically backed LBJ's sweeping Domestic War on Poverty. Many other facets of the War on Poverty took precedence, and of course the Vietnam War gripped the nation and led to the downfall of LBJ's presidency. Throughout this time, though, Kennedy formed the view that any attempt to address poverty issues would have to include minimum wage legislation. Kennedy espoused the view that government had to monitor the market and ensure that companies would not exploit workers by paying them menial wages, leaving them under the poverty level. This view, though, met with considerable resistance from numerous groups.

To many conservative free-marketers, minimum wage represents yet another attempt of big government to improperly regulate the economy. The minimum wage, they say, "hurts low income people" by raising unemployment rates.[1] Such individuals also point to the effect of depriving students from working at a lower rate, which they may gladly accept. Libertarians view the minimum wage as a regulation imposed by big government that distorts the marketplace. To many Democrats, mostly union workers or leaders of the labor movement, the minimum wage had its pitfalls as well. Must union workers made enough so that any increase in the minimum wage did not help them personally economically. Indeed, many unions feared the adoption of a subminimum training wage. This, they argued, would keep wages down by employers like fast food restaurants that did no real training but had high turnover.

The poverty problem and need for a minimum wage increase, however, became particularly vital in the 1970s and 1980s. Finding jobs for the many millions of women and baby boomers looking for employment posed particular difficulties. Mechanization in struggling sectors of the economy, notably coal mining and cotton textiles, resulted in a dearth of jobs in those areas. Residents in pockets of rural poverty suffered badly. Native Americans on reservations continued to experience severe poverty. Many jobs moved abroad. Unemployment rates, which had averaged 4.7 percent in the late 1960s to 1973, rose to an average of 7.4 percent between 1973 and 1986.[2]

The number of persons at poverty level increased between 1970 and 1980 from 25 to 29 million. Meanwhile, the minimum wage could not make a dent into the rising poverty issue. Methodically, Congress, with the support of then President Jimmy Carter, hiked the federal minimum wage in stages to $3.35 an hour by 1981. These modest increases, however, failed to keep up with rapidly rising prices. The real wages of full-time production workers stagnated. Household debt shot up, particularly as inflation soared and the economy suffered from one of the longest and harshest bear markets. Workers complained bitterly that corporations held down wages. Some workers embraced protectionism, urging folks to "buy American." By the late 1970s, with high double-digit inflation, steep gas price hikes and an ever increasing cost of living, the increases to the minimum wage did not make a dent into the economic struggles of millions of low-wage earners. Carter's infamous call for Americans to tighten their belts led to profound dissatisfaction of his and Democratic policy and sealed Reagan's sweep into the White House. Blue collar Americans, finding no help on the economic horizons, voted for a Republican presidential candidate in record numbers.

During the Reagan years, quests for minimum wage reform legislation met persistent resistance. With campaign promises of tax cuts and supply side economics, the Reagan conservatives did not believe in increased government regulation. These tax cuts for high-income wage earners, supporters said, would result in a stimulated economy and more opportunities for the poor. To the contrary, the cuts in marginal tax rates for the wealthy that the Reagan administration had secured contributed to an already rising economic inequality between the wealthy and the poor. Millions of Americans continued to live in households below the poverty line. Millions more, including hosts of low-wage workers, tethered on the brink of poverty.[3]

While many wealthy people in the Reagan era prospered as never before, the real wages of full time production workers continued to stagnate. Job seekers complained that the fastest growing sectors in the job market paid the lowest. All of these trends augured for an increase in the minimum wage.

While Reagan attracted blue collar workers in his resolving defeat of Carter, soon his pledges turned at least some around. Cutting of social programs assisting the poor did not help the common worker. Kennedy in stump speeches made the case against the Reagan administration's cuts in the budgets for food stamps and the Women, Infants and Children feeding program.

Kennedy attacked Reagan over hunger. Kennedy called for large expansions in the food stamp programs and other methods for feeding the young and the elderly. But Reagan, speaking to teenagers at the White House, argued, "I don't think there is anyone going hungry in America simply by reason of decision or inability to feed them." Instead, "where there is hunger," Reagan said, "that is probably because of a lack of knowledge on the part of people as to what is available."[4]

Reagan's views on hunger displayed to the public at large the philosophical divide on the propriety of the minimum wage, and other social programs as well. To Reagan and his followers, the minimum wage was unnecessary because with hard work anyone could find a decent paying job in the free-market economy. To Reagan, the minimum wage represented an evil entitlement. Under this view, lazy workers could expect a wage no matter what. They did not need to work hard, nor could employers do anything about it. Equating this to those engaging in welfare fraud, Reagan and his supporters ardently opposed the minimum wage.

History bears little credence to these philosophical views. To begin, most low-income wage earners were hard working immigrants and children of immigrants who came to America in the early 1900s, and particularly after World War I. Mostly hard working individuals seeking to eke out a living, and often working exceedingly long hours and more than one job, these individuals did not fit into the "lazy worker" stereotype. Indeed, exploitation of such individuals stood as the norm rather than the isolated (but real) instances of welfare fraud. Then, having endured the Great Depression, such families did not have the means to complete a high school education, much less higher education. This led to an insidious pattern of poverty through generations. Reagan adherents did not see it this way and instead viewed the minimum wage as a convenient excuse to protect individuals who failed to seek the best jobs.

Obviously such patent philosophical differences meant that Kennedy had little clout on economic policy, and particularly efforts to boost the minimum wage, during Reagan's presidency. While Reagan did not carry out some of his colorful campaign denunciations of big government, such as dismantling the Education Department, he nonetheless encouraged advocates of deregulation and wanted nothing to do with minimum wage legislation. Indeed, Reagan tried to reduce expenditures for federal agencies assisting the poor, such as the Housing and Urban Development (HUD) and Health and Human Resources (HHS). None of these initiatives helped the "new Democrats" who fled to support Reagan in the 1980 presidential election. Still, with an economy decidedly better than the inflationary Carter era, despite the 1987 stock market crash, many "Reagan Democrats" stayed aboard.

In truth, Kennedy recognized that he needed to bide his time on economic issues. On a personal note, Ted had ended his marriage with Joan Kennedy following the 1980 election. Some attribute his lack of effort on the economic front to yet another personal woe. But Kennedy knew when and how to fight. In truth, he had no way of stemming Reagan's conservative economic agenda on the minimum wage issue. One cannot make a connection between Kennedy's marital issues with his relative silence on certain economic issues. The times simply did not dictate such efforts.

Confirmation of this occurred in 1984. Walter Mondale, running as the Democratic presidential nominee met resounding defeat in historical measures against the affable Reagan. Facing Reagan's popular mandate, Mondale, as the then-disgraced Carter's former vice president, could hardly have had a chance for success. Instead of nominating a candidate not identifiable with Carter's legacy of double-digit inflation and high unemployment, the Democratic party backed Mondale. Results of the election confirmed what polls predicted: Reagan won in a landslide. He took every state except Mondale's home state of Minnesota and the District of Columbia. Reagan won the electoral college by a staggering margin of 525–13.

Kennedy did not back Mondale at the start. Mondale sought his endorsement after winning the Iowa caucuses and chafed that Kennedy would not actively campaign for him. Kennedy stayed neutral, as Jesse Jackson and Gary Hart fought Mondale in the primary. But when Mondale had enough delegates, Kennedy endorsed Mondale. At the Democratic convention, Kennedy did his best by attacking Reagan and providing soaring rhetoric as to Mondale's skills. But his tepid approach early on surely presaged his discomfort with the nominee. Regardless, Mondale never stood a chance, even if he had had early backing by Kennedy and even if Kennedy would have actively campaigned. The economy in 1984 had significantly improved since 1980. Reagan received credit for the release of the American hostages in Iran. Reagan portrayed a strong military presence. Many Americans reveled in his taking on the air traffic controllers.

Reagan also held the sympathy factor. A nation witnessed yet another assassination attempt. Reagan gamely survived John Hinckley's attempt on his life. Exuding strength from his hospital room, Reagan gave many Americans what they wanted: an almost superhero-type character who epitomized the dream of a strong leader. The contrast between Reagan's image and Carter's could scarcely have been more stark.

But behind the scenes, in what his cabinet and advisors surely knew but kept hidden from Americans, Reagan's memory had faded dramatically. The oldest president upon his reelection, Reagan governed through largely symbolic means. He could still deliver carefully scripted one-liners and quip with the best of them. Still photogenic, Reagan as he began his second term had a clear mandate.

Given Reagan's popular mandate and Congressional majority, the years 1984–88 proved especially difficult for Kennedy on the economic legislation front. With supply side adherents remaining firm in their convictions, minimum wage reform stood little chance. No doubt this explains Kennedy's activism on the Judiciary Committee regarding

Bork's nomination and his involvement in the Comprehensive Anti-Apartheid Act of 1986.

In 1987, with the hope that Democrats could end the eight-year Republican stranglehold on the presidency, a number of hopefuls announced primary runs, including Richard Gephardt of Missouri, Al Gore, Jr. of Tennessee, and Senator Paul Simon of Illinois. Delaware Senator Joe Biden, former Colorado Senator Gary Hart and the Reverend Jesse Jackson led the pack. However, well before 1988 aggressive investigative reporters increasingly dug into the personal lives of major candidates. Soon reports of Biden's plagiarism of speeches ended his candidacy. (Interestingly, the plagiarism scandal did not surface after Obama chose Biden as his vice presidential running mate in 2008.) In May 1987, the *Miami Herald* broke a story that Hart, who had dared reporters to pry into his personal life, had an extramarital affair. Newspapers featured a picture of Hart sitting on a yacht, named *Monkey Business*, in a revealing pose with model Donna Rice. Yet another aspirant, therefore, dropped out of the race.

Reverend Jackson fared well for a while, winning five southern primaries. But Jackson had his own skeletons in his closet. Four years earlier he had referred to New York City as "Hymietown," an obvious anti–Semitic slur. Then, when Louis Farrakhan, head of the Nation of Islam, described Judaism as a "gutter religion," Jackson refused to criticize the statement.[5] The so-called "rainbow coalition" did not welcome all comers. Despite Jackson imploring "keep hope alive," he could not with his divisive stances command the Democratic party's backing.

Michael Dukakis of Massachusetts emerged as the primary winner. With a decisive victory in the early New Hampshire primary, Dukakis achieved a tremendous fundraising advantage. Ted Kennedy's son Patrick, then a twenty-year-old Providence College sophomore, ran for election in March 1988 as a Rhode Island delegate for Dukakis. With his first political victory Patrick Kennedy pledged to Dukakis as a Rhode Island delegate at the Democratic National Convention.[6]

Ted Kennedy campaigned earnestly for Dukakis all year. Dukakis praised Kennedy's efforts, expressing his gratefulness for Kennedy's active fundraising and appearances. Like Bush, Dukakis took the nomination on the first ballot at the convention. Kennedy spoke at the convention and ridiculed Bush for hiding from the Reagan administration's Iran-Contra debacle. Mimicking Bush, Kennedy repeatedly queried "where was George."[7]

The problem, ultimately, resided in Dukakis' wooden speaking style and passionless personality. Squandering a 17-point lead at the close of the Democratic convention Dukakis blundered in a well-remembered ad showing him riding a military tank. His vice presidential nominee, Lloyd Bentsen of Texas, tried gamely to turn the tide. In a televised debate with Republican vice presidential nominee Dan Quayle, Bentsen got the best of his younger and outmatched foe. When Quayle made reference to John F. Kennedy, Bentsen hit him head on, stating, "I knew Jack Kennedy, Jack Kennedy was my friend. You are no Jack Kennedy." Indeed, Quayle's utter ineptitude and lack of qualifications for the vice president position should have emboldened a strong Democratic candidate to run. The thought of Quayle occupying the White House in the case of an emergency, many Democrats thought, would sway the election. Yet, this seeming gift to Dukakis never came to fruition.

This teaches an important historical lesson. While much fanfare accompanies the decision-making process for appointment of the nominee for the vice president, in truth it has scarcely ever mattered. Mondale's historic appointment of the first female nominee, Geraldine Ferraro, made absolutely no difference. Quayle's lack of a grasp of national issues, to the point of utter mockery on Saturday Night Live, watched by millions, ultimately would have no effect. Only JFK's strategic appointment of LBJ in the 1960 election, which resulted in LBJ delivering Texas on election day, ever turned a presidential election. In the end, then, Americans historically vote for the president. The vice president does not sway the voting. This may well explain Obama's choice of Joe Biden of Delaware as his nominee, by then a bland candidate who could not deliver any state and has served as a silent vice president.

Thus, even with the good fortune of attacking Quayle, Dukakis continued to lose ground. A particularly negative ad criticized Dukakis' revolving door prison policy during Dukakis' governorship. This program, instituted by a Republican predecessor, enabled prisoners to the take brief furloughs. One Massachusetts prisoner, Willie Horton, on a weekend furlough had repeatedly beaten and stabbed a man and raped his fiancée. Though Bush's national committee disavowed knowledge of dissemination of pictures of an ominous-looking Horton, no doubt the Bush team knew and approved of the ads.

During the campaign, in 1988, Kennedy lost a major fight in an effort to raise the minimum wage, then $3.55 per hour, for the first time in seven years.[8] It took Kennedy over a year, until June 29, 1988, to even get the bill out of committee. It called for a modest increase to $4.55 per hour over a three-year period.

But Senate Republicans remained firm, calling for a subminimum wage for training of workers in their first 90 days. Kennedy would not agree, and the bill never made it out of committee.[9]

Kennedy, seemingly, would have to wait until a more favorable political environment to push the minimum wage agenda. But in 1989 he renewed his efforts to increase the minimum wage. The concept of minimum wage had deep roots with Ted Kennedy:

> Minimum wage legislation was something Kennedy always associated with his brother Jack, who had pushed it unsuccessfully in the Senate in 1960, and then, as President, had secured an increase from $1 to $1.25 that was enacted in 1961.[10]

With the threat of a veto, Kennedy nonetheless in 1989 co-sponsored a bill with the new majority leader Senator George J. Mitchell of Maine. It would have raised the minimum wage, over three years, from $3.35 per hour to $4.65. Bush's Secretary of Labor, Elizabeth Dole, wife of then minority leader Senator Bob Dole, said the administration would go no higher than a $4.25 wage after three years, with a six month training wage at $3.35. On March 23, 1989, the House passed a $4.25 per hour bill, with a two month subminimum training period.[11]

When the Senate took up the bill again, Kennedy challenged the major argument against it, the contention that an increase in the minimum wage would cause employers to fire workers. Kennedy told the Senate that "these are the same old tired arguments."[12] With Kennedy's speech the Senate trimmed back the bill to the same $4.55 per hour and two month training period as the House bill. On April 12, 1989, the Senate adopted the modified Kennedy bill 62–37.[13]

On June 13, 1989, Bush vetoed the bill and insisted on no more than $4.25 per hour over three years and no less than a six month training wage. The House did not have enough votes to override the veto. Nonetheless, Kennedy reintroduced the bill, seeking a compromise. Kennedy proposed $4.25 after two years and a 60-day training wage. Kennedy enlisted the aid of Lane Kirkland, president of the AFL-CIO. Kirkland met with John Sununu, Bush's chief of staff, and urged a compromise on the training wage.[14]

On October 31, the administration agreed to $4.25 an hour over two years. Democrats and unions accepted a six-month training period at 85 percent of the minimum wage ($3.61 per hour). "The minimum wage," Kennedy said, "was one of the first and is still one of the best anti-poverty programs we have."[15]

Kennedy's critics, most prominently Thomas Sowell, set forth quite a different view of the minimum wage. According to Sowell, the minimum wage leads to rampant unemployment:

> The net economic effect of minimum wage laws is to make less skilled, less experienced or otherwise less desired workers more expensive-thereby pricing many of them out of jobs. Large disparities in unemployment rates between the young and mature, the skilled and unskilled, and between different racial groups have been common consequences of minimum wage laws.[16]

Sowell viewed minimum wage regulations as an evil of government intervention:

> Minimum wage laws make it illegal to pay less than the government specified price for labor. By the simplest and most basic economics, a price artificially raised tends to cause more to be supplied and less to be demanded than when prices are left to be determined by supply and demand in a free market. The result is a surplus, whether the price that is set artificially high is that of form produce or labor. Minimum wage laws are almost always discussed politically in terms of the benefits they confer on workers receiving those wages. Unfortunately, the real minimum wage is always zero, regardless of the laws, and that is the wage that many workers receive in the wake of the creation or escalation of a government-mandated minimum wage, because they lose their jobs or fail to find jobs when they enter the labor force.[17]

Sowell also opposes local "living wage" measures. According to Sowell, "what the so-called living wage really amounts to is simply a local minimum wage policy requiring much higher rates than the federal minimum wage."[18]

More recent critics of the minimum wage echo Sowell's criticism. According to one of them,

> the economic case against minimum wage laws is simple. Employers pay a wage no higher than the value of an additional hour's work. Raising minimum wages forces employers to dismiss low productivity workers. This policy has the largest effect on those with the least education, job experience and maturity. Consequently, we should expect minimum wage laws to effect teenagers and those with less education. Eliminating minimum wage laws will reduce unemployment and improve the efficiency of low productivity labor.[19]

This critic acknowledged that other than left-wing economists supported the minimum wage. The economic case for minimum wage increases has gained from public and professional opinion. As MacKenzie writes, "even some free market leaning economists, like Steven Landsburg, have conceded that minimum wage increases do not affect employment significantly."[20] Landsburg noted that, clearly, minimum wage laws have a disproportionate effect on teens and blacks. But he dismissed these critics because "minimum wages have mostly a tiny impact on employment … the minimum wage obstacles were lousy jobs anyway. It is almost impossible to maintain the old argument that minimum wages are bad for minimum wage workers."[21]

Writing for the Mises Institute, a well known Austrian journal, MacKenzie attempts to rebuke Landsburg's opinion. MacKenzie cites statistics which the author contends makes the critics of minimum wage laws right all along. Acknowledging that minimum wages should not drive the national employment rate to astronomical levels, MacKenzie argues that it does adversely affect teenagers and minorities. The article points to The Bureau of Labor Statistics. The unemployment rate for everyone over the age of 16 was 5.6 percent in 2005. The unemployment rate was 17.3 percent for those ages 16–19 years. For those ages 16–17 it was 19.7 percent. In the 18 to 19-year age group unemployment was 18.4 percent. MacKenzie argues that minimum wage laws do affect ethnic minorities more than others. The unemployment rate for white teens in the 16–17 age group was 17.3 percent in 2005. The same figures for Hispanic and black teens were 25 percent and 40.9 percent, respectively. Blacks ages 18–19 had unemployment rates of 25.7 percent, and those ages 20–24 19.75 percent in 2005. The Hispanic unemployment was slightly lower—17.8 percent at age 18–19 and 9.6 percent at 20–24.[22]

Contrasting these statistics, MacKenzie observed that "supporters of minimum wage laws do not realize that prior to minimum wage laws the national unemployment rate fell well below 5 percent. According to the U.S. Census, national unemployment rates were 3.3 percent in 1927, 1.8 percent in 1926, 3.2 percent in 1925, 2.4 percent in 1923, 1.4 percent in 1918, 2.8 percent in 1907, 1.7 percent in 1906 and 3.6 percent in 1902.[23] Writing in 2006, MacKenzie noted that some states had an unemployment rate of approximately 3 percent. Virginia then had an unemployment rate of 3.1 percent. Wyoming had an unemployment rate of 2.9 percent. Hawaii had an unemployment rate of 2.6 percent. The article states, "given these figures, it is quite arguable that minimum wage laws keep the national unemployment rate 3 percent points higher than would otherwise be the case."[24] Given that the federal minimum wage has not increased since 2006 and unemployment rates now hover at 9 percent, MacKenzie's argument can be easily challenged. Moreover, his citation to *pre*–Depression statistics, not including 1929–1940, raises an obvious flaw in his methodology.

Yet, as Obama presses for minimum wage increases, critics have again attacked the policy.[25] Mike Flynn argues that like all government mandates, a wage hike sets off unintended consequences and ends up harming the very people politicians say they are trying to help. Flynn's article sets forth five myths regarding minimum wage that he could ascribe to that policy. According to Flynn, Myth one is that hiking wages for those at the lowest rung of the job market will boost the economy. Flynn vehemently disagrees. He states there are not enough people earning minimum wage for minimum wage increases to make sense. In 1979, almost 14 percent of hourly wage workers earned minimum wage. According to Flynn, today just around 4 percent of hourly workers earn it. Among all wage and salary employees, only a little over 2 percent earn minimum wage. Among the entire labor force, that number is even smaller. In 2012, just 1.6 million were paid the minimum wage.[26]

The article continues with Myth two: minimum wage workers are poor. Flynn again disagrees. Citing a study as to who would benefit from the increase in minimum wage from $7.25 to $9.50, comparable to the level recently proposed by President Obama, Flynn says that just 11 percent of workers that would gain from the increase live in poor households. Over 63 percent of the workers who would gain are second or third earners in families making below the federal poverty line. According to Flynn, 43 percent of workers who would benefit live in households with income over $50,000. Flynn posits that most minimum wage workers are teens, young adults starting in the labor force or spouses providing a second income to the household. If the federal minimum wage increases, Flynn contends, these workers become the larger share of the minimum wage workforce as they crowd out those workers with fewer skills.[27]

Flynn describes Myth three, that minimum wage workers are supporting a family, as implausible. According to Flynn, the vast majority of Americans earning a minimum wage are not trying to raise a family. About half of those earning minimum wage, Flynn asserts, are under 25. A recent study by Dr. Bradley Schiller, Professor Emeritus at American University, found that among families where an adult was earning the minimum wage, 94 percent had a spouse who was also employed, often far above the minimum wage. And among half of these families the spouse was earning over $40,000 a year. That small subset of adults trying to raise a family on a minimum wage have very low skill levels, Flynn said. It is these workers, Flynn argues, that are most vulnerable to any contraction in employment caused by a minimum wage hike.[28]

Both myths four and five, according to the article, state that a mandated wage hike is the best way to improve income for minimum wage workers who are poor. Again, Flynn argues the contrary. He states that the number of minimum wage workers who are poor and struggling to raise a family is "thankfully" very small, a proposition resoundingly debunked by actual Department of Labor Statistics. Flynn favors the Earned Income Tax Credit (EITC) that was signed into law by President General Ford based on the negative income tax concept first developed by famed free market economist Milton Freedman. Low-income households receive a refundable tax credit, the amount of which is based on their other income. It acts as a guarantee of a minimum income rather than minimum wage, Flynn contends. If the worker's wages rise, the amount of EITC they can claim goes down. Their wages may go up, but the overall household income may stay the same. If, however, a mandated wage hike has a disemployment effect on these low-wage workers, they may be far worse off than before the wage hike, according to Flynn.[29]

Flynn then describes the reasons why he favors the EITC rather than an increase in minimum wage:

> The benefit of increasing the EITC, rather than a simple minimum wage hike, is that you can concentrate the benefits on those politicians claim they want to help: low income, poor workers struggling to raise a family. If a minimum wage causes people to lose their jobs, it is those workers, with lower skill sets, most vulnerable to the job loss. They reap the fall out of those politicians trying to help.[30]

Flynn concludes the article by boldly stating, "If our goal is to help those workers who are trying to raise a family on a minimum wage, a federal mandated wage increase is the worst thing we can do."[31]

Kennedy and others, of course, have a decidedly different view. Kennedy repeatedly throughout his time in the Senate sought increases in the minimum wage. Kennedy's ally on the Health Care legislation of 1996, Republican Nancy Kassebaum, vigorously opposed any increase in the minimum wage in 1994. On December 15, 1994, Kassebaum held a hearing and opened by stating, "I think it is terribly important for us at this juncture to keep the level that it is at $4.25 an hour, where low skilled workers can move into jobs and then advance."[32] Kennedy contested this view, arguing that the minimum wage deprived hard-working Americans of a chance to gain a decent wage.

Following the disastrous midterm 1994 elections, in which many Democrat stalwarts lost their office, including Tom Foley, Jim Sasser, Jack Brooks and New York governor Mario Cuomo, Kennedy approached Clinton to reinvigorate some traditional Democratic causes. Kennedy felt that the midterm elections created false fear on behalf of Democrats. He detected a conviction that took hold that the electorate had embraced the conservative cause.

Kennedy never accepted this. He realized that Republicans had made gains in the midterm elections largely due to the failure of Clinton's health care reform team and the short-lived ascendancy of Newt Gingrich's Contract with America. But Kennedy, rightly so, did not feel that conservatives now had a national mandate. Kennedy noted the trend in midterm elections, and observed that Republicans had gained control of Congress by the narrowest of margins.

After the midterm elections, Kennedy spoke with President Clinton on several occasions. Clinton advised Kennedy that he felt "bone tired" from his ceaseless campaign-trail efforts. Feeling despair, Clinton wished to turn to the right. Kennedy reiterated that he felt that the Democrats still had a national majority of those voting nationwide.

In this context, Kennedy continued his advocacy for an increase in the minimum wage. To some extent, President Clinton agreed, supporting the increase in his State of the Union address. Other voices in the Clinton administration, including Dick Morris, advised Clinton of avoiding such measures. By adopting "triangulation," Morris urged, Clinton could gain a safe middle ground by co-opting ideas from both the left and the right.

Kennedy relented to a great extent, but not on the minimum wage. In January 1995, Kennedy advocated his minimum wage increase proposal to a joint meeting of House and Senate Democratic leaders. He expected considerable opposition from senators like John Breaux of Louisiana and Wendell Ford of Kentucky. Instead his junior colleague Senator John Kerry of Massachusetts had taken up the cause. Through a joint effort, senators such as Daschle said that he would support the initiative if Kennedy could get more conservative Democrats to back it. Kennedy thus sought a package of leaders, the White House and labor to support a bid to increase the minimum wage.

Thus, while minimum wage legislation had stalled for years, it surfacing again in January 1995 during President Bill Clinton's State of the Union address. Clinton implored, "You can't make a decent living on $4.25 an hour."[33] On January 31, 1995, Kennedy presented his idea of increasing the minimum wage to a joint meeting of House and Senate Democratic leaders. Kennedy determined he needed to get a package that the leaders, the White House and labor would all support. Kennedy unified these different factions by proposing a $1.50 increase over three years, with indexing, and 90 cents over two years, without indexing.[34] Yet, additional bargaining ensued, and on July 31, 1996, a group of conferees assigned to settle differences between House and Senate versions of the bill agreed to provide a 50 percent increase to $4.75 that October 1, and another 40 cents, up to $5.15, on September 1, 1997.[35]

On August 2, 1996, Congress sent the minimum wage bill to President Clinton for his signature. Notably, for the first time since the Immigration Act of 1965, a bill signed by the president bore Ted Kennedy's name as a co-sponsor.[36]

The fact that Kennedy did not ultimately have a bill in his name signed into law for 31 years is revealing in many respects. First, it demonstrates that Kennedy did not occupy his Senate seat for the purposes of political aggrandizement. Rather, through this period Kennedy continually compromised and allowed others to eventually have their names stamped on the bill sent to the president. Notably, though, this ability to create consensus fostered Kennedy's causes, such as cancer legislation, antidiscrimination provisions in education, campaign finance reform, anti-apartheid legislation, health care reform and an increase in the minimum wage.

Second, the lack of Kennedy-sponsored legislation signed into law does call into question his nickname, coined by recent biographers, as "the lion of the Senate." Indeed, a very different conclusion emerges. Most of Kennedy's initial bills in these areas were far too liberal in scope for passage. Rather, it took other senators to propose compromise legislation for eventual passage, whether through Republican or Democratic presidents. Kennedy may have left a more visible stamp on his Senate legacy with respect to Legislative accomplishments if his bills had more modest goals in the first instance.

Third, a review of all of these prominent bills fortifies the notion that not one single senator can press bills into law. The sheer length of these legislative enactments, often diverging from the main topic, illustrates the hardship of passage of simple, clean legislation on discrete issues.

Still, by 1996, Kennedy stood as one of the most senior senators, commanding respect from many of his colleagues and indeed many Republicans. Interestingly, Senator Kassebaum's joinder with Kennedy in passage of the increase in minimum wage in 1996 came right before she retired.

Following passage of the minimum wage bill in August 2006, Kennedy's and Democratic attention turned to the presidential election campaign. The GOP chose Senator Bob Dole as its candidate. A World War II veteran who had earned two Purple Hearts and a Bronze Star, Dole had lost use of his arm while fighting in Italy. A longtime Kansas Senator, Dole ran in 1976 as President Gerald Ford's vice presidential running mate. Dole, however, seemed old and out of step compared to the young and vibrant Bill Clinton. Moreover, while a moderate conservative, he sought to placate right-wing Patrick Buchanan, who surprisingly defeated Dole in the New Hampshire primary.

Dole therefore embraced an anti-abortion plank in the party platform. Dole also named former New York congressman Jack Kemp, a strong pro-life advocate, as his running mate. Dole called for across-the-board tax cuts at 15 percent, while at the same time seeking a balanced budget. These stances proved incompatible, particularly when coupled with Dole's eagerness to increase defense spending.

Dole also campaigned in an uninspiring fashion. At 73 years old, Dole was the oldest person ever nominated to run for president for the first time. He neither exuded energy nor motivated the masses. Not a compelling speaker, especially toward the end of the campaign, Dole appeared dispirited.

To the contrary, Clinton campaigned vigorously and positioned himself as a centrist. Clinton's 1996 State of the Union address highlighted the preservation and expansion of family values. Clinton championed the curbing of teen gangs, reduction of youth pregnancies and smoking, and community policing. Later in the campaign he emphasized his support for school uniforms. In short, Clinton, having suffered the devastating midterm election defeats in 1994, ran as a decidedly more moderate candidate in 1996 than he did in 1992.

Polls increasingly showed Clinton widening his margin over Dole. Clinton also claimed credit for the surging economy. In his vigorous campaign, he reminded Americans of the help he had directed their way in the past three years, including the increase in the minimum wage by supporting and signing the Kennedy-Kassebaum bill.

In November 1996, Clinton won with ease an election that featured the lowest voter turnout since 1948, when Truman beat Dewey after newspapers declared a Dewey victory. Clinton captured 49.2 percent of the vote compared to 40.7 percent for Dole. Ross Perot, who initially gripped the nation in 1992 with his third-party candidacy, garnered 9 percent of the vote. Clinton triumphed in the electoral college by a 37 percent to 15 percent margin. Still, even though House Democrats picked up 9 seats, Republicans still enjoyed a majority of 19. In the Senate, Republicans gained two seats for a 55–45 margin. Kennedy, while not at the forefront, supported Clinton and relished the idea of working for four more years with an activist president.

The momentum gained in 1996 through passage of the Health Insurance Portability Act and Minimum Wage legislation would soon wane as President Clinton found himself in a tawdry scandal with his political life on the line. Interestingly, Kennedy's next most visible efforts in the passage of legislation would come after George Bush's razor thin victory to the presidency, in the controversial No Child Left Behind legislation.

10

The Lewinsky Scandal, Bush's Controversial Election and the No Child Left Behind Act of 2001

Following Kennedy's two legislative accomplishments in 1996, the Health Insurance Portability Act and Minimum Wage legislation, Kennedy seemed primed for greater achievements. Clinton sailed through the Democratic primary and awaited news of the Republican nominee. Bob Dole emerged as the Republican nominee. The two portrayed to the public a decidedly different image. Clinton, young and vibrant, exuded confidence and determined leadership. Dole seemed old and uncomfortable in the limelight. His speeches, highly scripted, were uninspiring. President Clinton won reelection in a landslide, and presumably Kennedy had the forum to press into passage significant legislation.

But a Patient's Bill of Rights failed to even make it into debate in the Senate. A further proposal to increase the minimum wage met with defeat. Kennedy pushed for education reform, calling for 100,000 additional well-trained teachers over the next ten years.

All these efforts, however, took a back seat once the news broke that Clinton may have obstructed justice and committed perjury with respect to an affair with an intern, Monica Lewinsky. Clinton's brash tactics, including going on national television, pointing his finger and telling a nation "I never had sexual relations with that woman," surely backfired. Hillary Clinton did not help either, proclaiming that this all stemmed from a "vast right-wing conspiracy." Indeed, in a much more profound way, the nation's obsession with impeachment proceedings doomed any further meaningful legislation during the second Clinton term.[1]

As noted in Steven M. Gillon's book *The Pact*, "Monica Changed Everything." On January 21, 1998, Erskine Bowles arrived at his office in the White House at 7:00 a.m. He generally spent two hours preparing for his daily 9:00 a.m. briefing with the president. While some White House officials learned the prior evening of a *Washington Post* report that Clinton had had an illicit affair with an unnamed White House intern, Chief of Staff Bowles learned about it for the first time when he read the newspaper headline.

The story, and investigations that followed, brought the Clinton presidency down after such promise following the 1996 landslide victory over Dole. Clinton's first encounter with Monica Lewinsky, it soon became revealed, occurred on November 15, 1995. Clinton and Lewinsky continued their clandestine meetings over the next 20 months. After Lewinsky transferred to work at the Pentagon, a conniving Monica Tripp befriended her and cajoled her to share tales of her sexual encounters with Clinton. Tripp, for reasons unknown, secretly taped these conversations. Tripp also told the attorneys for Paula Jones, who had a sexual harassment lawsuit pending against Clinton. Thus, on January 17, 1998, when Clinton testified in deposition in the Jones case that he never had a sexual relationship with Lewinsky, he heaped upon himself trouble. The tapes, turned over to Special Prosecutor Kenneth Starr, became the subject of a lurid, detailed report published for all Americans to see on the internet.

While Clinton continued to deny the allegations, every day the situation grew bleaker amid the uncovering of new evidence. Word surfaced of the existence of a blue dress containing Clinton's semen. Through all this, Clinton delivered his State of the Union speech, which received high marks from many observers. After the speech, Clinton went on a campaign-style trip to sell his initiatives.

However, Special Prosecutor Kenneth Starr tenaciously pursued the issue. By March 1998, though, Clinton's approval rating soared to over 70 percent, while only 11 percent of the public had a favorable view of Starr. At least for the moment, Democrats had shifted the focus to a sex scandal rather than an issue of potential obstruction of justice and perjury in a court proceeding. However, Starr proceeded deliberately and the nation awaited the so-called Starr report. Gingrich, trying to placate Republican party moderates as well as the conservative base that urged moving full speed ahead on impeachment proceedings, pronounced that all needed to wait because the law required the independent counsel to inform the House of substantial and credible information that could serve as grounds for impeachment.

Until July 1998, the Lewinsky scandal focused on the abstract question of whether a sexual encounter had even taken place. Clinton repeatedly denied it. That changed on July 28 when Lewinsky reached an agreement with Starr to tell all about her relationship with Clinton. Lewinsky also turned over to Starr the blue dress. On the evening of August 15, Clinton confessed the details of his tryst with Lewinsky to his wife Hillary.

Faced with conclusive DNA evidence, Clinton testified by closed circuit television before a grand jury investigating the Lewinsky affair. After seven months of denial, Clinton admitted that he had had a sexual relationship with Lewinsky. But Clinton tried to blur the issue, obscuring what constituted "sexual relations." According to Clinton, that meant intercourse, which never occurred, so he had told the truth in the Jones deposition.

That evening, though, Clinton went on national television to tell the nation about his testimony. Clinton admitted that he had misled his wife and the country, and confessed to inappropriate physical contact with Lewinsky. Clinton admitted to a critical lapse in judgment and took responsibility for a personal failure on his part. Clinton, though, remained defiant, complaining it was a private matter and the investigation had gone on way too long.

However, even members of his own party started to raise grave issues of possible impeachment. On August 25, Senator Richard Gephardt gave a speech regarding the possibility of impeachment. Former close aide George Stephanopoulos, now a commentator on television, derided Clinton for his actions. Democratic Senator Joseph Lieberman of Connecticut, who would eventually accept the 2000 vice presidential nomination with Al Gore, denounced Clinton as well. With all this, Clinton met with the House and Senate to apologize to them personally.

Such an apology could not stave off the political dynamic Clinton had placed in force. While a majority of the country supported a vote for censure and opposed impeachment, Republicans widened the scope of the Starr report to other Clinton scandals, including Whitewater and Travelgate.

On October 8, Gingrich, as Speaker of the House, commenced House debate to authorize the Judiciary Committee to undertake a formal impeachment investigation. By the time the debate over whether to proceed with impeachment had ended, Clinton joined Andrew Johnson and Richard Nixon as only the third American president to face an impeachment inquiry. The House voted, largely among partisan lines, to do just that. By a vote of 256 to 178, Clinton now faced impeachment proceedings. Many confuse impeachment with ultimate dismissal as president. Impeachment merely means further proceedings toward a vote whether a president should face removal from the White House. Even so, such proceedings unleashed a divisive and inflammatory attack on the Clintons. Clinton haters, so fervent in their desire for revenge, accused Clinton of all types of conspiracies, including murdering Vince Foster.

While the midterm elections in 1998 proved the public did not wish a prolonged impeachment trial, nonetheless partisan forces prevailed. Polls showed that a majority of Americans opposed impeachment. While it seemed absolutely clear the Senate would never muster the two-thirds vote to convict the president, still the House proceedings continued. On December 19, 1998, the House passed two articles of impeachment against Clinton. The first alleged that the president had committed perjury in his Grand Jury testimony on August 17. The other stated that he had obstructed justice.

Without question, the impeachment fight sapped Clinton of efficacy in the last two years of his presidency. Even though the Senate acquitted Clinton on the two impeachment charges, the damage had already occurred.

This, of course, impacted Kennedy, who relegated his role to counseling Clinton through this troubling time. "I continued to be supportive. I met with him nearly every day as 1998 wound down."[2] The scandal, coupled with the lame duck status of Clinton, spoiled the end of any major legislative accomplishments for Ted Kennedy in the twentieth century.

Y2K ushered in a new century, filled with fear on the one hand, and expectations for an unparalleled future on the other hand. As television stations across the country spanned New Year's celebrations worldwide, the much feared Y2K crash, predicted by some to destroy our computers and even our banking system, never happened. Also, on the bright side, the stock market had barreled to unprecedented highs, fattening millions of Americans' 401 (k) accounts, raising expectations of early retirements and fueling lavish lifestyles. Yet, many Americans fretted as the twenty-first century embarked, fearing that bitter partisanship in Washington would divide the nation in ways reminiscent of the 1960s.

Certainly, the country had experienced unprecedented turmoil since the Watergate years with the impeachment proceedings against President William Jefferson Clinton over his irresponsible lies under oath regarding a tawdry sex scandal involving a young intern, "that woman," Monica Lewinsky. A two-term successful presidency by all other measures flamed out as Democrats sought to regroup for a bitter 2000 election against the Bush family dynasty.

To be sure, family dynasties in presidential politics were nothing new. At the inception of our nation, John Adams and his son John Quincy Adams governed the United States through tumultuous years. The Kennedy dynasty, beginning with the Camelot era under John F. Kennedy, shortened by his untimely assassination, the tragic presidential run of Robert Kennedy, and the 37 years of Edward Kennedy in the Senate, marked an unparalleled stamp on familial governance. Now, yet a new dynasty, the Bush family, stampeded America with the nomination of the son of former president George Herbert Walker Bush (1988–1992), George W. Bush, as the Republican candidate against incumbent Vice President Al Gore.

By the time of the election, a fractured and divisive United States Supreme Court was the court of last resort in our tripartite scheme of government. The Senior Justice, John Paul Stevens, appointed by Republican Gerald Ford, now stood ironically as the leader of the Court's "liberal" wing. Joining him was an improbable nominee, the loner David Souter, appointed by George H.W. Bush and sworn in on October 8, 1990. The two Clinton nominees, Ruth Bader Ginsburg in 1993 and Stephen Breyer in 1994, filled out the so-called left portion of the Court.

On the right, Chief Justice William Rehnquist, Richard Nixon's former Assistant Attorney General, could count on Reagan strict constructionist 1986 appointee Antonin Scalia and the controversial Clarence Thomas nominated by Bush in 1991. Anthony Kennedy, a 1987 Reagan appointee from the largely liberal Ninth Circuit Court of Appeals, veered mostly to the right. This left the first female Justice, Stanford law graduate Sandra Day O'Conner, on the Court since 1981, as the ever powerful swing vote.

This highly fragmented Court would leave its indelible mark on American history in perhaps the most partisan and important decision of all time, *Bush v. Gore*.[3] Never before had the United States Supreme Court selected a president, and it is doubtful it will ever happen again. By a 5–4 margin, this previously states' rights Court overturned the Florida Supreme Court and stopped vote recounts, thus handing Bush the election.

Beside its unrivaled impact of choosing a president, the *Bush v. Gore* decision did much more. In the next eight years, President Bush replaced the retiring swing vote Sandra Day O'Connor with archconservative Samuel Alito, and with the death of Chief Justice Rehnquist, appointed his former clerk, the young John Roberts as Chief Justice. In so doing, Bush snubbed sitting Senior Justices and shifted the Court markedly to the right.

The 2000 election had all the drama of an action movie. Proving that reality can become stranger than fiction, nobody could have predicted the remarkable twists and turns of the 2000 election.

First consider the nominees. Both patricians, Bush and Gore came from privileged families who had long served the country in various political capacities. "W," the son of President George Herbert Walker Bush, had never succeeded in anything. But, startling to his ill-equipped opponents, Bush proved an affable candidate who could connect with many Americans. Gore, son of a former longtime senator from Tennessee and then vice president to Bill Clinton, had certainly earned the nomination. However, while known as an excellent debater, Gore appeared too intellectual and failed to connect with mainstream America.

Gore also made an early controversial campaign decision. Rather than ride on the coattails of a successful Clinton presidency from a political standpoint, Gore veered away from Clinton and vowed to campaign without his help. Some attribute Gore's decision to his disdain for Clinton's public infidelities, particularly with Monica Lewinsky. Others speak of Gore's ego, wishing to carve out his own place in history without Clinton taking credit. Clinton stood ready to help, but honored Gore's wishes to campaign on his own terms.

In the end, Gore grossly miscalculated in his campaign. Desperately needing help in the Southern states, Gore could well have swept to victory had he allowed Clinton to campaign actively there. Instead, even in Clinton's home state of Arkansas, Gore had Clinton take a backseat. Gore thought that his nomination of Joe Lieberman as vice president would help carry the critical swing state of Florida, where many Jewish residents would identify with the Jewish Lieberman.

Many expected Gore to leap ahead in the polls when he engaged in televised public debates with Bush. They hearkened back to the Kennedy/Nixon debates in 1960, which historians and political pundits have often described as the turning point in that close election. Gore played up the debates, and an interested American populace turned in with high expectations for a decisive Gore victory in the debates. By raising expectations, though, Gore again miscalculated. He led many Americans to believe he would clobber Bush in a debate on the facts, making him look ill informed and ill equipped to serve as president.

To the contrary, Gore came across horribly in the first debate. Using debate tactics that backfired, Gore seemed too gleeful to try to teach Bush a historical lesson on many topics Americans could care less about. Bush, to the contrary, came across as likeable and confident, as opposed to the condescending Gore. Gore failed miserably in the first debate, and while he fared better in the others, the damage had been done.

Still, the election remained strikingly close. Polls showed no decisive victory. The outcome would depend on a number of so-called swing states, and if Gore could pull out a victory in any of the Southern states.

On election day, it all came down to Florida, home of George Bush's brother Jeb Bush. Without Clinton, not only did Gore fail to take his home state of Tennessee, but he lost in Arkansas as well. This left the election to one state: Florida. Shortly before 8:00 p.m. the major television networks projected, based on exit polls, that Gore had won Florida and thereby the election.[4] Within a few hours of this call, they retracted the projection and called the state too close to call. At approximately 2:15 p.m. on November 8, the networks declared George W. Bush had won Florida and hence won the presidency, despite Gore's leading the popular vote. Official tallies later showed that Gore had won the popular vote by capturing 50,992,335 votes (48.4 percent) to Bush's 50,455,156 (47.9 percent).[5]

The vote count in Florida turned out, surrealistically, too close to call. On Wednesday, the first complete election figures showed Bush ahead by a slim margin of 1,784 votes. Under Florida law, results this close required all counties in the state to do an immediate automatic recount.[6] That process, which meant running all the ballots through the counting machines, took a day. This time, the new results announced Thursday November 9, cut Bush's margin to 327 votes.

Gore, not surprisingly, asked for manual recounts, most prominently in Palm Beach, where the layout of the ballots led a largely liberal population to mistakenly vote in high numbers for archconservative third-party candidate Patrick Buchannan. This so-called "butterfly ballot," plus the so-called "hanging chads," soon became household words as the nation stood transfixed in a tight election that the courts, not the people, would eventually decide.

The Bush legal team struck first, led by Washington lawyer Theodore Olsen. Olsen filed suit on Saturday, November 11, asking Miami Federal Judge Donald M. Middlebrooks to stop the recounts before they even started. Judge Middlebrooks rejected Bush's position and allowed the recounts to proceed.[7]

Despite this initial legal victory, the Bush team had the benefit of Republican Secretary of State Katherine Harris, who took the position that under Florida law the recounts could last no longer than seven days after the election. On November 18, Harris vowed to certify the state election for president in Bush's favor, but on November 17, the Florida Supreme Court intervened on its own initiative and stepped into the fray to overrule Harris. The Florida Supreme Court ruled that Harris could not certify the recounts until Sunday, November 26. The Bush team, furious at the Florida Supreme Court decision, decided to seek review of a State court construing state election laws with the United States Supreme Court. This shocked many, as Republican ideology normally followed states' rights, meaning that state courts should interpret their own state election laws. Remarkably, the United States Supreme Court sent the case back to the Florida Supreme Court, asking it to explain whether it had "considered the relevant portions of the federal constitution and law."[8] In oral argument, the United States Supreme Court justices focused on Article II of the Constitution as argued by the Bush team. The Bush team argued that, under Article II, the Florida legislature did not have the authority to overrule federal law. The justices said nothing about Bush's argument under the Equal Protection clause of the Fourteenth Amendment.

Split with mixed messages, the Florida Supreme Court issued its next ruling on December 8 and ordered an immediate tabulation of 9,000 Miami-Dade ballots, relying explicitly on the standards established by the Florida Legislature in previously interpreting Florida's Election Code in counting as legal a vote based on a "clear indication of the intent of the vote."[9]

Republicans wasted no time in urging the U.S. Supreme Court to stay such a recount. This time, the Court acted immediately, voting five to four on the afternoon of December 9 to stay such a recount and setting the morning of December 11 as the time for oral argument.

The day after oral argument, the U.S. Supreme Court delivered a five to four opinion. To the surprise of many observers the justices did not maintain, as many Bush lawyers had expected, that the Florida Supreme Court had violated Article II of the United States Constitution. Rather, the five conservative justices, all Reagan-Bush appointees, for the first time focused on the issues of equal protection. They stated that the recounts ordered by the Florida Supreme Court violated the rights of the voters to have their ballots evaluated consistently and fairly, and that the recounts therefore ran afoul of the equal protection clause.

Few defend the reasoning of the opinion, and its plainly partisan stamp has sullied the Court. A particularly vehement critic, Professor Alan M. Dershowitz of Harvard, resorts to considerable hyperbole in a book written in 2001 out of anger less than a year after the election. According to Dershowitz, "the five justices who ended Election 2000 by stopping the Florida hand recount have damaged the credibility of the U.S. Supreme Court, and their lawless decision in *Bush v. Gore* will have a more enduring impact on Americans than the outcome of the election itself."[10] Dershowitz slams the five conservative justices not only as partisans, but questions their ethics, labeling the decision as fraudulent. An ardent critic, though more measured in his analysis, Jeffrey Toobin also decried the decision. In Toobin's view, "the opinion did not reflect any general legal principles; rather the Court was acting only to assist a single individual—George W. Bush."[11]

Ted Kennedy's reaction to the Bush/Gore electoral debate seems measured. According to Kennedy himself, "I was naturally dismayed by the ambiguities of the 2000 election, and disturbed by the Supreme Court's role and decision-making process in it."[12] This was hardly a stinging rebuke of the Court or a critical analysis of the United States Supreme Court's decision. A recent biography of Ted Kennedy, remarkably, sheds absolutely no light on Kennedy's reaction or involvement in the electoral crisis.[13] According to yet another recent biography, Bush's election in 2000 had ushered in an era of bad feelings on Capitol Hill. According to the biography, Democrats seethed at what they viewed as a stolen election in the State of Florida, allowing Bush to defeat Gore. But according to a Kennedy biographer "Ted wasted little time being disappointed by Gore's loss or agonizing over his party's quandary in the Senate. Adept after nearly four decades in office at adjusting to the frequent power changes in Washington, Ted came to a simple conclusion: he was going to try to work with George Bush on education."[14]

The inauguration of George W. Bush in January 2001 certainly ushered in a new era in Washington. Bush came with a socially conservative platform. Relying perhaps most heavily than any other president on his Vice President, Dick Cheney, some wondered who really ran the country. Kennedy made the best of Bush's election, and tried to forge bipartisan consensus. The most controversial effort, the No Child Left Behind Act, passed in January 2002.

> Over the objections of some fellow Democrats, Kennedy helped pass President Bush's No Child Left Behind Act in 2001, a sweeping law that required more rigorous testing of public school students and makes it easier for parents to transfer their children from low performing schools.[15]

Reviewing Kennedy's role in the legislation, the legislation itself and the aftermath of the act yields insight into this bipartisan enactment. During the 2000 presidential campaign, George W. Bush made educational reform a major plank in his domestic platform, saying that he wanted especially to end the "soft bigotry" of low expectations for minority students. The test-based system of accountability he proposed appealed to many Republicans. However, the vastly increased role for the federal government in an arena traditionally left to the states ran into opposition from some conservatives. Interestingly, many civil rights groups rallied to the cause of the No Child Left Behind Bill. In the Senate, Ted Kennedy became the Chief Democrat spokesperson in favor of the bill.

Like so many of his legislative efforts in the past, the impetus behind Kennedy's support of the act stemmed from his desire to address discrimination. Kennedy thought "the bill would inject billions of new dollars per year into the nation's school systems, most of the money aimed at the weakest districts."[16] Indeed, the actual act contains provisions for addressing minority children issues.[17] The act also provided educational opportunities for "Indian, Native Hawaiians and Alaska Natives."[18] Further, the act provided for improved education for homeless youth.[19]

No doubt these provisions stirred Kennedy's support, for they represented causes he had backed for years. In Kennedy's words, "President Bush had signaled a willingness to tackle education reform, and I was certainly willing to work together on something that would make a difference."[20] The No Child Left Behind Act, Kennedy thought, had tools of reform such as "standards and accountability with a high emphasis on testing and with the federal government taking the dominant role in measuring the results."[21]

When the No Child Left Behind Act emerged, crafted by the White House with Kennedy's close involvement, many Democrats chafed at the bill. It met with significant and well-intentioned opposition by teachers and their unions. Many Democrats argued that the provision in the bill to punish schools that did not meet annual standardized test yearly progress markers failed to take into account the challenges many poor districts faced with at-risk children. Steadily improving standardized tests scores, these opponents argued, did not measure students' learning or educational skills.

Kennedy, though, argued to both his colleagues and teachers' unions that the testing standards would identify struggling schools and assist in getting help to children in need. According to Kennedy, the bill would inject billions of new dollars per year into the nation's school systems, with most of the money aimed at the weakest districts.

Kennedy's belief in the bill was bolstered by his counterpart in the House, George Miller of California. Miller was the new ranking Democrat of the House Education and Labor Committee. He commanded considerable power on many progressive issues, with education foremost among them. Miller conveyed to Kennedy that he felt Bush had a grasp of educational matters. Miller and Kennedy worked closely together on the act, along with Republican Senator Judd Gregg of New Hampshire and Congressman John Boehner (now Speaker of the House).

In the No Child Left Behind Act, Bush proposed a 46.7 billion dollar authorization of the Elementary and Secondary Education Act, a leading feature of Lyndon Johnson's War on Poverty, enacted in 1965. Partisan fighting in Congress had stunted the Education Act's effectiveness for many years, with Republicans demanding more emphasis on block grants and voucher programs. Democrats, on the other hand, pushed for reduced class size and teacher training.

Bush's tools for reform included so-called standards and accountability, with a high emphasis on testing. Ironically, this supposed conservative president urged that the federal government take the dominate role in measuring standardized testing results. Kennedy, in his memoir, unequivocally states that he studied the testing measures and found the approach promising. Kennedy expressed public enthusiasm for the measure and complimented Bush. Kennedy, in his memoir, emphasized that he pressed the areas where Republicans and Democrats agreed while downplaying the voucher issue.

By early April 2001, Kennedy felt enough compromise had occurred to push the bill forward. The Democrats had agreed to use federal funds for private tutoring of students at failing schools. Republicans, on the other hand, agreed to relinquish their insistence on vouchers for private schools. To the consternation of many Democrats, Kennedy proclaimed his support for the bill and praised Bush for keeping education a priority.

Full Senate debate began on the bill in May 2001. Kennedy felt emboldened by several Republican compromises, such as an agreement for targeting resources to children in the neediest schools, increased support for teachers and stronger parent involvement in schools. Kennedy's support of Bush soon diminished, when the Republican-controlled Congress announced the budget resolution in early May and appropriations for the No Child Left Behind Act fell far short of Kennedy's expectations.

Kennedy trudged on, backing the Senate's reauthorization of the Elementary and Secondary Education Act. Kennedy remained optimistic, pointing to the funding levels to make sure children who need extra help get it. With Senate passage, the bill headed to a conference committee that would try to bring it and the House bill into alignment. Kennedy felt that increasing funding could be tackled once the bill came to law.

Exhaustive negotiations regarding testing requirements and funding issues continued for over two months among designated numbers of the House and Senate. Finally, on December 12, 2001, the parties reached agreement on the specifics of the legislation. It was the only bipartisan measure to pass that year. The following January, Bush signed the No Child Left Behind Act into law. According to Kennedy, the Democrats had scored a major victory. According to Kennedy, the negotiations resulted in an appropriations agreement of $22.6 billion for education in fiscal year 2002, an enormous increase over Bush's original goal of a $685 million increase. Kennedy truly felt the No Child Left Behind Act was the most significant advance in public education in the past quarter century.

Unfortunately, though, the legacy of the act is dominated by the unintended side effects of the mandatory testing requirements, beginning with students in the second grade. Unhappy teachers' unions, at the time of consideration of the act, "argued that the provision to punish schools that did not meet 'adequate yearly progress markers,' as defined by steadily improving test scores, was arbitrary and unfair, and failed to take into account the challenges many districts faced with at-risk children."[22] Empirical data abounds with accounts of the dominant effect the testing requirements had on the efficacy of the No Child Left Behind Act. Faced with potential loss of federal funds, many schools and teachers resorted to teaching to the test, instead of ensuring students received a broad range of learning and instruction. This lessened the quality of education in previously highly regarded schools.[23]

Yet another more devastating side effect involved scandals in which schools cheated to present high tests scores. Schools in Georgia, for example, became involved in such practices, leading to widespread calls for reform.[24]

Another undesirable feature of the testing aspects of the act stems from the tremendous pressure placed on students as young as seven years old. Children that age, and at most ages, develop learning skills at wildly different rates. Such testing results do not provide useful information as to a student's learning skills and development.

Moreover, even well esteemed higher education institutions now eschew SAT results and instead rely on student essays, teacher recommendations and grades. Perhaps most prominently, liberal arts college Sarah Lawrence in Bronxville, New York, 30 minutes outside of New York City, has adopted a policy of not utilizing SAT scores in their consideration of collegiate applicants. Lewis and Clark, a rising school six miles outside of Portland, Oregon, now has a program where students can present important high school projects in lieu of the SAT or ACT.

Almost immediately after passage of the No Child Left Behind Act in January 2002, Kennedy and his colleagues began to regret their decision to back it. "Some Democrats would grumble that Kennedy's love of the deal had obscured his better judgment—that in this case he gave away too much, especially with the testing requirements."[25] Tom Harkin, who said Kennedy had convinced him to back the bill, would eventually state that he felt "sorry I voted for the darn thing."[26] As Kennedy notes, "the President never fought for the funds he promised."[27]

Rather than defend the bill, Kennedy soon denounced it and blamed Bush for reneging on his side of the bargain. "Within a year after No Child Left Behind took effect, Kennedy's office would claim that the Bush administration had shortchanged the program by $9.6 billion—a big chunk that was authorized for the program that year."[28] As Kennedy puts it, "No Child has struggled on through the ensuing years, effective in some ways, but never the transformative tool it could have been; underfunded, mismanaged, and poorly implemented ... a spectacular broken promise of the Republican administration and Congress."[29]

While the act remains in effect, Kennedy distanced itself from it. "America's children deserved better," he said.[30] It does not stand as a shining moment in Kennedy's history in the Senate.

11

From Bush, to Immigration Reform Attempts, to Obama and the Passing of the Senator

On the morning of September 11, 2001, Ted Kennedy sat in his Senate office with Senator Judd Gregg, awaiting the arrival of Laura Bush. The First Lady had prepared to give testimony before the Education Committee on the subject of early education. President Bush read to a young elementary school class in Sarasota, Florida, as part of his tour to publicize his administration's commitment to education reform. As Kennedy waited for Mrs. Bush, his wife Vicki called and told him an airplane had crashed into one of the World Trade Center towers in New York City. According to Kennedy, Senator Gregg, he and Mrs. Bush kept the television off and simply talked for a while.[1] Kennedy biographer Cannelos describes Kennedy and Mrs. Bush glued to the TV coverage until Secret Service agents hustled Mrs. Bush away to a secure location.[2]

Regardless, 9/11 had a profound impact on an entire nation that day and thereafter. For the purposes of history, America had experienced its first terrorist attack and the first invasion of its borders since Pearl Harbor. A Kennedy biographer describes Kennedy's phone call with a constituent, Cindy McGinty, the next day. While Kennedy does not mention it or anything else about 9/11 in his biography, Cannelos states that Kennedy placed a phone call to console Ms. McGinty, who lost her husband the day before on the ninety-ninth floor of the World Trade Center during a business meeting.[3] Cannelos waxes philosophically about Kennedy's intervention on this issue.

In any event, immediately following the September 11 attack by Al-Qaeda, Bush sent in troops to Afghanistan to hunt down the terrorists responsible and to try to capture or kill Osama Bin Laden. However,

Kennedy felt the administration lost no time exploiting the trust he had gained in Congress and from Americans in changing the subject to Iraq. Led by Vice President Richard ("Dick") Cheney, Secretary of Defense Donald Rumsfeld and Rumsfeld's deputy Paul Wolfowitz, Bush embarked on a plan to try to democratize Islamic nations.

Kennedy states that he found no just cause for the invasion of Iraq. Iraq posed no threat that justified an immediate preemptive war. Moreover, Kennedy saw no pattern of relationships between Saddam and Al-Qaeda.[4] Along with West Virginia's Senator Robert Bryd, Kennedy soon emerged as one of the most vocal critics of the Bush administration's march to war in Iraq. His stance put him at odds with a then-popular president, as well as his fellow Massachusetts Senator John Kerry.

Many Democrats, fearful of losing seats in the midterm 2002 elections, accepted the Bush administration's approach. On September 26, Democratic Senate leaders announced a deal with Republicans on a war resolution that gave Bush what he desired: authority to use force against Iraq to enforce United Nations resolutions. Kennedy formally announced on October 4 that he would vote against the war resolution. Yet, a total of 77 senators, including Kerry and Hillary Clinton, supported the authorization of force.

Using the authority granted in the October vote, Bush went to war in Iraq on March 20, 2003. After the invasion began, Kennedy took the Senate floor to express his support for the troops, but not the war. Soon Kennedy referred to Iraq as "Bush's Vietnam." The Iraq war, bolstered by a televised presentation by Secretary of State Colin Powell showing areas of supposed stockpiles of weapons of mass destruction, gripped a fearful nation. Powell later regretted the presentation, claiming convincingly that he had relied on inaccurate and unreliable data.

Kennedy's voice against the incursion in Iraq would soon obtain additional backing. In addition, a new presidential election loomed large in 2004. This time Kennedy backed John Kerry. He campaigned for him in the Iowa caucuses, but noticed sluggishness in his campaign. Howard Dean of Vermont had taken a passionate stance against the war in Iraq, and at least initially galvanized many Democrats. Kerry, though, went on to win the Iowa caucuses, New Hampshire, and rang up nine victories on Super Tuesday. Dean hurt himself with a bizarre "scream," mocked by many, after losing the Iowa caucuses.

Kerry went on to win the primary and nominated now-disgraced John Edwards as his vice president. Hopeful that Edwards, from South

Carolina, would capture Southern votes, the plan ultimately failed. Bush won reelection, this time not in as close a fashion as his campaign four years earlier with Gore. While Kerry fell short of the White House, Kennedy felt that through his campaigning experience he still had political clout on a national landscape.

Despite Bush's reelection, he emerged as a damaged and vulnerable president. The worsening conditions in Iraq sapped his credibility. Then, a slow and inept government response to Hurricane Katrina, which devastated New Orleans in 2005, sullied Bush's reputation further. The nation began to think that we had a presidency spiraling out of control. Democrats rode the wave of voter displeasure with Bush and took back control of Congress in 2006.

Kennedy remained active, agreeing with Bush and Senator McCain that solving illegal immigration required multiple changes in existing laws. Contrary to many attacks on Kennedy, he first sought to take stronger steps to seal the border with Mexico.[5] Kennedy also plainly sought a solution to dealing with undocumented workers. Kennedy, who eschewed mass deportation, looked into the poverty-ridden circumstances that led many to cross the border. He supported a temporary visa for workers if they paid a fine and passed a background check. This latter feature answered many criticisms from anti-illegal immigrant proponents who rightfully pushed an agenda where illegals had murdered American citizens and fled across the border. But the Kennedy initiative helped to assist bona fide workers and screen questionable illegal aliens.

Kennedy's last major legislative effort following the No Child Left Behind Act of 2001, and in the wake of 9/11 security concerns, the Comprehensive Immigration Bill, symbolizes both his efforts at securing allies across the aisle and the ultimate disappointment of failing to pass into law important reform. Ironically, following his death in 2009, "Obamacare," encompassing much of his ideas of health care reform spanning 40 years, became the law. Now, Obama battles Congress to enact immigration reform. These latest reform attempts stem from efforts preceding Obama's presidency by Kennedy and John McCain.[6]

Kennedy and McCain took several stabs at implementing immigration reform in the 2000s. The first, titled the Service and Orderly Immigration Act (S. Bill 1033) reached the Senate in 2005. Contrary to its critics, the bill started in Title I with an emphasis on border security. It was not an amnesty bill in the slightest. Section III directed the Secretary of Homeland Security to protect the international borders of the United States. According to the text of the bill,

> the strategy *must* include: (1) identification and evaluation of points of entry and portions of the border *must* be protected from illegal transit; (2) a design for the most appropriate and cost effective means of likely defending the border against threats, including advancements in technology, equipment, personnel and training needed to address security vulnerability; (3) risk based priorities for assuring border security, including deadlines for addressing security and enforcement needs; (4) coordination of federal, state, regional, local and tribal authorities to provide for effective border management and security enforcement; (5) a prioritization of research and development objectives to enhance border security and enforcement needs; (6) an update of the 2001 Port of Entry Infrastructure Assessment Study that was conducted by the legacy U.S. Customs Service and General Services Administration; (7) strategic interior enforcement coordination plans with personnel of Immigration and Customs Enforcement; (8) strategies enforcing coordination plans with personnel of the Department of Homeland Security and State to end human smuggling and trafficking activities; (9) any other appropriate infrastructure, security plans or reports the Secretary deems appropriate for inclusion; (10) the identification of low-risk travelers and how such identification would facilitate cross-border travel; and (11) ways to ensure that U.S. trade and commerce are not diminished by efforts, activities, and programs to secure the homeland.[7]

The bill goes on to have a long Section 133, titled "Improving the Security of Mexico's Southern Border." Once again it establishes mandates "to prevent the use and manufacturing of fraudulent traffic documents."[8] It further stated that Homeland Security and appropriate officials of Central American countries "control alien smuggling and trafficking and to prevent the use and manufacturing of fraudulent travel documents."[9]

Only after these strong security measures does the bill, in Section 302, addressed the "Admission of Essential Workers." This involved granting a temporary visa to aliens who demonstrate they can perform work in the United States. The visa was to last for three years, with an extension for one additional three-year period if the alien remained employed. Finally, the bill provided for permanent resident status for eligible aliens on self petition.[10]

Having set forth the actual text of the bill itself, critics of the 2005 Senate bill are large on rhetoric and short on substance. Interestingly, although the bill began with border security, those opposing it resorted to the amnesty accusation. In an article published by the Heritage Foundation, the bill was described as "in effect amnesty—which undercuts the rule of law by rewarding those who have acted wrongly and will only encourage further illegal entry."[11] Finding border security not enough, co-authors James J. Carafano, Janice L. Kephart and Paul Rosenzweig argued for mass deportation: "Any effective deterrent must require individuals to leave and apply for admission without prejudice or advantage."[12]

Summarizing the perceived deficiencies in the bill, the Heritage Magazine article argued that Congress needs a better bill that does not grant amnesty to illegal aliens, provides the infrastructure to properly implement a guest worker program, ensures internal enforcement of immigration laws, effectively engages the cooperation of states in Latin America and requires an effective border control strategy.[13]

To the contrary, the *Washington Post* described the bill, introduced on May 14, 2005, as an "attempt to forge a realistic, comprehensive and bipartisan national immigration policy."[14] The editorial accurately begins by noting that the bill requires new investment in "border security and technology." At the same time, the editorial observes that the bill allows employers to hire foreigners under a temporary visa program if they are able to prove they cannot hire American workers for the same job. Under the compromise bill, visa holders would have been entitled to change jobs, and apply to stay, thereby eliminating a potential source of illegal immigration, and would have been issued tamper-proof identity (ending the use of fake Social Security cards).

Further commenting on the bill, the editorial concluded that "most controversially—but ultimately sensible—the bill allows illegal immigrants already here to regularize their status, but not easily; they would have to go to the end of the line, and only by paying a hefty fine ($1,500), staying employed for a prescribed period and paying back taxes would they be allowed to stay in the United States."[15]

McCain and Kennedy argued that the bill did not provide for amnesty because it required a recognition of wrongdoing. They also argued that establishing the temporary visa would prevent a new pool of illegal immigration from arriving. It would become more politically realistic to fine employers who continued to employ illegals. While not completely endorsing the bill, the *Washington Post* dubbed it a "common sense and hard-nosed approach."[16]

The bill, however, stalled in Congress in 2006. The measure was blocked primarily by House Republican leaders adamantly opposed to provisions that could have allowed undocumented immigrants to become citizens. Shortly after the bill stalled, the *Boston Globe* reported plans by Kennedy and McCain to introduce a revised version of the bill in consultation with President Bush.[17] The *Boston Globe*, in describing the early negotiations for the new measure, reported that the bill would likely keep in the 700 mile border fence, and would double the size of the U.S. Border Patrol. The planned bill would also add new means to crack down on employers who hire undocumented workers, a further attempt to assuage the concerns about the nation's porous borders.[18]

The article correctly observed that the new bill would likely enrage advocates of a tough approach to immigration by allowing most undocumented immigrants already in the country to earn legalized status. Early drafts of the bill allowed those here illegally to become citizens after 12 years if they met requirements such as learning English, passing a criminal background check, paying back taxes and paying a $2,000 fine.[19] Commenting on the new bill, Kennedy stated:

> Those who have lived here, who have basically played by the rules, worked hard ... they, I believe, ought to be able to adjust their status. This is a complex issue and demands a comprehensive approach. I don't expect it to be easy sledding.[20]

McCain also viewed White House backing as a chance to make history: "There's active participation. There's a window of opportunity. I don't know when it becomes impossible but I know this is the greatest opportunity—right now in the next several months."[21]

McCain's hopes proved wrong. On May 9, 2007, S. 1348, titled the Comprehensive Immigration Reform Act of 2007, was introduced in the Senate by Senator Harry Reid. McCain and Kennedy strongly backed the bill. Aiming to address the critics on loose borders, virtually the entire act focused on border enforcement. Title I of the bill focused solely on border issues. Section 1502, for example, set forth an "increase in full time border patrol agents." The bill provided for 20,000 more border patrol agents. The bill included funding for 300 miles for vehicle barriers and 105 camera and radar towers. Indeed, the bill is dominated with border security measures and strong employer sanctions for employing illegal immigrants. Section 1502, for example, sought the increase of 2,000 border patrol agents for 2008, and 2,400 each for 2009 through 2012.[22] At least 20 percent of additional agents were to be assigned to northern borders.

The bill also authorized "permanent check points on roadways in patrol sections that are located in proximity to the international border between the United States and Mexico."[23] The bill also addressed increased security at ports of entry.[24] As for fences, the bill addressed replacing and extending fences in Tucson, Yuma, San Diego, and other high-traffic areas. It provided a strict two year deadline for fixing and constructing all new fencing.[25]

With all this in mind, the bill went far further. It enabled significant surveillance security not later than six months from the enactment of the act.[26] The bill also would have enacted a national strategy for border security. This included funding for an assessment of "the threat posed by terrorists and terrorist groups that may try to infiltrate the United States at locations along the international land and maritime borders."[27] These and other critical border control issues were to be implemented no later than *one year* from the enactment of the act.[28]

Section 114 was entirely devoted to "improving the security of Mexico's southern border."[29] If enacted the bill would have accomplished the following: (1) specific implementation of programs to deter smuggling of illegal immigrants from Mexico, Belize and Guatemala; (2) tracking of Central American gangs which have so affected Los Angeles and other western states; (3) combatting human smuggling; and (4) attacking deaths at the United States border in cooperation with Mexico including those due to drug smuggling.[30]

The bill contained a myriad of other features that, without partisan politics, should have appealed to Republicans. It included border patrol training, document fraud detection, and significant criminal penalties for arriving illegally. It included three years of prison for those evading immigration, ten years if the evasion resulted in bodily harm and life imprisonment under certain circumstances.[31]

The proposed bill's border initiatives are staggering, thus making it difficult to comprehend the continued criticism on it being lax on security. The actual text of the act defies such criticism. Section 115 addressed combatting human smuggling. The bill placed a one year requirement for the Secretary to submit to Congress a report to combat human smuggling.[32] Section 116 dealt with deaths at the Mexico/United States border. It again gave a one year window for the Commissioner of the Border of Customs and Border Protection to recommend actions to reduce deaths at the border.[33]

The efforts to stave off illegal immigrants from arriving in the United States did not end there. In Subtitle C, the bill had a number of technological and other provisions to enhance border security. Section

121, titled "Biometric Data Enhancement," required no later than October 1, 2008, for the Secretary to "collect all fingerprints from each alien to provide fingerprints during the initial enrollment in the integrated entry and data exit system."[34] The bill also mandated a plan to use satellite communications to assist border agents at ports of entry, in remote areas along the international land borders and between all border security areas.[35]

In direct response to the events of September 2011, the bill would have provided comprehensive border control training. Such training, if implemented, would surely have assisted in controlling the flood of illegal immigration critics wished to stop. To that end, Section 125 set up document fraud detection, creating a Forensic Document Laboratory to detect false immigration papers.[36]

Hopefully, by spending time going through the actual text of the bill, it sheds light on the extensive efforts to respond to legitimate border control concerns while also addressing the difficult problem of how to treat hard-working individuals who entered illegally, many decades ago. Before getting to the so-called "amnesty" provisions, further description of the strong border control measures remains essential.

Section 131 provided for mandatory detention of aliens apprehended at or between ports of entry. And consider Section 132, titled "Evasion of Inspection or Violation of Arrival, Reporting, Entry or Clearance Requirements." The provision would have imposed *three* years of imprisonment for an offense and imprisonment for life or a death sentence for any conduct resulting in a death.

While critics have reviled the federal government for controlling enforcement and purportedly precluding states from taking action, Section 133, titled "Temporary National Guard Support for Securing the Southern Land Border of the United States" allowed "the Governor of any State may order any units or personnel of the National Guard of such state to ... provide command, control and continuing of support for units or personnel performing annual training duty."[37] It authorized ground reconnaissance activities, airport reconnaissance activities, emergency medical support and services and "construction of roadway, patrol road, fences, barriers, and other facilities to secure the southern land border of the United States."[38]

As a further border enforcement mechanism, Section 134 provided incentives for members of the armed forces to serve in the Bureau of Customs and Border Protection.[39] The bill also contained an emergency deployment of border patrol agents, permitting an additional 1,000 additional agents to be provided to any state for the purpose of patrolling and defending the international border.[40] In addition, the bill empowered the Secretary to increase by not less than 100 the number of helicopters to perform various missions. Further, the Secretary was required to increase by no less than 250 the number of power boats under the control of the United States Border Patrol.[41] Additional motor vehicles, portable computers, hand-held global positioning system devices, night vision equipment, border armor, weapons and uniforms were added features of the bill designed to provide stringent border patrol. In fact, the act placed no limitations as to the funds to be appropriated for the extra equipment.[42]

In addition to stringent border control measures, the Comprehensive Immigration Reform Act of 2007 contained important provisions for internal enforcement. Title II began with a section for removal and denial of benefits to terrorist aliens.[43] At the same time, the act sought to amend Section 249 and provide a record of lawful admission for permanent residence for aliens who entered the United States before 1972. It required continuous residence since entry as well as demonstration of good character.[44] In other words, far from complete amnesty, the bill differentiated between aliens who presented a danger to United States citizens and those who had displayed good character for an extensive period of time.

Provisions also addressed detention of aliens ordered removed if the alien refused to make all reasonable efforts to comply with the removal order, including failing to make timely application in good faith for travel or other documents necessary to the alien's departure. It provided the Secretary the discretion to parole such aliens who had applied for admission and not deport the alien unless violations of the terms for parole occurred.[45] The latter portion of this part strikes a balance by attempting to avoid deportation of those of questionable character who, like American citizens, comply with parole conditions.

Amendments increasing criminal penalties related to gang violence and alien smuggling were proposed as additional controls. Any alien who had been a member of a criminal street gang or who participated in the activities of any street gang, or who had reason to know of such activities, were deportable.[46] Alien smugglers faced a similar fate. Designed to apply to those who facilitated or induced a person lacking lawful authority to enter the United States or who harbored, concealed, or shielded from detection such a person, such individuals faced varying criminal penalties depending on the offense, up to and including deportation.[47] Employers who knowingly employed ten or more individuals with actual knowledge of illegal status faced stiffened criminal penalties as well.[48]

Heightened criminal penalties for illegal entry also applied to aliens who illegally crossed the border or eluded examination or inspection by an immigration officer. Civil penalties and fines also were increased.[49] Other internal controls included reform of passport, visa and immigration fraud offenses. These offenses, ranging from forgery of passports to unlawful production of passports, carried hefty imprisonment sanctions as well as civil penalties and fines.[50] The act also cracked down on marriage fraud, providing up to ten years in prison and fines for knowingly entering into a marriage for the purpose of evading the immigration laws or knowingly misrepresenting the existence or circumstances of marriage.[51]

Further internal controls included amendments for removal of aliens for passport and immigration fraud offenses. There was also a provision to ensure that aliens incarcerated in prison are not released to the community after completion of their sentences.[52] This provision, if enacted, would have answered the criticisms of many, including in Los Angeles, who have rightfully complained about several circumstances where aliens got released from prison, committing murder, and fled to Mexico. Indeed, Section 210(a)(2) provided for expansion of these rules so that such aliens would be removed from the United States after the completion of their sentences. In addition, aliens who could post a bond and demonstrate they had the means to depart voluntarily could leave the United States. Upon proof of departing they would have the bond returned.[53]

Additional internal measures included allocation of field agents to conduct background checks.[54] Such background checks were required to be completed and assessed on any alien suspected of fraud relating to his or her status in the United States. Most importantly, for the period of 2008–2012, the act authorized appropriation to the Director of the Federal Bureau of Investigations $3,125,000 for each of the fiscal years for improving the speed and accuracy of background checks.[55] As for critics that the federal government did not apply proper resources to the states, Section 218 mandated reimbursement for costs associated with processing criminal illegal aliens to reimburse states and local governments for costs associated with dealing with undocumented aliens through the criminal justice system. These reimbursements included the costs of indigent defense, criminal prosecution, autopsies, translators, interpreters and court costs.[56] The amount of such appropriations were massive. For each of the fiscal years from 2008 to 2012, the Federal Government was authorized to provide states up to $400,000,000.[57]

Critics of the current immigration system argued that the lack of authority of the states have provided so-called "sanctuary cities," such as Los Angeles.[58] Yet Section 240D stated that "notwithstanding any other provision of law, law enforcement personnel of a State or a political subdivision of a State have authority of a sovereign entity to investigate, apprehend, arrest, detain or transfer to federal custody, including the transportation across state lines to detention centers" an alien for the purpose of assisting in the enforcement of the criminal provisions of the immigration laws in the United States in the normal course of carrying out the law enforcement duties of such personnel.[59] The provision made clear that "State authority has never been displaced or preempted by Federal law."[60]

The act also provided for the increase in federal detention space. Under Section 233, "the Secretary shall construct or require, in addition to existing facilities for the detention of aliens, at least 20 facilities in the United States that have the capacity to detain a total of not less than 20,000 individuals at any time for aliens detained pending removal or a decision on removal of such aliens from the United States subject to available appropriations."[61] In addition to the construction of the centers, the bill called for expansion of justice prisoner and alien transfer systems. This included the daily operations of such systems with buses and airhubs in three geographic regions, allocating a set number of seats for aliens for each metropolitan area, allowing metropolitan areas to trade seats allocated in the system for such aliens to other areas based on the transportation needs of such areas and requiring an annual report that analyzes the number of seats in each metropolitan area as allocated under the system for such aliens.[62]

Title III of the act dealt with unlawful employment of aliens. In addition to the measures discussed earlier, these additional provisions required strict document verification. An employer hiring, recruiting or referring for a fee an individual in the United States was required to verify that the individual was eligible for such employment by attesting, under penalty of perjury and on a form prescribed by the Secretary, that the employer verified the employee for eligibility for employment. This required not simply an examination of passports or a permanent resident card, but rather a declaration under penalty of perjury that the document examined is genuine and relates to the employee being eligible for employment in the United States. Under Section 274A(c)(1), employers had to retain attestation of such documents for five years after the date of hiring. Employers also needed to retain all documents from workers for the same period and the act gave the Department of Labor (DOL) the authority to investigate such claims and assess appropriate penalties. For first time offending employers, assessment of civil penalties of not less than $500 but not more than $4,000 for each unauthorized alien employed would have been imposed. The act also provided for penalties of not less than $200 and not more than $2,000 for each record-keeping violation. For employers found to have engaged in a pattern of such violations, a criminal penalty involving a fine of $20,000 for each unauthorized alien and imprisonment for not more than three years provided teeth to prevent employers from hiring illegal aliens.[63]

As this lengthy discussion of the Comprehensive Immigration Act of 2007 demonstrates, major portions of the proposed bill dealt with homeland security issues involving secure borders and strict internal controls with respect to both identifying and imprisoning illegal aliens that had committed a crime. The act also strictly prohibited employers from hiring illegal aliens. The final part of the act, called by some the "amnesty" provision, is contained in Title IV, "Non-Immigrant and Immigrant Visa Reform." Subtitle A involved temporary guest workers. Section 403 pertained to the admission of temporary workers intending to perform jobs in the United States for a specified period of time and then return to their country of origin.[64] Individuals needed to pay a $500 application fee, and pay penalties for overstaying their admission period. Employers also had recording obligations with respect to hiring employees in the United States with visas.[65] Combatting the notion that the federal government policy was to encourage low-income temporary foreign workers, Section 407, titled "Recruitment of United States Workers," established an electric job registry on the internet website of the Department of Labor that provides "a single internet link to each State Workforce Agency's statewide electronic registry for jobs available throughout the United States to United States Workers."[66] Section 407 required that the employer attest that the employer has posted opportunities at a prevailing wage level and required the employer to maintain records not less than a year after the date of hiring any temporary foreign worker that describes the reasons for not hiring any United States workers who may have applied for such position. In this new program, the bill appropriated funds for not less than 2,000 compliance investigators dedicated to enforcing compliance of this new portion of the act.[67]

The bill's "backlog reduction" section sought the elimination of backlogs in those attempting to enter the United States legally. Section 503 provided for an allocation for immigrant visas for preference allocation for family-sponsored immigrants. The visas were provided to unmarried sons and daughters of citizens, spouses and unmarried sons and daughters of resident aliens, sons and daughters of citizens and brothers and sisters of citizens.[68]

Section 504 provided relief for minor children and widows. The primary provision of that section states:

> An alien who is a spouse of a citizen of the United States for less than two years at the time of the citizen's death or if married for less than two years at the time of the citizen's death who proves by a preponderance of the evidence that the marriage was entered in good faith and not solely for the purpose of obtaining an immigration benefit, and was not legally separated at the time of the citizen's death, and each child of such alien, shall be considered, for purposes of this subsection to remain an immediate relative at the time of the citizen's death.[69]

Under this clause, anyone who had filed a proper petition remained an immediate relative if the United States citizen's spouse or parent loses United States citizenship on account of domestic abuse. Aliens born to an alien lawfully admitted for permanent residence during a visit abroad also would remain lawfully within the United States. The act provided similar relief for orphans of those lawfully admitted to the United States.[70]

Similarly, the proposed act provided for exemptions for students and individuals seeking advanced degrees.[71] Section 510 provided for expedited adjudication of employer petitions for aliens with extraordinary artistic ability.

In Subtitle B, known as the "Securing Knowledge, Innovation, and Leadership Act of 2007" (SKIL Act of 2007), the bill provided to those who had received a Masters degree from a United States institution of higher education the ability to stay in the United States.[72] The United States-educated immigrants, including immigrants who had earned Masters or higher degrees, or had been awarded medical specialty certification based on doctoral training and experience in the United States, and spouses and minor children also earned exemptions under the act.[73] Section 525 sought student visa reform. The Section allowed bona fide students qualified to pursue a full course of study in mathematics, engineering, technology or sciences leading to a bachelor's degree and who seek to enter the United States with such a course of study consistent with the above to have a right to remain in the United States unless the institution reported the termination of attendance of the immigrant student. The Section further allowed an alien admitted under these circumstances to work off campus if the alien had enrolled full time at the education institution and maintained good academic standing. If the employer provided the education institution and Secretary of Labor with attestation that the employer had spent at least 21 days recruiting United States citizens to fill the position, then aliens could be employed 20 hours a week during the academic term and 40 hours during vacation periods and between academic periods.[74]

The proposed bill in Subtitle C, titled the "DREAM Act of 2007," another controversial part of the bill, provided for adjustment of status of long term residents who entered the United States as children.[75] The alien must have been physically present in the United States for a continuous period of not less than five years immediately preceding the date of enactment of the act and not yet reached the age of 16 years at the time of initial entry. The alien also must have been a person with a good moral character at the time of the application.[76]

The conditional permanent resident status would have been valid for a period of six years, subject to termination if the alien did not maintain good character.[77] Section 631 provided for higher education assistance to an alien who adjusted his or her status to that of a lawful permanent resident. It allowed such individuals to apply for student loans, federal working programs, or higher education assistance.[78] The proposed act also provided a supplemental immigration fee of $500 for any alien who received any immigration benefits under the bill.[79] The act also provided for certain nonimmigrant victims of terrorism to remain in the United States.[80]

The proposed bill also provided relief for widows and orphans of aliens. They needed to be an immediate relative or family-sponsored relative.[81] Any alien wishing to stay needed to declare that English is the common and unified language of the United States.[82] Along with other provisions requiring English proficiency, such features countered opposition that adjusted individuals would not embrace the United States as their homeland. The proposed act also provided automatic acquisition of citizenship of adopted children from outside the United States.[83] The parent of the child needed to be a citizen of the United States either by birth or by naturalization who had been physically present for a period of not less than five years in the United States.[84]

The most controversial provision of the proposed bill, the Z visa, had been formally proposed in predecessor bills. The Z visa would have only been issued to undocumented workers. The purpose of the Z visa was to permit all undocumented workers to be assigned a visa category—allowing them to work and live in the United States while their cases were being reviewed. In order to qualify for the proposed Z visa, applicants would have had to prove that they arrived in the United States before January 1, 2007. The Z visa was renewable in four-year increments, and could have led to a permanent resident "Green Card."[85]

On June 7, 2007, three Senate clotures (move to end discussion) occurred on the bill with the first losing 33–63, the second losing 34–61 and the third losing 31–50. This had been thought by some to signal the end of the bill's chances, since on that day, after the first failing bill, Senator Harry Reid had told reporters that, if another vote failed, "the bill's over with. The bill is gone." However, at the urging of President Bush, the bill was brought back for the session in the Senate as Bill S.1639 on June 25. On June 26, a motion to proceed in the Senate succeeded by a margin of 64–35. A number of amendments to the bill were considered and rejected. On June 28, the bill failed to get the 64 votes needed to end the debate. The final vote was lost 54–43. The Senate had its chances and President Bush said he was disappointed at Congress's failure to act on the immigration reform issue.[86]

Recently, McCain hailed Kennedy for his immigration efforts:

> If we do succeed, and I think we will, it will be a testimonial to Ted Kennedy's efforts years ago that laid the groundwork to this agreement.... You will find that this agreement had very little difference from the legislation that was led by Senator Kennedy some years ago.[87]

McCain honored his old ally, despite lingering antipathy in the Republican party for the Kennedy name. The degree to which the Arizona's senator gesture gets replayed in conservative media will likely signal how Congress responds to the latest efforts for immigration reform, the article noted.[88]

Obama's efforts in immigration reform led to what many called the "Gang of Eight" to recently draft new legislation. Comprised of four Democrats and four Republicans, the bill made its way to the Senate floor on May 28, 2013.[89] Supporters of U.S. Immigration Reform are hoping that this passage of the legislation through the committee will boost the likelihood of winning full Senate approval.

The McCain/Kennedy bipartisan bill and its successor bills stalled back in 2007 when Senator John McCain of Arizona ran for president, making an improbable comeback after his campaign literally planned to close down within days. He won the Republican presidential nomination. McCain forged an unlikely coalition, placating the Republican right just enough to gain enough votes to outflank right wing candidates such as Mike Huckabee. He also staved off Mitt Romney of Massachusetts, who appealed to the moderate wing of the party.

In January 2008, Ted Kennedy endorsed Barack Obama for president of the United States. At the time it seemed like a risky move. He did not merely express a marginal preference for Obama over Hillary Rodham Clinton, who had emerged as the overwhelming favorite of the Democratic party. It pitted Kennedy, with his vast fund-raising resources, against the powerful and equally well-funded Clintons in a battle for the leadership of the Democratic party.

Some ascribe Kennedy's support of Obama to his disdain that the Clintons had worked on behalf of his rival Jimmy Carter at the 1980 Democratic National Convention.[90] Kennedy himself, though, discards such a notion. He referred to Hillary Clinton as a long-term friend and someone he could have "enthusiastically supported." Kennedy felt that Obama had the "capacity to inspire."[91] Kennedy therefore not only endorsed Obama but enthusiastically campaigned for him.

The campaign for the presidency in 2008 had its fair degree of drama on both the Democratic and Republican side. Hillary Clinton began as the prohibitive favorite for the Democratic nomination. Amassing a formidable political machine, Clinton in the beginning underestimated Obama, a novice senator with no public name recognition. Yes, he had made a splash with the publication in October 2006 of *The Audacity of Hope*. Still, even though a best seller, writing a book stood on a far different footing than running for the presidency. Besides the daunting task of raising money, Obama would have to rely on an experienced campaign team. He had a number of advisors who felt that many members of the party would not work for Hillary in the first four critical primaries: Iowa, New Hampshire, Nevada and South Carolina. The proximity of Chicago, Obama's home base, to Iowa, would work in his favor, his advisors implored.

Of course, part of the calculus on deciding whether to run for Obama depended on race. Could Obama overcome deep-seated prejudice and carry enough states to become the first African American nominee of the Democratic party for the presidency? And even if so, many primary voters wondered whether an African American could win a general election against any Republican nominee. Obama also wondered whether Al Gore would become part of the mix; when Gore assured Obama he would not run, Obama effectively launched his campaign on February 10, 2007, on the steps of the Old State Capitol in Illinois.[92]

Clinton had started her campaign a month earlier, and seemed much more organized. She proclaimed that her campaign intended to raise $15 million in the first three months of 2007, and $75 million by the end of the year. Clinton, at the beginning, clearly emerged as the front runner, and appeared formidable indeed. But pieces began to crumble. Hollywood icon David Geffen, in a well-publicized televised interview, disavowed Hillary Clinton and her campaign.

By October 2007, seven candidates emerged on the Democratic side. The five additional individuals consisted of John Edwards, Joe Biden, Chris Dodd, Bill Richardson, and Ohio congressman Dennis Kucinich. All took the stage for a debate on October 30 at Drexel University just before 9:00 p.m. This debate in Philadelphia changed everything. While Obama did not shine, five of the candidates attacked Clinton on a variety of issues. Clinton equivocated on New York's decision to provide driver's licenses to illegal immigrants, and her opponents had a field day pointing out her inconsistent positions.

Obama utilized the debate to point himself as a force for change. More and more, Obama depicted Clinton as a Washington insider who would not answer the hard questions. Obama seized on his youth and exuberance to gain precious respect among young voters.

Soon, it became apparent that endorsements from the Kennedy clan, particularly Ted Kennedy, loomed large in the primary. John Edwards, Clinton and Obama all courted Ted Kennedy's backing. A longtime friend of Senator Chris Dodd from Connecticut, however, Kennedy made it clear he would he not endorse anyone while Dodd remained in the race. Kennedy also had long-standing ties to Clinton and Edwards, but increasingly found himself smitten by Obama.

Following Obama's stunning victory in the Iowa caucuses, Dodd bowed out. However, Caroline Kennedy felt shunned by Hillary Clinton's lack of personal effort to obtain her endorsement. Bill Clinton made similar miscalculations with Ted Kennedy. The day after the Iowa results, Bill called Ted seeking his endorsement. Former President Clinton, however, belittled Obama in a way that offended Ted Kennedy. Kennedy's displeasure with the Clintons continued to grow through New Hampshire and Nevada. Kennedy became increasingly to believe that the Clintons improperly played up race.

Kennedy also appreciated Obama's soft-pedaled approach to seeking his endorsement. Obama, during the campaign, had not actively courted endorsements. He felt differently, however, about Kennedy: "Barack didn't generally give a fig about endorsements. But the backing of Edward Moore Kennedy was an entirely different matter."[93] Along with Edwards and Clinton, Obama avidly but in a restrained fashion sought Kennedy's endorsement. Obama understood that Kennedy had long-standing ties to Clinton and Edwards. Obama interacted with Kennedy by showing his vision. Obama's youth, vigor and idealism that appealed across generational and racial lines reminded Kennedy of JFK. In addition, some attributed women in his life as influencing his endorsement decision. His brother Bobby's widow, Ethel, had publicly anointed Obama two years earlier, calling him "our next President."[94] Ted's wife Vicki adored Obama and so did JFK's daughter Caroline.

Caroline Kennedy Schlossberg weighed in heavily on a Ted Kennedy endorsement of Obama. Famously reserved, Caroline had never taken part in politics with great relish. Caroline liked and admired Hillary Clinton. They moved in similar circles in New York and had more than a cordial relationship. But Caroline leaned toward Obama, taking note of how he had inspired his daughters.

As the Iowa caucuses drew near, Caroline felt torn. Many of her colleagues flew out to canvas there for Clinton. Caroline dreaded a call from Clinton asking her to go. She would have found it impossible to refuse, and once she had campaigned for Clinton, a subsequent endorsement of Obama would have no meaning.

Hillary miscalculated badly. Rather than calling Caroline herself and asking for her support, she had a staffer call. Caroline felt chagrin by Hillary assigning the task to a staffer, and Caroline ducked the call. Caroline felt relieved to follow her heart, and once Obama's Iowa primary victory conferred credibility on his campaign, Caroline informed him of her support. Obama then started planning when to unveil her endorsement for maximum impact.[95]

The Iowa results, with Dodd's departure, also fortified the Clintons' view that Hillary would land Kennedy's endorsement. Surely, Kennedy knew that no one would fight harder for his dreams of universal health care than Hillary. Indeed, during the campaign courtship process, Kennedy had taken the Clintons sailing on his fifty-foot schooner across Nantucket Sound. This, the Clintons thought, had cemented their relationship.

The Clintons underestimated several things. Ted felt fierce family devotion and took seriously Caroline's intention to back Obama. Kennedy also discerned a clearer path to the presidency with Obama than with Clinton. Obama sensed this and asked Kennedy for his support. But he gave Kennedy space, and also had Daschle, with whom Kennedy had a close relationship, check in with him regularly.

To the contrary, Bill Clinton took the opposite approach. In a series of follow up calls, Clinton went from heatedly arguing with Kennedy to pleading desperately with Kennedy. Obama, meanwhile, kept his cool and told the senator to take his time. He made it clear how much a Kennedy endorsement would mean, but never attempted to force his hand.

Bill Clinton, on the other hand, continued an increasingly combative tact with Kennedy. In the end, Kennedy chose to endorse Obama. The day after the South Carolina primary, Ted Kennedy and Caroline stood on a stage at American University with Obama and endorsed his candidacy. This signaled a decided shift from Hillary Clinton's previous front runner role. Kennedy said at the time: "There was another time when another young candidate was running for president and challenged America to cross a New Frontier.... So it is with Barack Obama. He has lit a spark of hope amid the fierce urgency of now."[96]

On Super Tuesday, Clinton did carry California, New York, New Jersey and even Massachusetts, despite Kennedy's backing. But Obama carried more states and delegates. The Kennedy effect on Obama's fortunes is hard to overstate. Ted's endorsement dominated the news and led Maria Shriver to join the Obama bandwagon.

Kennedy continued to campaign for Obama, playing a prominent role. Soon, it became clear Obama had an insurmountable lead over Clinton. While on the crest of victory, Obama soon lost the benefit of Kennedy's campaign efforts.

Those campaign efforts for Obama ended when Kennedy suffered a seizure. Soon, he learned, he had cancer and a huge brain tumor. Fighting through, he did give a pathos-filled speech at the Democratic convention and made it to Obama's inauguration in January 2009.

On August 25, 2009, however, Ted Kennedy succumbed to brain cancer at the age of 77. Painted as the "last lion of the Senate"[97] in contemporary reports, Kennedy's passing, as it should, garnered national attention. Citing Kennedy as the "liberal standard bearer,"[98] the *Los Angeles Times* went on to eulogize Kennedy both for his perceived accomplishments and perceived failures.

Senator Orrin Hatch, the conservative Republican from Utah, lamented Kennedy's passing, noting that the Senate sorely needed his presence for passage of a comprehensive national health care reform bill. Echoing that sentiment, President Obama stated: "He could passionately battle others and do so peerlessly on the Senate floor for the causes he held dear, and yet maintain warm friendships across party lines."[99]

Liberal stalwart Senator Barbara Boxer of California similarly reflected: "He had an amazing ability to find the glimmer of common ground that might be elusive to a lot of us because we don't have deep relationships with people on the other side, or we don't know everything that makes them tick."[100]

Similar recognition of Kennedy's skills at compromise came from the GOP. Kenneth M. Duberstein, a former chief of staff in the Reagan White House and one of the wise elders in Washington observed: "What Senator Kennedy profoundly understood was that we are a nation of incrementalists who like our progress in bite size pieces…. He made the art of compromise not a four letter word."[101]

Michael S. Steele, chairman of the Republican National Committee, credited Kennedy's long term tenure in the Senate: "For close to five decades, Senator Kennedy followed in his family's long tradition and served his country with great distinction. His legacy should serve as an inspiration to anyone interested in public service."[102]

But a far different message echoed from the cacophony of the talk radio and across the conservative blogosphere. Such right wingers excoriated Kennedy upon his death for his liberal politics and the 1969 death of Mary Jo Kopechne. Some said good riddance and even wished Kennedy eternal damnation: "If you can't say something nice about a person then say something mean about them instead. Especially if they are unapologetic manslaughters."[103]

The response to Kennedy's passing illustrates a profound political change during his years in the Senate. Kennedy came from an era that recognized courtesy and negotiation as a valued skill. The divergent response to his death points to an age when public conversation has coarsened and many of the loudest voices in both major parties treat compromise as surrender.

Perhaps the most valuable insight into Kennedy's career in the Senate comes from Republican John McCain, a man Kennedy worked with on many bills, including the failed immigration act reforms of 2005 to 2007. Even though Kennedy vigorously opposed McCain's presidential run, the Republican senator from Arizona noted: "He had this unique capability to sit people down and at a table together—and I've been there on numerous occasions—and really negotiate concessions. And so, he not only will be missed, but he has been missed."[104]

Conclusion

This book has analyzed ten pieces of Ted Kennedy's major legislative efforts plus his 2005–2007 efforts at immigration reform. In so doing, it describes the path of such legislation from the time of enactment through the present.

With this perspective in mind, and with Senator Kennedy's passing, an examination of some of the recent writings regarding his legislative accomplishments seems appropriate.

Kennedy biographer Edward Klein recently wrote before his death:

Ted had compiled a legislative record unsurpassed by any living senator. Among the scores of bills bearing his name, or imprint, he could take credit for the Civil Rights Act of 1964; the Voting Rights Act of 1965; the expansion of the voting franchise to eighteen-year-olds; the 1997 Kennedy-Hatch law providing health insurance to children; the 1982 Voting Rights Act extensions; the 1996 Kennedy-Kassebaum bill, which made health insurance portable for workers; the 1998 law that allocated billions for AIDS testing, treatment, and research; the 1990 Americans with Disabilities Act; the 1993 Family Medical Leave Act, and the 2001 No Child Left Behind Act.[1]

Historian Michael Beschloss, in a speech at the Russell Senate Office Building declared:

I don't need to tell anyone in the room that if you had to choose one of the greatest historical figures in the U.S. Senate in the past two centuries, Edward Kennedy would be at the top of the list.... I often think of President Kennedy, who in the 1950s had to choose some of the great senators whose portraits would be painted on a wall here on Capitol Hill. I think that if he were to do that today, his brother would be on the wall as a master legislator.... If you want to write the history over the last 70 years, you couldn't do better than to study Edward Kennedy's life. Often times the presidency gets more attention than many Senators who have served, and when you have a Senator who has served for years, it's a very good example of the fact that ... a Senator who makes that much impact can do more to change American history than some Presidents of the United States.[2]

Are these glowing assessments by Klein and Beschloss accurate? This study establishes that a balanced assessment of Senator Kennedy's accomplishments in the Senate falls short of these pronouncements, yet deserve considerable historical attention.

With respect to Klein's listing of Kennedy's "legislative record," as a nascent scarcely two year Junior senator when the Civil Rights Act passed in 1964, Kennedy did not play a major role in its passage. While he gave his maiden speech in support of the bill, the historical evidence shows it had little, if any, bearing on the bill's passage.

As for Klein crediting Kennedy with the passage of the Voting Rights Act of 1965, he simply has it wrong. Kennedy lost the vote eliminating the poll tax in the Senate, and only through a subsequent United States Supreme Court decision did the proposed enactment become law.

Klein omits in his laundry list of legislative accomplishments Kennedy's Immigration Act of 1965. To be sure, this act represented Kennedy's first true sponsored legislative achievement. While the aftermath of the act demonstrates unintended consequences, such as the rise in illegal immigration, the omission of the act seems indefensible. As late as 2008, Kennedy worked with Republican Senator John McCain to attempt to address the ill effects of the act.

While Kennedy played a role in the other legislative efforts mentioned by Klein, he ignores the very controversial Title IX Amendments to the Education Act of 1972, which created a flurry of court controversies over collegiate athletics for years. And Klein mentions the No Child Left Behind Act of 2001, but fails to discuss the very controversial testing aspects of the act and its current consequences on school children.

Beschloss, too, drastically overstates Ted Kennedy's role in history. Does Kennedy deserve to "be at the top of the list" of senators in the past two centuries? Surely, Lyndon B. Johnson had a far more dramatic impact in pushing through actual legislation than Ted Kennedy. One can scarcely compare the two, albeit Johnson had an entirely different style than Kennedy. Nonetheless his effectiveness may remain unequalled by any other senator.

Indeed, Kennedy's effectiveness in the Senate requires two measurements. The first measurement involves an assessment, done in this book, of the nine pieces of "major" legislation listed by the *Boston Globe*. This study shows that Ted Kennedy's actual legislative record, while solid, is somewhat modest. Consider the ten acts analyzed in this book:

1. The Immigration Act of 1965 eliminated a racist quota system. However, to this day its unintended consequences, including a flood of illegal immigrants draining overall services, have eluded reform efforts and remain unaddressed.

2. The National Cancer Act of 1971 greatly increased funding for cancer research. Still, despite dramatic improvements, cancer strikes and kills thousands of Americans a year.

3. The Title IX Education Amendments of 1972 eradicated discrimination in public institutions. However, it spawned divisive litigation regarding sports programs, which nobody anticipated at the time, resulting in elimination of key men's sports teams.

4. The Campaign Reform Act of 1974 addressed some of the ills of the Watergate era. However, the historical evidence shows Kennedy, as requested by the Democratic leadership, took a back seat and played virtually no role in its passage.

5. The Comprehensive Anti-Apartheid Act of 1986, much overlooked by historians and passed remarkably during the Reagan presidency, stands as a shining moment in Kennedy's career. Within two years, Nelson Mandela became a free man and played a profound role in South African and international politics.

6. The Americans with Disabilities Act (ADA) helped curb discrimination against the disabled in the workplace. Title II of the ADA greatly impacted the accessibility of public accommodations. Yet disability discrimination lawsuits have skyrocketed, demonstrating that discrimination in the workplace against the disabled remains a significant problem.

7. The Family and Medical Leave Act of 1993 provided much-needed relief for employees requiring unpaid leave to care for an ill family member or themselves. However, some employers loathe the act because many employees have abused it, often to avoid discipline based on preexisting performance deficiencies.

8. The HIPPA Act of 1996 served as a watershed in health care reform. Its primary feature—to allow employees to keep their insurance after leaving their job and placing limitations on refusals to renew coverage based on preexisting conditions—helped millions of Americans. However, the act did not go far enough. Kennedy, if alive, would no doubt have attempted to broker a better deal with respect to Obama's current health care reform law.

9. The Minimum Wage legislation of 1996 attempted to provide low-income workers with a decent wage, placing them above poverty level.

Critics of the legislation argue it leads to higher unemployment, but few mainstream historians deny the import of the legislation.

10. The No Child Left Behind Act of 2001 sought to assist disadvantaged students in achieving educational quality, in Kennedy's eyes. Instead, it institutionalized a system of standardized testing of students at a very young age which, according to many, has stifled learning opportunities and fostered "teaching to the test."

11. Immigration Reform efforts in 2005–2007 failed to make its way to vote in the full Senate, yet those efforts served as the basis for Obama's immigration law.

Looking at this body of work, certainly some achievements jump out. However, given Ted Kennedy's 47 years in the Senate, the legislation described above seems modest indeed.

One cannot divorce, however, a complete assessment of Kennedy's effectiveness as a senator without looking at his successful efforts to reach across the aisle to compromise. And while the fringe right may disagree, the uniform historical consensus is that this "wild-eyed liberal" devoted his years to achieving incremental changes through bipartisan efforts.

While Ted Kennedy will forever be remembered for his personal flaws, his actual record as a senator stands, deservedly so, among the highest of any senator in his era. While the eulogies following his passing overestimate his influence, nonetheless Ted Kennedy is one of the most influential senators of the twentieth century.

Chapter Notes

Introduction

1. *The Boston Globe*, May 21, 2008; *The Seattle Times*, May 21, 2008.

2. Edward Klein, *Ted Kennedy: The Dream That Never Died* (New York: Crown, 2009), at pp. 184–185.

3. Adam Clymer, *Edward M. Kennedy: A Biography* (New York: Harper Perennial, 2000), at p. 42; Doris Kearns Goodwin, *The Fitzgeralds and Kennedys* (New York: St. Martin's Press, 1987), at p. 933; James Mc-Gregor Burns, *Edward Kennedy and the Camelot Legend* (New York: W.W. Norton, 1976), at p. 96; Theo Lippman, Jr., *Senator Ted Kennedy: The Career Behind the Image* (New York: W.W. Norton, 1976), at p. 23; Lester David, *Ted Kennedy: Triumphs and Tragedies* (New York: Award Books, 1975), at p. 147.

4. Edward Klein, "The Lion and the Legacy," *Vanity Fair*, June 2009, at p. 126.

5. *See generally* Peter S. Cannelos, *Last Lion: The Fall and Rise of Ted Kennedy* (New York: Simon & Schuster, 2009).

6. Peter Collier and David Horowitz, *The Kennedys: An American Drama* (New York: Warner Books, 1984); Joe McGinnis, *The Last Brother: The Rise and Fall of Teddy Kennedy* (New York: Simon & Schuster, 1993).

7. Klein, *Ted Kennedy*, at p. 164.

8. *The Philadelphia Inquirer*, July 21, 1969, at p. A1 ("Massachusetts authorities have cleared Sen. Edward Kennedy of negligence in connection with the fatal automobile accident he was involved in Friday night but will seek a citation against him Monday for leaving the scene of the accident"). *See also* David, *Ted Kennedy*, at p. 286 ("The newest Kennedy tragedy did not receive the biggest headline and little wonder: the story broke in the nation's newspapers the same Sunday morning that man set foot on the moon"). The incident would have more far reaching effects when Kennedy later sought the Presidency in the 1980 Democratic primary against embattled incumbent Jimmy Carter. James T. Patterson, *Restless Giant* (New York: Oxford University Press, 2005), at p. 128 ("Kennedy could not shake people's memories of Chappaquiddick … it left him politically vulnerable as he sought the nation's highest office").

9. Conservative talk show hosts, most prominently Sean Hannity of Fox and syndicated radio, have misrepresented the content of the McCain/Kennedy bill. Senator Kennedy clearly states that he did *not* support illegal immigration: "I strongly support legislation today to keep America open to *legal* immigrants, to enable them to use their talents and apply their skills in our economy and in all other aspects of our nation's life" (Edward M. Kennedy, *America Back on Track* [New York: Penguin, 2007], at p. 8).

10. Other major bipartisan efforts include The Immigration Act of 1965, healthcare reform in 1996 eliminating preexisting medical condition restrictions with Republican Nancy Kassebaum of Kansas and support of President Bush's extremely controversial No Child Left Behind initiative in 2001. *See The Boston Globe*, May 21, 2008.

11. Kennedy describes his reasons for backing Obama, instead of Hillary Clinton, in his recent memoir. *See* Edward M. Kennedy, *True Compass* (New York: Hachette Book Group, 2009), at p. 503 ("I was

among the millions moved as well as by Senator Clinton's powerful and uplifting appeal, but I came to believe that Obama was the candidate we needed now at this time in our history... I felt more and more certain that history had landed us the rarest of figures, one who could truly carve out new frontiers").

12. Chris Smith, "The Brief Bizarre Political Career of Caroline Kennedy," *New York Magazine*, February 2, 2009, at p. 18 ("Barack Obama's campaign was surging—largely thanks to the stunning endorsements received one week earlier from Ted Kennedy and, more surprisingly, Ted's niece Caroline").

13. Verbatim text of Kennedy Democratic convention speech, August 26, 2008.

14. *Ibid.*

15. Robert Dalleck, *An Unfinished Life: John F. Kennedy, 1917–1963* (Boston: Little, Brown, 2003), at pp. 480–482.

16. James T. Patterson, *Grand Expectations: The United States, 1945–1974* (New York: Oxford University Press, 1996), at p. 489.

17. Carl M. Brauer, *John F. Kennedy and the Second Reconstruction* (New York: Columbia University Press, 1979), at p.11.

18. Collier and Horowitz, *The Kennedys*, at *passim.*

19. Canellos, *Last Lion*, at *passim.*

20. Jeff Shesol, *Mutual Contempt: Lyndon Johnson, Robert Kennedy and the Feud That Defined a Decade* (New York: W.W. Norton, 1997).

Chapter 1

1. Arthur Schlesinger, Jr., *A Thousand Days* (Boston: Houghton Mifflin, 1965), at p. 15.

2. *The New York Times*, January 22, 1961; Thurston Clarke, *Ask Not: The Inauguration of John F. Kennedy and the Speech That Changed America* (New York: Henry Holt, 2005), *passim.*

3. Doris Kearns Goodwin, *The Fitzgeralds and Kennedys*, at p. 933. *See also* Burns, *Edward Kennedy and the Camelot Legend*, at pp. 74–75 ("Amid this indecision only one man had a definite conviction as to what should be done, and a determination to achieve it," Joe Kennedy said. "Now its

Ted's turn"). Ted Kennedy disputes that he ever heard his father urge he run for the Senate. Lippman, *Senator Ted Kennedy*, at pp. 14–15; Burton Hersh, *The Education of Ted Kennedy* (New York: William Morrow, 1972), at p. 147.

4. *Ibid.* A Ted Kennedy biographer, Adam Clymer, disagrees with Goodwin's analysis of Kennedy's reluctance to enter politics and describes Kennedy as not only ambitious but seizing the opportunity. Clymer, *Edward M. Kennedy*, at p. 31. Burns quotes Kennedy as saying, "Nobody told me to run, I wanted to" (Burns, *Edward Kennedy and the Camelot Legend*, at p. 75). Burns, however, gives credence to Joseph Kennedy's influence on his son Ted's decision to run.

5. Kennedy, *True Compass*, at pp. 162, 166.

6. Dalleck, *An Unfinished Life*, at p. 497.

7. Canellos, *Last Lion*, at p. 75.

8. Clymer, *Edward M. Kennedy*, at p. 37.

9. Thurston Clarke, *The Last Campaign: Robert F. Kennedy and 82 Days That Inspired America* (New York: Henry Holt, 2008), at p. 31. Less objective accounts of Ted Kennedy's early Senate years gush with considerable hyperbole about Kennedy's performance. David, *Ted Kennedy*, at p. 149 ("Kennedy amazed everyone. From the beginning his behavior was exemplary").

10. Dalleck, *An Unfinished Life*, at p. 503, *quoting* pre-presidential papers at the John F. Kennedy Library, at p. 276 (1962).

11. Peter Collier and David Horowitz, *The Kennedys*, at pp. 412–413. A Kennedy biographer agrees that in his first year, he focused on local issues: "The Soviet threat he worried about was the menace to the Massachusetts fishing industry from Soviet travelers. He battled the Civil Aeronautics Board when it took away the valuable right to fly to Florida away from Boston-based Northwest Airlines, and he looked for ways to protect the declining textile and shoe industries" (Clymer, *Edward M. Kennedy*, at p. 47).

12. Collier and Horowitz, *The Kennedys*, at p. 413.

13. Jeffery Toobin, *The Nine: Inside the Secret World of the Supreme Court* (New York: Doubleday, 2007), at p. 60.

14. Clymer, *Edward M. Kennedy*, at p. 51; Kennedy, *American Back on Track*, at p. 10 ("In 1963, with the approval of Congress, President Kennedy signed the first nuclear ban treaty with Nikita Khrushchev of the Soviet Union.") Accordingly, Lippman's assessment, without citations or reference to Senate records, misses the mark. Lippman, *Senator Ted Kennedy*, at p. 425 ("His performance in the [first] two years is barely visible in any records of government activity.").

15. Clarke, *The Last Campaign*, at p. 34; David, *Ted Kennedy*, at p. 159 ("Throughout the summer and fall of 1963, Kennedy continued in the role he had created for himself: to listen carefully, say as little as possible and learn the business.").

16. Dalleck, *An Unfinished Life*, at pp. 480–482. Kennedy also served on the immigration subcommittee, as well as on the subcommittee on constitutional issues. Clymer, *Edward M. Kennedy*, at p.46 ("While not influential the first year, Kennedy brushed up against the three paramount issues of a momentous time: civil rights, nuclear arms, and Vietnam.").

17. Shesol, *Mutual Contempt*, at p. 203. For an incisive view of LBJ's respect for the Senate as an institution *see* Robert A. Caro, *The Years of Lyndon Johnson: Master of the Senate* (New York: Alfred A. Knopf, 2002).

18. Shesol, *Mutual Contempt*, at p. 461, quoting *The Washington Post*, January 18, 1969 A1.

19. Remarks of Senator Edward M. Kennedy Upon Receiving an Honorary Degree, Harvard University, December 1, 2008.

20. Clymer, *Edward M. Kennedy*, at p. 31.

21. Goodwin, *The Fitzgeralds and Kennedys*, at p. 933.

22. *Ibid.* at pp. 18–19.

23. Clymer, *Edward M. Kennedy*, at p. 57 quoting *Congressional Record* 88:11, at pp. 7375–80. The *Congressional Record*, the daily transcript of senatorial debates and speeches on the floor, remains in printed volumes in the Federal Depository Library from 1962 to 1973. After that online access to the contents of the *Congressional Record* capture the history of Kennedy's debates and legislative accomplishments. Historians must take care, however, in citing the *Congressional Record* because not only can members of Congress insert changes, they can also add pre-written speeches not even given on the floor.

24. *See* Taylor Branch, *Pillar of Fire: America in the King Years, 1963–65* (New York: Simon & Schuster, 1998), at p. 388 ("Johnson completed a brief national address: My fellow citizens, we have come to a time of testing. We must not fail. Let us close the springs of racial tension").

25. James T. Patterson, *Brown v. Board of Education: A Civil Rights Milestone and Its Troubled Legacy* (New York: Oxford University Press 2001), at p. 124.

26. J.W. Peltason, *Fifty-eight Lonely Men: Southern Federal Judges and School Desegregation* (Carbondale: University of Illinois Press, 1978), at p. 244 ("The Supreme Court had declared public school segregation unconstitutional, but many federal judges had permitted the evasion of consequences of these decisions.").

27. Harvard Sitkoff, *The Struggle for Black Equality, 1954–1980* (New York: Hall & Wang, 1981), at p. 166.

28. Juan Williams, *Eyes on the Prize: Americas Civil Rights Years, 1954–1965* (New York: Penguin,1988), at p. 253 ("The Civil Rights bill offered no comprehensive remedy for discrimination in voting rights.").

29. Kennedy, *America Back on Track*, at pp. 6–7 ("I made my maiden speech in the Senate in support of the Civil Rights Act of 1964, and I was proud to be part of the great battle for equality."). Kennedy did, in fact, give a stirring speech. David, *Ted Kennedy*, at p. 175 ("My brother was the first President of the United States to state publicly that segregation was wrong. His heart and soul are in this bill. If his life and death had any meaning it was that we should not hate but love another. We should use our powers not to create conditions of oppression that lead to violence, but conditions of freedom that lead to peace. It is in that spirit that I hope the Senate will pass this bill.").

30. Clymer, *Edward M. Kennedy*, at pp. 57–58. Kennedy admirer Lester David, without citation, offers a different version. According to David, Hubert Humphrey commended Kennedy "for his steadfastness

of purpose and his willingness to be present during these difficult trying days in handling the chores of handling certain parts of the Bill" (David, *Ted Kennedy*, at p. 176). In a recent book collaborated by writers from *The Boston Globe*, the main author describes Kennedys speech as "his first major speech in the Senate" (Cannellos, *Last Lion*, at p. 98). The latest book about Kennedy improperly suggests that "he could take credit for the Civil Rights Act of 1964" (Klein, *Ted Kennedy*, at p.184).

31. Patterson, *Grand Expectations*, at p. 544.

32. *Ibid.* at pp. 544–45.

33. Kennedy makes no mention in his memoir of the lack of attention paid to his Maiden speech. Rather, Kennedy touts that he "was increasingly involved in both the substance of the discussion and the debate" (*Kennedy, True Compass*, at p. 216).

34. Patterson, *Grand Expectations*, at p. 545.

35. California's antidiscrimination law, called FEHA, has no damage limitations unlike Title VII of the Civil Rights Act of 1964, as amended. *See* California Government Code 12900 *et seq.*

36. Edward Lazarus, *Closed Chambers: The First Eyewitness Account of the Epic Struggles Inside the Supreme Court* (New York: Times Books, 1998), at p. 451.

37. Lazarus, *Closed Chambers*, at pp. 453–54.

38. Curiously, Ted Kennedy made little public efforts to block Thomas' Supreme Court nomination, even though he stood to eviscerate the very law Kennedy proclaims to have embraced. Clymer, *Edward M. Kennedy*, at pp. 481–82 ("[H]is examination had been perfunctory. He took less than ten minutes on February 6 to probe the views of Clarence Thomas, the head of the Equal Opportunity Commission").

39. Shesol, *Mutual Contempt*, at p. 229; David, *Ted Kennedy*, at p. 197 ("It was an historical occasion. It marked the first time that two brothers had taken the oath as U.S. senators together"); Kennedy in his memoir reveled that Bobby became a senator with him. Kennedy, *True Compass*, at p. 229 ("Bobby and I took office together on January 4, 1965 – me, for my first full

term ... having my brother as a colleague in the Senate was wonderful.").

40. Clymer, *Edward M. Kennedy*, at p. 65.

41. Shesol, *Mutual Contempt*, at p. 253; Lippman, *Senator Ted Kennedy*, at p. 29 ("Almost immediately from the minute he was sworn in a junior senator of New York, Robert was impatiently looking for greater different challenges"). *See also* Canellos, *Last Lion*, at p. 11 ("It didn't help that Bobby's temperament was wholly incompatible with the Senate."); Kennedy, *True Compass*, at p. 229 ("My brother found the Senate's pace infuriatingly slow in relation to make changes he wanted to make.").

42. Canellos, *Last Lion*, at p. 113 ("Ted decided to take up the cause against the poll tax."); Clymer, *Edward M. Kennedy*, at p. 65.

43. Shesol, *Mutual Contempt*, at p. 238.

44. *Ibid.* at p. 239.

45. Burns, *Edward Kennedy and the Camelot Legend*, at p. 110.

46. Clymer, *Edward M. Kennedy*, at p. 65.

47. Kennedy, *America Back on Track*, at p. 7. Kennedy sympathizer Lester David also lauds Kennedy's efforts. David, *Ted Kennedy*, at p. 198 ("Edward reached another milestone when he led an effort for legislation banning poll taxes.").

48. Patterson, *Brown v. Board of Education*, at *passim*.

49. Kennedy biographer Adam Clymer suggests Ted Kennedy chose to fight the poll tax "as a way to show Robert his skill" (Clymer, *Edward M. Kennedy*, at p. 65). This type of rivalry finds no support in either the legislative record or other historical accounts. Rather, as a reelected senator, Ted Kennedy began to veer away from local legislation to legislation of national impact.

50. *Ibid.* at p. 68.

51. *Congressional Record* 89:1, at pp. 7882ff.

52. Clymer, *Edward M. Kennedy*, at p. 69. Not understanding that indeed the Constitutional issue required a court decision, Lester David writes: "In the tense roll call that followed, the Johnson forces defeated Kennedy 49–45, but it was an honorable defeat" (David, *Ted Kennedy*, at p. 195). The most recent biography of Ted

Kennedy incorrectly states that Kennedy's legislation led to the Voting Rights Act of 1965. Klein, *Ted Kennedy*, at pp. 184–85.

53. Burns, *Edward Kennedy and the Camelot Legend*, at p. 130 ("In 1966, the U.S. Supreme Court declared state and local poll taxes unconstitutional.").

54. *The Boston Globe*, May 21, 2008; Lippman, *Senator Ted Kennedy*, at p. 36 ("Kennedy managed the hearings with grace as well as professionalism.").

55. *Three Decades of Mass Immigration: The Legacy of the 1965 Immigration Act* (Washington, D.C.: Center for Immigration Studies, 1995), at p. 1. The Center for Immigration Studies describes itself as a non-partisan think tank.

56. P. L. 89 236: 79 stat 911, amending the Immigration Act of 1952. The Act exempted such individuals—referred to as "immediate relatives" – from the numerical limitations of this Act. *See* Section 201(b).

57. Joyce Vialet, *The Immigration and Nationality Act: Questions and Answers* (Washington, D.C.: Congressional Research Service, March 11, 1982), at p. 14. The CRS works for Congress, providing non-partisan research for committees, members and their staff.

58. Clymer, *Edward M. Kennedy*, at p. 71.

59. *Ibid.* Lippman, therefore, incorrectly describes the scope of the legislation in his book. Lippman, *Senator Ted Kennedy,* at p. 35 ("The bill enacted in 1965 *abolished* national origin quotas and allowed immigration on a first come-first served basis with skills and family ties to United States citizens taken into account.").

60. U.S. Senate, Subcommittee on Immigration and Naturalization of the Committee of the Judiciary, Washington, D.C., February 10, 1965, at pp. 1–3.

61. Kennedy, *True Compass*, at p. 233 ("The quota system since 1924 had allowed masses of northern Europeans to enter the United States, while keeping stringent limits on Asians, Africans, and people of color generally.").

62. *Ibid.*

63. John F. Kennedy, *Public Papers of the Presidents of the United States* (Washington, D.C.: U.S. Government Printing Office, 1964), at pp. 594, 597. Ted Kennedy also

makes the salient point that JFK felt deeply about the plight of immigrants once arriving in the United States. Kennedy, *True Compass*, at p. 233 ("Jack had cared about immigration reform, but it was what happened to newcomers once they had been allowed in that stirred his conscience; the indignities heaped on the boatloads of poor Irish disembarking at Boston, for instance.").

64. Edward M. Kennedy, "The Immigration Act of 1965," *The Annals of the American Academy of Political and Social Science* 367.

65. *Congressional Record*, 89:1, at pp. 24776–24778.

66. Clymer, *Edward M. Kennedy*, at p. 71.

67. Burns, *Edward Kennedy and the Camelot Legend*, at p. 130 ("Ted's courtesy with his elders helped him through the maze of legislative maneuvering.").

68. *Three Decades of Mass Immigration*, at pp. 6–7.

69. *Ibid.* at p. 2.

70. *Ibid.* at p. 3.

71. The article also suggests that illegal immigration increased as a result of the bill, with no supporting data or a suggestion of a nexus between the two.

72. Vialet, at p. 14.

73. Center For Immigration Studies, at p. 13.

74. Public Law 89–236 stat at p. 921.

75. Public Law 89–236, stat at p. 921, Section 21(e).

76. *Three Decades of Mass Immigration*, at p. 3.

77. *Ibid.*

Chapter 2

1. George C. Herring, *America's Longest War: The United States and Vietnam, 1950–1975* (New York: John Wiley & Sons 1979), at p. 258.

2. Kennedy, *America Back on Track*, at p. 69.

3. Kennedy admits this in his memoir. Kennedy, *True Compass*, at p. 238 ("I supported this war when I arrived in Vietnam on that October 1965 visit. I still supported it upon my return.")

4. Clymer, *Edward M. Kennedy*, at p. 78.

5. James Carroll, "Ted Kennedy, the Champion," *The Boston Globe* December 1, 2008.

6. Kennedy, like virtually all senators, voted in favor of the war in Afghanistan following 9/11. Kennedy, *America Back on Track*, at p. 89.

7. Clymer, *Edward M. Kennedy*, at pp. 79–80.

8. Clymer, *Edward M. Kennedy*, at pp. 79–80.

9. Shesol, *Mutual Contempt*, at p. 284.

10. *Ibid. at* p. 284.

11. Clymer, *Edward M. Kennedy*, at p. 80.

12. Meet the Press, March 6, 1966. *See also* Lippman, *Senator Ted Kennedy*, at p. 51 ("Publicly in 1966 Ted Kennedy was saying things like I am eighty-nine percent in favor of the Johnson administrations policies in Vietnam").

13. Shesol, *Mutual Contempt*, at p. 286.

14. Clymer, *Edward M. Kennedy*, at p. 84.

15. Shesol, *Mutual Contempt*, at p. 299.

16. Clarke, *The Last Campaign, passim.*

17. Clymer, *Edward M. Kennedy*, at p. 83 ("Ted Kennedy's advisors on the subcommittee and senatorial staff were urging him to join in with public attacks on the refugee problems... for some reason Kennedy was relatively low key on the criticism and prodding"); Lippman, *Senator Ted Kennedy*, at p. 52 ("During 1966 and 1967, Kennedy held more hearings on the refugee situation and raised his voice more sharply against the meager help given to civilian war victims... "); Burns, *Edward Kennedy and the Camelot Legacy*, at p. 134.

18. Clymer, *Edward M. Kennedy*, at p. 83.

19. *Ibid.*

20. Shesol, *Mutual Contempt*, at p. 620.

21. *Ibid.*

22. Patterson, *Grand Expectations*, at p. 684.

23. Burns, *Edward Kennedy and the Camelot Legend*, at p. 137, quoting *Congressional Record*, at pp. 34190–34192.

24. *Ibid.* at p. 680; Kennedy, *True Compass*, at p. 260 ("On January 31, less than two weeks after I returned from Vietnam the Tet offensive erupted. As Bobby breakfasted with members of the National Press Club in New York ... more than eighty thousand North Vietnamese and Vietcong troops broke an announced religious holiday cease fire and rose up along a front throughout the South, attacking villages, towns, and cities. The communists paid a terrible price in casualties for this surprise offensive ... U.S. forces won the battle, but its initial severity outraged the American public").

25. Clymer, *Edward M. Kennedy*, at p. 104; Lippman, *Senator Ted Kennedy*, at p. 58 ("In March 1968 Robert Kennedy entered the presidential race and Kennedy was swept up in that").

26. Clarke, *The Last Campaign*, at p. 20.

27. Kennedy in his memoir discusses Bobby's decision to run, and says nothing about any disagreement as to timing. Instead, he takes credit for assigning key people to the campaign. Kennedy, *True Compass*, at pp. 262–264.

28. *Ibid.* at pp. 20–21.

29. Shesol, *Mutual Contempt,* at pp. 401–402.

30. Kennedy in his memoir discusses Bobby's decision to run, and says nothing about any disagreement as to timing. Instead, he takes credit for assigning key people to the campaign. Kennedy, *True Compass*, at pp. 262–264.

31. *Ibid.* at p. 111.

32. Clymer, *Edward M. Kennedy*, at p.109; David, *Ted Kennedy*, at p. 207 ("But with Bobby in, Ted was in too. In the next two and a half months, Ted was to be on the road all but five nights").

33. Clarke, *The Last Campaign*, at pp. 172–175.

34. *Ibid.* at pp. 121–122. *Congressional Record* 91:1, at p. 13003.

35. *Congressional Record* 91:1, at p. 13003.

36. BBC on this Day, October 11, 1969.

37. Clymer, *Edward M. Kennedy*, at p. 130

38. *Ibid.* at p. 129.

39. David, *Ted Kennedy*, at p. 230; Burns, *Edward Kennedy and the Camelot Legend*, at p. 154 ("The venture was to run for whip-assistant Democratic leader of the Senate").

40. Kennedy, *True Compass*, at p. 279.

41. Clymer, *Edward M. Kennedy*, at p. 131.

42. Lippman, *Senator Ted Kennedy*, at p. 113.

43. David, *Ted Kennedy*, at p. 231.

44. Clymer, *Edward M. Kennedy*, at p. 132

45. Lippman, *Senator Ted Kennedy*, at p. 114.

46. Clymer, *Edward M. Kennedy*, at p. 132.

47. Lippman, *Senator Ted Kennedy*, at p. 105. Kennedy's memoir does not shed light on his decision to run for the Whip post. Kennedy, *True Compass*, at pp. 279–280.

48. Burns, *Edward Kennedy and the Camelot Legend*, at p. 157.

49. Caro, *Master of the Senate*, at pp. 355–356; Goodwin, *LBJ and the American Dream,* at pp. 113–115.

50. David, *Ted Kennedy*, at p. 232.

51. Clymer, *Edward M. Kennedy*, at p. 135.

52. Lippman, *Senator Ted Kennedy*, at p. 117.

53. Clymer, *Edward M. Kennedy*, at p. 139.

54. *Ibid.* at p. 145.

55. David, *Ted Kennedy*, at pp. 248–249.

56. Collier and Horowitz, *The Kennedys*, at pp. 468–469.

57. Burns, *Edward Kennedy and the Camelot Legend*, at p. 167; Kennedy, *True Compass*, at p. 288 ("That night on Chappaquiddick Island ended in a horrible tragedy that haunts me every day of my life .... This night I was irresponsible").

58. *The Philadelphia Inquirer*, July 21, 1969, at p. A1.

59. Lippman, *Senator Ted Kennedy*, at p. 120.

60. Clymer, *Edward M. Kennedy*, at p. 160.

61. David, *Ted Kennedy*, at p. 275.

62. Clymer, *Edward M. Kennedy*, at pp. 158–159.

63. *Ibid.* at p. 160.

64. Bob Woodward, *The Brethren: Inside the Supreme Court* (New York: Simon & Schuster, 1979), at pp. 56–57; Lazarus, *Closed Chambers*, at p. 101; Toobin, *The Nine*, at p. 28.

65. Woodward, *The Brethren*, at p. 56.

66. *Ibid.* at 74.

67. *Congressional Record* 91:11, at p. 10366 (March 19, 1970).

68. Woodward, *The Brethren*, at p. 75.

69. Lippman, *Senator Ted Kennedy*, at pp. 122–123.

70. *Washington Evening Star*, January 22, 1971.

71. *The Boston Globe*, May 21, 2008; *The Seattle Times,* May 21, 2008.

72. James T. Patterson, *The Dread Disease: Cancer and Modern American Culture* (Cambridge: Harvard University Press, 1987), at p. 237.

73. Clymer, *Edward M. Kennedy*, at p. 173.

74. *Ibid.* at p. 174.

75. *Ibid.*

76. Patterson, *The Dread Disease*, at p. 242.

77. *Ibid.* at p. 243.

78. *Ibid.*

79. Clymer, *Edward M. Kennedy*, at p. 174.

80. *Ibid.* at p. 175.

81. Patterson, *The Dread Disease*, at pp. 248–249.

82. Clymer, *Edward M. Kennedy*, at p. 176.

83. *Congressional Record* 92:1, at p. 23768.

84. Committee Report No. 92–247 (June 28, 1971), accompanying S.1828, 92nd Congress, 1st Session.

85. Public Law 92–218, Section 407(b)(2), December 23, 1971.

86. *Ibid.* at Section 409(a),(b).

87. *Ibid.* at Section 408(a),(b).

88. *Ibid.* at Section 410c.

89. *Ibid.* at Section 410 c(b)(1).

90. Patterson, *The Dread Disease*, at p. 249.

91. *Ibid.*

Chapter 3

1. Cannellos, *Last Lion*, at p. 184.

2. Clymer, *Edward M. Kennedy*, at p. 197. Kennedy in his memoir does not address Mansfield at all. Instead he writes that he exhorted Senator Sam Ervin "to get things going through his constitutional rights subcommittee." He also takes credit for obtaining banking and telephone records. Kennedy, *True Compass*, at p. 372.

3. *The Seattle Times*, May 21, 2008.

4. Pub. L. 92–318, Title IX, June 23, 1972.

5. Pub. L. 92–318, Summary of Bill.

6. 20 U.S.C. § 1681 (a).

7. Allison Kasic and Kimberly Schuld, *Title IX*, Independent Women's Forum 2008, at p. 1.

8. 20 U.S.C. § 1681(c).

9. Clymer, *Edward M. Kennedy*, at p. 185.

10. Cannellos, *Last Lion*, at p. 185.

11. *The Boston Globe*, May 21, 2008.

12. United States Commission on Civil Rights Equal Opportunity Project Series, Vol. 1, at pp. 152–153 and appendices (Washington, D.C., 1996).

13. *Ibid.*

14. Pub. L. 92–318, Summary of Bill.

15. Kasic and Schuld, *Title IX*, at p. 1 ("Title IX policy also undermines equal opportunity by forcing colleges and universities to eliminate men's sports opportunities in order to provide few or no new opportunities for women").

16. *Ibid.* at p. 2.

17. *Cohen v. Brown University*, 991 F.2d 888, 892 (1st Cir. 1993). The First Circuit is the appellate court that reviewed the District Court (trial court's) decision.

18. *Ibid.*

19. *Cohen*, 991 F.2d at p. 892.

20. *Ibid.* at pp. 892–93.

21. *Cohen v. Brown University*, 809 F. Supp 978, 980 (D.R.I. 1992).

22. *Ibid.*

23. *Ibid.*

24. *Ibid.*

25. *Cohen*, 991 F.2d at p. 893.

26. *Ibid.*

27. *Ibid.*

28. *Ibid.* at p. 894.

29. 34 C.F.R. §106.41(a) (1992).

30. *Ibid.* at p. 897.

31. *Ibid.* at p. 905.

32. *Ibid.* at p. 906.

33. *Ibid.* at p. 907.

34. Kasic and Schuld, *Title IX*, at p. 416.

35. David Aronberg, "Crumbling Foundations: Why Recent Judicial and Legislative Challenges to Title IX May Signal Its Demise," *Florida Law Review* 1995, at p. 47.

36. *Ibid.* at p. 1099.

37. *Ibid.*

38. *Ibid.* at p. 1102.

39. *Ibid.*

40. Department of Education Office for Civil Rights, "Clarification of Intercollegiate Athletic Policy Guidance: The Three Part Test (1996)," available at http://www.ed.gov/about/offices/list/OCR/box/clarific.html.

41. *Mansourian*, at p. 1103.

42. *Ibid.* at p. 1,108.

43. *Ibid.*

44. *Ibid.*

45. "40 Years of Change," *Sports Illustrated*, May 7, 2010, at pp. 49–57.

46. *Ibid.* at p. 3.

47. *Ibid.* at p. 45.

48. *Ibid.* at p. 49.

49. *Ibid.*

50. *Ibid.*

51. *Ibid.*

52. *Ibid.*

53. *Ibid.*

54. *Ibid.* at pp. 52–53.

55. *Ibid.*

56. *Ibid.* at pp. 53–54.

57. *Ibid.* at p. 54.

58. *Ibid.*

59. *Ibid.* at p. 59.

60. *Ibid.*

61. *Ibid.* at p. 59.

62. *Ibid.* at p. 60.

63. *Ibid.* at pp. 60–61.

64. *Ibid.* at p. 64.

65. *Ibid.* at p. 65.

66. *Ibid.*

67. *Ibid.* at p. 66.

68. *Ibid.*

69. *Ibid.*

70. *Ibid. See* Kasic and Schuld, *Title IX*, at p. 1 (arguing that Title IX has discriminated against male athletes in it application).

71. Diane Pucin, "Title IX Complaint Names Irvine Schools," *Los Angeles Times*, November 10, 2010.

72. *Ibid.*

73. *Ibid.*

74. *Ibid.*

Chapter 4

1. Clymer, *Edward M. Kennedy*, at p. 200.

2. Patterson, *Grand Expectations*, at pp. 756–57.

3. *Ibid.* at 771.

4. *The Boston Globe*, October 21, 1973.

5. Klein, *Ted Kennedy*, at p. 124.
6. *Ibid.*
7. Kennedy, *True Compass*, at pp. 331–332.
8. *The Boston Globe*, May 21, 2008.
9. "The Federal Election Campaign Laws: A Short History," http://www.fec.gov/info/appfour.htm.
10. *Ibid.*
11. The FEC and the Federal Campaign Finance Law (Federal Election Commission, 2009), http://www.fec.gov/pages/brochures/fecfeca.shtml.
12. Congressional Quarterly Weekly Report, Vol. XXVII, No. 49, December 5, 1969, at p. 2435; Clerk of the House, The Annual Statistical Report On Contributions And Expenditures Made During the 1972 Election Campaigns (1974), at p. 161.
13. Clymer, *Edward M. Kennedy*, at p. 202.
14. S.B. 4496.
15. Statutes at Large, Vol. 88, at pp. 1263–1304.
16. Digest Public General Bills And Resolutions, 93rd Congress, p A-194 -A-195.
17. *Ibid.*
18. *Ibid.*
19. *Ibid.*
20. Thomas (Library of Congress), Summary of S.3094
21. *Ibid.* at pp. 3–4.
22. Jo Freeman, "Political Party Contributions and Expenditures Under the Federal Election Campaign Act: Anomalies and Unfinished Business," *Pace Law Review*, Vol. 4, No. 2 (1984), at p. 207.
23. *Ibid.* at p. 1.
24. *Ibid.* at p. 1.
25. John T. Wooley and Gerhard Peters, *The American Presidency Project*.
26. Pub. L. No. 93-443, 88 Stat 1263, 1265.
27. *Ibid.*
28. *Congressional Record* 93:1, at pp. 38177, 38281.
29. Andrew J. Cowin, *A Campaign Finance Reform That Protects Incumbents* (The Heritage Foundation, 1990), at p. 65.
30. *Ibid.*
31. *Ibid.* at p. 2.
32. *Buckley v. Valeo*, 424 U.S 1 (1976).
33. Peterson, *Political Party Contributions*, at n.3.

34. *Ibid.*
35. *Ibid.*
36. *Ibid.*
37. Cowin, *A Campaign Finance Reform That Protects Incumbents*, at p. 2.
38. *Ibid.*
39. *Ibid.* at p. 3.
40. *Citizens United v. IEC*, 130 S. Ct. 876 (2010).
41. *McConnell v. Federal Election Committee*, 540 U.S. 93, 203–209 (2003); *Austin v. Michigan Chamber of Commerce*, 494 U.S. 652 (1990).
42. *Citizens United*, 130 S. Ct. at p. 886.

Chapter 5

1. *Boston Globe*, May 21, 2008.
2. Clymer, *Edward M. Kennedy*, at p. 363.
3. *Ibid.* at p. 225.
4. Kennedy hedges on this subject in his memoir, stating, "At the 1976 Democratic convention that nominated him for president, Carter chose not to offer me a speaking role. Still, as his administration began in 1977, our relationship was harmonious enough" (Kennedy, *True Compass*, at p. 353).
5. *Baltimore Sun*, October 1, 1976.
6. Patterson, *Restless Giant*, at pp. 108–109.
7. Clymer, *Edward M. Kennedy*, at p. 254.
8. James Fallows, "The Passionless Presidency II," *Atlantic Monthly* (June 1979), at pp. 75–81.
9. Patterson, *Restless Giant*, at p. 39.
10. *Ibid.* at pp. 115–116.
11. Kennedy, *True Compass*, at p. 357.
12. Clymer, *Edward M. Kennedy*, at p. 280.
13. Patterson, *Restless Giant*, at p. 110.
14. Clymer, *Edward M. Kennedy*, at p. 284; Kennedy, *True Compass*, at p. 367 ("It was in the aftershock of this speech that I began thinking seriously about running for the presidency in 1980").
15. Patterson, *Restless Giant*, at p. 128.
16. Cannelos, *Last Lion*, at p. 214.
17. Patterson, *Restless Giant*, at p. 128.
18. Cannelos, *Last Lion*, at p. 225.
19. *Ibid.*
20. Kennedy, *True Compass*, at p. 384.

21. Garry Wills, *The Kennedy Imprisonment* (Boston: Little, Brown, 1981), at p. 295.

22. Cannelos, *Last Lion*, at p. 236.

23. Clymer, *Edward M. Kennedy*, at p. 358.

24. *Ibid.* at p. 359.

25. Clymer, *Edward M. Kennedy*, at p. 361.

26. Margaret K. McMillion, *Morality and Grand Strategy: The Executive Branch And The Anti-Apartheid Act* (National Defense University Library Special Collections, December 15, 1989), pp.1–2.

27. Clymer, *Edward M. Kennedy*, at p. 363.

28. *Ibid.* at p. 366.

29. Committee on Banking, Housing and Urban Affairs, Legislative Calendar Ninety-Ninth Congress (1985), at p. 14.

30. *The New York Times*, June 6, 1985.

31. Brenda M. Branaman, *South Africa: U.S. Policy After Sanctions* (Washington, D.C.: Congressional Research Service May 1, 1987), at p. 1.

32. *Congressional Record* 99:1, at p. 7334.

33. Clymer, *Edward M. Kennedy*, at p. 378.

34. Patterson, *Restless Giant*, at p. 173.

35. McMillion, *Morality and Grand Strategy*, at p. 1.

36. *Ibid.* at pp. 2–3.

37. Branaman, *South Africa*, at p. 1.

38. *Ibid.* at p. 2.

39. Clymer, *Edward M. Kennedy*, at p. 402.

40. *Ibid.* at p. 470.

41. Patterson, *Restless Giant*, at p. 337.

Chapter 6

1. Clymer, *Edward M. Kennedy*, at p. 405.

2. Cannellos, *Last Lion*, at p. 250.

3. Senate Judiciary Hearings on nomination of William H. Rehnquist, July 29, 1986, at p. 14.

4. Klein, *Ted Kennedy*, at p. 156.

5. Cannellos, *Last Lion*, at p. 251.

6. Clymer, *Edward M. Kennedy*, at p. 417.

7. Klein, *Ted Kennedy*, at p. 156.

8. *Ibid.* at p. 157.

9. Patterson, *Restless Giant*, at p.171.

10. Kennedy, *True Compass*, at pp. 404–405.

11. Cannellos, *Last Lion*, at p. 251.

12. *Ibid.* at p. 21.

13. Clymer, *Edward M. Kennedy*, at pp. 205–206.

14. *Congressional Record* 101:I, at p. 19807.

15. 42 U.S.C. § 12010 *et. seq.*

16. *Ibid.* at Section 101 (5)(A).

17. *Ibid.* at Section 2(b).

18. For the discussion below, refer to M. Kirby Wilcox, *California Employment Law* (New York: Matthew Bender 2010).

19. For these reasons, employees in California subjected to disability discrimination should sue under California's antidiscrimination law, FEHA, Cal. Gov't Code §12900 *et. seq.* FEHA does not have any such punitive damage caps.

20. *See, e.g., Schultz v. Spraylat Corp*, 866 F. Supp 1535, 1539 (C.D. Cal 1994) ("Since Schultz's psychological condition does not prevent him from participating in major life activities, the Court finds that he is not physically disabled").

21. P.L. 110.325.

22. 42 U.S.C. § 12102(4)(D).

23. *Congressional Record*s 101:II, at p. 17369.

24. Clymer, *Edward M. Kennedy*, at p. 472.

25. *Congressional Record* 101:II, at p. 17370

26. 129 S.Ct. at p. 2350.

27. *Ibid.* at p. 2352.

28. *Ibid.* at p. 2353

29. 42 U.S.C. § 12183(a)(1).

Chapter 7

1. *Congressional Record* 101:11, at p. 26726.

2. Patterson, *Restless Giant*, at p. 234.

3. Clymer, *Edward M. Kennedy*, at pp. 503–505.

4. *Ibid.* at p. 514.

5. *The Boston Globe*, May 21, 2008.

6. Judith Stadtman Tucker, "Hands Off My FMLA," *The Huffington Post*, January 2, 2007.

7. Patterson, *Restless Giant*, at p. 326.

8. Clymer, *Edward M. Kennedy*, at p. 515.

9. *Ibid.*

10. *Ibid.*

11. 29 U.S.C 2612, 107 Stat 8–9.

12. *Ibid.* at 107 Stat 8.

13. *Ibid.* at 107 Stat 11.

14. *Ibid.* at 107 Stat 12.

15. *See* 29 U.S.C. § 2601(b).

16. 29 U.S.C. § 2651(b); see also 29 C.F.R. § 825.701(a).

17. 29 C.F.R. § 825.702(a).

18. *See generally* Wilcox. Much of the following discussion derives from the Wilcox Section on FMLA, beginning at § 8.20.

19. 29 U.S.C. § 2615(a)(1); *see Liu v. Amway Corp.* 347 F. 3d 1125, 1133–1135, (9th Cir. 2004) (employee presented triable issue of fact that employer denied employee's right to FMLA leave by rejecting her requests for additional leave and forcing her to take shorter extensions of additional leave and by mischaracterizing FMLA protected leave as personal leave); *Bachelder v. America West Airlines, Inc.* 259 F. 3d 1112, 1124 (9th Cir. 2001) (employer actions deterring employees' participation in protected activities constitute interference or restraint with employees' exercise of their rights); *Faust v. California Portland Cement Co.* 150 Cal. App. 4th 964, 879, 58 Cal. Rptr. 3d 729 (2007) (interference claim under FMLA and thus under CFRA does not involve burden-shifting analysis of *McDonnell Douglas*).

20. See 29 U.S.C. § 2614(a); 29 C.F.R. § 825.216(a)(1). *See also Gambini v. Total Renal Care, Inc.* 486 F. 3d 1087, 2007 (9th Cir. 2007) (any arguable error in instructing jury as to employer's burden of proving that employee's federally-protected leave was not factor in its decision to terminate her employment was harmless in light of employer's uncontroverted evidence it would have fired employee for her conduct regardless of her leave status).

21. *Funkhouser v. Wells Fargo Bank, N.A.* 289 F. 3d 1137, 1141 (9th Cir. 2002). *See* 29 C.F.R. § 825.700(b) (nothing in Act prevents employer from amending existing leave and employee benefit programs, provided they comply with Act).

22. 29 U.S.C. § 2612(a)(1)(A); 29 C.F.R. § 825.112(a)(1). Effective January 16, 2009, the Department of Labor moved the language from former 29 C.F.R. § 825.207(d)(2), addressing the interaction between worker's compensation, light duty and the FMLA, to 29 C.F.R.§ 285.207(e) with no change.

23. *See* 29 C.F.R. § 825.120 *et seq.*

24. *See* Cal. Code Reg. § 7291.13(a).

25. 29 U.S.C. § 2612(a)(1)(D); 29 C.F.R. § 825.112(a)(4); Gov. Code § 12945.2(c)(3)(C). *see Rowe v. Laidlaw Transit, Inc.* 244 F. 3d 1115, 1118 (9th Cir. 2001) (serious ankle injury qualified employee for coverage under FMLA and reduced schedule qualified as FMLA leave, because it was undisputed that physician restricted her activities, including those that had been essential part of her job and she presented request for temporary part-time duty on that basis).

26. *Wilcox,* § 8.21.

27. *See Marchisheck v. San Mateo County,* 199 F 3. 1068, 1076 (9th Cir. 1999), *cert. denied,* 530 U.S. 1214, 120 S. Ct. 2217, 147 L. Ed. 2d 250 (2000).

28. *Tellis v. Alaska Airlines, Inc.,* 414 F. 3d 1045, 1045, 1046–1048 (9th Cir. 2005).

29. *Pang v. Beverly Hospital, Inc.,* 79 Cal. App 4th 986, 996, 94 Cal. Rptr. 2d 643 (2000).

30. *Scamihorn v. Gen. Truck Drivers, Local 952,* 282 F. 3d 1078 (9th Cir. 2002).

31. 29 C.F.R. § 825.122(c)(2). See 29 C.F.R. § 1630.22(h).

32. Wilcox, § 8.21(2)(c).

33. *Ibid.*

34. Tucker, "Hands Off My FMLA," at p. 1.

35. Susan Freilich Appelton, *The Networked, Yet Still Hierarchical Family,* *Virginia Law Review,* September 1, 2008, at p. 2.

36. Deborah Walker, *Mandatory Family Legislation: The Hidden Costs* (Washington, D.C.: The Cato Institute, 1988), at p. 3.

37. *Ibid.*

38. *Ibid.*

39. Tucker, "Hands Off My FMLA," at p. 3.

Chapter 8

1. Clymer, *Edward M. Kennedy,* at p. 253.

2. Michael D. Shear, "Jimmy Carter Attacks Ted Kennedy," NYTimeswww, September 16, 2010.

3. *Ibid.*

4. Kennedy, *True Compass*, at p. 453.

5. Patterson, *Restless Giant*, at p. 328.

6. *Ibid.* at p. 329.

7. *Ibid.* at p. 538

8. *Ibid.* at p. 539.

9. *The New York Times*, May 19, 1994.

10. *Ibid.*

11. *Congressional Record* 103:II, at pp. 20414 ff.

12. *Ibid.* at p. 25597.

13. Gillon, *The Pact*, at p. 117.

14. *The Boston Globe*, May 21, 2008.

15. Aug. 21, 1991 [H.P. 3103]

16. 29 U.S.C. 1181, Section 701 (a).

17. 29 U.S.C. 1181, Section 702.

18. Mark Leibovich, *New York Times*, July 17, 2009.

19. *Ibid.*

Chapter 9

1. Milton and Rose Friedman, *Free to Choose* (New York: Harcourt Brace Jovanovich, 1980), at pp. 237–38.

2. Patterson, *Restless Giant*, at p. 63.

3. *Ibid.* at p. 164.

4. Clymer, *Edward M. Kennedy*, at p. 355.

5. Patterson, *Restless Giant*, at p. 220.

6. Clymer, *Edward M. Kennedy*, at p. 436.

7. *Official Proceedings of the Democratic National Convention* (Washington, D.C.: DNC Services Corporation, 1988), at p. 313.

8. Clymer, *Edward M. Kennedy*, at p. 442.

9. *Ibid.*

10. *Ibid.* at p. 446.

11. *The New York Times*, March 9, 1989.

12. *Congressional Record* 101:1, at pp. 5710f.

13. Clymer, *Edward M. Kennedy*, at p. 448.

14. *New York Times*, November 1, 1989.

15. *Congressional Record* 101:1, at p. 27878

16. Thomas Sowell, "What Causes Unemployment," *Capitalism Magazine*, November 14, 2005, at p. 2.

17. Thomas Sowell, *Basic Economics* (New York: Basic Books, 2000), at pp. 210–211.

18. Thomas Sowell, "Living Wage Kills Jobs," *Jewish World Review*, November 5, 2003, at p. 2.

19. D. W. MacKenzie "Mythology of the Minimum Wage," Mises Institute May 3, 2006.

20. *Ibid.*

21. *Ibid.*

22. *Ibid.*

23. *Ibid.*

24. *Ibid.*

25. Mike Flynn, "Five Myths About the Minimum Wage," *Breitbart*, March 10, 2013.

26. *Ibid.*

27. *Ibid.*

28. *Ibid.*

29. *Ibid.*

30. *Ibid.*

31. *Ibid.*

32. Kassebaum, Senate Labor Committee, December 15, 1994, at p. 1.

33. Clymer, *Edward M. Kennedy*, at p. 565.

34. *Ibid.* at p. 566.

35. *The New York Times*, July 26, 1996.

36. Clymer, *Edward M. Kennedy*, at p. 581.

Chapter 10

1. For the best account of the halt in legislation due to the Lewinsky scandal, *see* Steven M. Gillon, *The Pact: Bill Clinton, Newt Gingrich and the Rivalry That Defined a Generation* (New York: Oxford University Press, 2008).

2. Kennedy, *True Compass*, at p. 468.

3. *Bush v. Gore*, 531 U.S. 98 (2000) (per curiam 5–4 decision).

4. Alan Dershowitz, *Supreme Injustice* (New York: Oxford University Press, 2001).

5. Patterson, *Restless Giant*, at p. 409.

6. Toobin, *The Nine*, at p. 144.

7. Dershowitz, *Supreme Injustice*, at p. 32.

8. Patterson, *Restless Giant*, at p. 415.

9. Dershowitz, *Supreme Injustice*, at p. 44.

10. *Ibid.* at p. 3.

11. Toobin, *The Nine*, at p. 173.

12. Kennedy, *True Compass*, at p. 487.

13. Klein, *Ted Kennedy.*

14. Cannelos, *Last Lion*, at p. 350.

15. *The Boston Globe*, May 21, 2008.

16. Cannellos, *Last Lion*, at p. 354.

17. Public law 107–110, 20 USC 6301, Title I, Sections 1001–1004.

18. *Ibid.* at Title VII, Sections 701–703.

19. *Ibid.* at Title X, Part D.

20. Kennedy, *True Compass*, at p. 489.

21. *Ibid.* at p. 490.

22. Cannellos, *Last Lion*, at p. 354.

23. Personal interview, retired school principal Hugh Gottfried (now deceased), September 12, 2009.

24. "Test Scores Raise Red Flags," *Los Angeles Times*, Feburary 17, 2010, A10 ("An extensive analysis of Georgia standardized test is raising fears that the exams have been altered by teachers and administrators worried about facing sanctions under the Federal No Child Left Behind Law… In one extreme case, an Atlanta middle school was flagged for abnormally high incidents of changed answers in 89.5% of its classes.")

25. Cannellos, *Last Lion*, at p. 355.

26. *Ibid.*

27. Kennedy, *True Compass*, at p. 491.

28. *Ibid.*

29. *Ibid.* at p. 494.

30. *Ibid.*

Chapter 11

1. Kennedy, *True Compass*, at p. 492.

2. Cannelos, *Last Lion*, at p. 436.

3. *Ibid.* at p. 357.

4. Kennedy, *True Compass*, at p. 496.

5. Cannelos, *Last Lion*, at pp. 376–77.

6. S. Bill 1033, Title I, Section 111.

7. *Ibid.*

8. *Ibid.* at Section 133.

9. *Ibid.* at Section 133.

10. *Ibid.* at Section 302.

11. James Jay Carafano, Janice L. Kephart and Paul Rosenzweig, "The McCain Kennedy Immigration Reform Bill Falls Short," *Executive Memorandum*, No. 975, July 26, 2005.

12. *Ibid.*

13. *Ibid.*

14. "Enter McCain-Kennedy," *The Washington Post,* Editorial, May 14, 2005.

15. *Ibid.*

16. *Ibid.*

17. Rick Klein, "Kennedy, McCain Try Again on Immigration," *The Boston Globe*, February 28, 2001.

18. *Ibid.*

19. *Ibid.*

20. *Ibid.*

21. *Ibid.*

22. S. Bill 1348, Section 5202.

23. *Ibid.* at Section 104.

24. *Ibid.* at Section 104.

25. *Ibid.* at Section 106.

26. *Ibid.* at Section 111

27. *Ibid.* at Section 112(b)(2)

28. *Ibid.* at Section 112(b)(1)

29. *Ibid.* at Section 114

30. *Ibid.* at Section 115–117.

31. *Ibid.* at Section 132

32. Section 115

33. Section 116(b)(2)

34. Section 121(12)

35. Section 122 (1–4)

36. Section 125, Senate Bill 1348

37. Section 133(c)

38. Section 133(b)

39. Section 134(a)

40. Section 151

41. Section 152(b)

42. Sections 152–158

43. Section 201.

44. Section 249

45. Section 202.

46. Section 205(a)(f)

47. Section 274

48. Section 274(b)

49. Section 275

50. Sections 1541–1546.

51. Section 1547.

52. Section 220.

53. Section 211.

54. Section 216.

55. Section 216(c).

56. Section 218.

57. Section 218(b)(1).

58. A vocal critic of the current immigration laws is KABC talk show radio host Doug McIntyre.

59. Section 240D(a).

60. *Ibid.*

61. Section 233(a).

62. Section 235.

63. Section 301.

64. Section 402.

65. Section 404.

66. Section 407.

67. Section 412.

68. Section 503.

69. Section 504(a)(iii).

70. Section 506.
71. Section 507 and 508.
72. Section 522-H-1-B Visa Holders.
73. Sections 523–524.
74. Section 505(a) and (b).
75. Section 624(a)(1)(A)
76. *Ibid.*
77. Section 625(a)(b)
78. Section 631
79. Section 644(a).
80. Section 742 and 743.
81. Section 761(d).
82. Section 767.
83. Section 821.
84. Section 320(a)(2).
85. "Z Visa" 2002 U.S. Support 2012.
86. Andrea Koppol, "Senate Immigration Bill Suffers Crushing Defeat," CN-Nwww, June 28, 2007.
87. Michael McCaulin, "John McCain Pays Homage to Ted Kennedy and Immigration Reform Push," *The Huffington Post*, January 28, 2013.
88. *Ibid.*
89. Richard Cowan, "Supporters of U.S Immigration Reform," Reuters, May 22, 2013.
90. Klein, *Ted Kennedy*, at p. 190.
91. Kennedy, *True Compass*, at pp. 502–03.

92. John Heilemann and Mark Halperin, *Game Change* (New York: HarperCollins, 2010).
93. Heileman and Halperin, *Game Change*, at p. 215.
94. *Ibid.* at p. 217.
95. *Ibid.* at p. 218.
96. *Ibid.* at p. 219.
97. *Los Angeles Times*, August 26, 2009, at p. AI.
98. *Ibid.* at p. A20.
99. *The Los Angeles Times*, August 27, 2009, at p. A16
100. *Ibid.*
101. *Ibid.* at p. A17.
102. *Ibid.*
103. Andrew Breitbart, *The Washington Times*, August 26, 2009.
104. CNN interview of John McCain, August 26, 2009.

Conclusion

1. Klein, *The Dream That Never Died*, at pp. 184–188.
2. Michael Beschloss remarks on launch of Edward M. Kennedy Oral History Project, December 5, 2004.

Bibliographical Essay

Secondary Sources

Biographies of Ted Kennedy abound. Very few represent balanced perspectives on the Senator.

Ted Kennedy Biographies

Unabashedly positive accounts include Edward Klein, *The Dream That Never Died* (New York: Crown, 1999), Peter Cannellos, *Last Lion: The Fall and Rise of Ted Kennedy* (New York: Simon & Schuster, 2009), Theo Lippman, Jr., *Senator Ted Kennedy: The Career Beyond the Image* (New York: W.W. Norton, 1996), and Lester David, *Ted Kennedy: Triumphs and Tragedies* (New York: Award Books, 1975). Of a similar nature is Burton Hersh, *The Education of Edward M. Kennedy* (New York: William Morrow, 1972).

Negative and sometimes vitriolic accounts of Ted Kennedy also abound. Without citing fringe and unreliable accounts, the most representative of such books are Joe McGinnis, *The Last Brother: The Rise and Fall of Teddy Kennedy* (New York: Simon & Schuster, 1993) and Peter Collier and David Horowitz, *The Kennedys: An American Dream* (New York: Warner Books, 1984). While the latter book focuses on the Kennedys in general, it contains its fair share of criticism of Ted Kennedy.

The most balanced biography of Ted Kennedy, by far, is Adam Clymer, *Edward M. Kennedy: A Biography* (New York: Harper Perennial, 2000). While Clymer generally provides a positive image of Senator Kennedy, the depth of his scholarship greatly exceeds any of the books listed above. His account ends in 1999, and therefore does not portray the last ten years of Ted Kennedy's life in the Senate. A less balanced account, but well worth reading due to its impeccable scholarship, is James McGregor Burns, *Edward M. Kennedy and the Camelot Legend* (New York: W.W. Norton, 1976).

Memoirs

A look at Ted Kennedy's accomplishments from his own perspective can be found in Edward M. Kennedy, *America Back on Track* (New York: Penguin, 2007). His more comprehensive memoir, completed near his death, supplies a surprisingly more balanced assessment of his life and record. Edward M. Kennedy, *True Compass* (New York: Hachett Book Group, 2009).

General Accounts of the Kennedy Family

More general accounts of the Kennedys shed some light on Ted Kennedy's career in the Senate. For such insight, the best source remains Doris Kearns Goodwin, *The*

Fitzgeralds and the Kennedys (New York: St. Martin's Press, 1987). For the best account of Robert F. Kennedy and the sharp contrast with his political style from his younger brother, see Jeff Shesol, *Mutual Contempt: Lyndon B. Johnson, Robert Kennedy and the Feud That Defined a Decade* (New York: W.W. Norton, 1997).

Other generalized accounts focus primarily on John F. Kennedy, including Robert Dalleck, *An Unfinished Life: John F. Kennedy 1917–1963* (Boston: Little, Brown, 1993) and Carl Brauer, *John F. Kennedy and the Second Reconstruction* (New York: Columbia University Press, 1976).

Broader Historical Accounts

Broader historical accounts touch on various aspects of Ted Kennedy's career. For an assessment of the effect of Chappaquiddick on Kennedy's presidential aspirations, see James T. Patterson *Grand Expectations: The United States, 1945–1974* (New York: Oxford University Press, 1996). Patterson echoes a similar theme in James T. Patterson, *Restless Giant* (New York: Oxford University Press, 2005).

Works on John F. Kennedy

Additional works about John F. Kennedy include the legendary Arthur Schlesinger, Jr., *A Thousand Days* (Boston: Houghton Mifflin, 1965) and Thurston Clark, *Ask Not: The Inauguration of John F. Kennedy and the Speech That Changed America* (New York: Henry Holt, 2005).

Legal Works

Since this book involved a legal analysis of legislative acts, several books have particular significance. For an incisive view of the shift of the United States Supreme Court to the right, see Jeffery Toobin, *The Nine: Inside the Secret World of the Supreme Court* (New York: Doubleday, 2007). For a behind the scenes look at the United States Supreme Court by a former law clerks perspective, see Edward Lazarus, *Closed Chambers: The First Eyewitness Account of the Epic Struggle Inside the Supreme Court* (New York: Times Books, 1998). The classic book about the inner workings of the Supreme Court is Bob Woodward, *The Brethren: Inside the Supreme Court* (New York: Simon & Schuster, 1979).

Civil Rights

While Ted Kennedy's biographers have overstated his role in passage of the Civil Rights Act of 1964, nonetheless he embraced the Act. For compelling narratives of the Civil Rights movement, see Taylor Branch, *Pillar of Fire: America in the King Years, 1963–68* (New York: Simon & Schuster, 1998), Juan Williams, *Eyes on the Prize: Americas Civil Rights Years, 1954–1965* (New York: Penguin, 1988) and Harvard Sitroff, *The Struggle For Black Equality, 1954–1980* (New York: Hall & Wang 1981).

Books discussing desegregation, another cause of Ted Kennedy, include James T. Patterson, *Brown v. Board of Education: A Civil Rights Milestone and Its Troubled Legacy* (New York: Oxford University Press, 2001) and J.W. Peltason, *Fifty-Eight Lonely Men: Southern Federal Judges and School Desegregation* (Urbana: University of Illinois Press, 1978).

Topical Secondary Sources

With his passing, several recent accounts praise Kennedy as the best Senator in history. Plainly other Senators deserve consideration. For Lyndon Baines Johnson's senate career, see Robert A. Caro, *The Years of Lyndon Johnson, Master of The Senate* (New York: Alfred A. Knopf, 2002).

Ted Kennedy's stance on Vietnam shaped perception of his days in the Senate. A complete view of Americas involvement in Vietnam is contained in George C. Herring, *Americas Longest War: 1950–1975* (New York: John Wiley & Sons, 1979).

Ted Kennedy fully embraced and backed the National Cancer Act of 1971. For the best book on the subject see James T. Patterson, *The Dread Disease: Cancer and Modern America Culture* (Cambridge: Harvard University Press, 1987).

Primacy Sources

This book has utilized numerous primary sources. The most useful primary sources, the text of the ten actual bills assessed in this book, form the best historical tool. Less helpful, although thoroughly reviewed, is the Congressional Record. The Congressional Record contains valuable information, but has limited value given the ability of Congressmen to amend it and include remarks not made on the floor.

Other types of primary sources permeate this book.

Newspaper Articles

Among the many newspapers referred to in formulating this book include *The Boston Globe, The Seattle Times, The New York Times, The Philadelphia Inquirer, The Washington Post, The Los Angeles Times, BBC, The Washington Evening Star,* and *The Baltimore Sun.*

Topical Sources

For each chapter on the ten pieces of legislation analyzed in this book, I started with primary sources regarding the legislation itself.

With respect to the Immigration Act of 1965, the actual law is P.L. 236:79 stat 911. For an analysis of the Act by the Congressional Research service, a non-partisan group working for Congress providing research for committees, members and their staff, see Joyce Violet, *The Immigration and Nationality Act: Questions and Answers* (Congressional Research Service, March 11, 1982). A piece to consider, although partisan, is *Three Decades of Mass Immigration: The Legacy of the 1965 Immigration Act* (Washington, D.C.: Center for Immigration Studies, 1965). Also included in assessing Kennedy'S role see Kennedy's contemporaneous speech regarding the act in Subcommittee on Immigration and Naturalization of the Committee on the Judiciary, Washington D.C., February 10, 1965. Also consider Ted Kennedy, "The Immigration Act of 1965," *The Annals of the American Academy of Political and Social Science,* Vol. 637.

For the National Cancer Act of 1971, the original Kennedy/Javits bill ceded to an administration sponsored bill S. 1828. Also good insight comes from Committee Report No. 92–247 (June 28, 1971). For a review of the final law, see Public Law 92–218, Sec. 407(b)(2) (December 23, 1971).

The Title IX amendments to the Education Act of 1972 is Public Law 92–318 (June 23, 1972). For a highly critical article on the unintended side effects of the amendments, see Allison Kasic and Kimbely Schuld, *Title IX*, (Independent Women's Focus, 2008). The case *Cohen v. Brown University*, 951 F. 2d 888 (1st Cir. 1917) provided an excellent history of the changes from the original intent of the Act. Also necessary to understand the history of interpretation of the act, see the regulations at 34 C.F.R. 106.41(a) (1992). Criticizing the expanded scope of Title IX, review of a law review article assisted in this chapter. *See* David Aronberg, "Crumbling Foundations: Why Recent Judicial and Legislative Challenges To Title IX May Signal its Demise," *Florida Law Review*, 1995.

Kennedy has received credit from many biographers about spearheading Campaign Finance Reform after Watergate. In fact, Kennedy had little to do with the Federal Campaign Act of 1972. The Kennedy/Scott bill, S.1496, never made it out of committee. A synopsis of the bill appears in *The Digest of Public General Bills and Resolutions*, 93rd Congress pages A-194–195. The bill that passed, Senate Bill 3044, can be found at Statutes at Large, Vol. 88, pp. 1263–1304. The summary of major action regarding the bill that passed is at Thomas (Library of Congress), Summary of S. 3094. For a good account of the benefits and flaws of the Act, see Jo Freeman, "Political Party Contributions and Expenditures Under the Federal Election Campaign Act: Anomalies and Unfinished Business," *Pace Law Review*, Vol. 4, No. 2 (1984). For a critical viewpoint of the campaign finance reform law, see Andrew J. Cowin, *A Campaign Finance Reform That Protects Incumbents* (The Heritage Society, 1990).

Historians have largely ignored Kennedys role in the passage of the Comprehensive Anti-Apartheid Act of 1986. For the Kennedy/Weicker bill, see Committee on Banking, Housing and Urban Affairs, Legislative Calendar Ninety Ninth Congress (1985). While that bill eventually failed in Committee, Kennedy had a stamp on the structure of the bill that passed. Useful accounts of the bill include Brenda M. Branaman, *South Africa: U.S. Policy After Sanctions* (Congressional Research Service, May 1, 1987) and Margaret K. McMillion, *Morality and Grand Strategy: The Executive Branch and the Anti-Apartheid Act* (National Defense University Library Special Collection, December 15, 1989).

The Family Medical Leave Act, vetoed twice by George H.W. Bush, passed under the new Clinton Administration in 1993, as Public Law 103, 29 U.S.C. 2617, 107 Stat 8–9. Defenders of the FMLA include Judith Stadtman Tucker, "Hands Off My FMLA," *The Huffington Post*, January 2, 2007. Some that denounce the modest reach of the Act include Susan Freilach Appelton, "The Networked, Yet Still Hierarchical Family," *Virgina Law Review*, September 1, 2008. Critics of the FMLA point to its hidden costs and abuse by employees. *See* Deborah Walker, *Mandatory Family Legislation: The Hidden Costs* (Washington, D.C.: The Cato Institute, 1988).

Health care reform, of course, permeated the career of Ted Kennedy. His historical stamp, the Kennedy/Kassebaum Act of 1996, allowed employees to keep their health care insurance after leaving their job. For the original Health Insurance Portability and Accountability Act, see 29 U.S.C. 1181. The narrowness of the scope of the Act, also known as HIPPA, has resulted in the current health care reform debate.

Minimum wage, another great passion of Ted Kennedy's, took years of legislative effort. For the first time since 1965, a bill signed by the President increasing the minimum wage bore Ted Kennedy's name as a co-sponsor, along with retiring Republican Nancy Kassebaum. Critics of minimum wage legislation argue it increases unemployment and hurts low income people. A sample of such works include Milton and Rose Friedman, *Free to Choose* (New York: Harcourt Brace Jovanovich, 1980) and Thomas Sowell, "What Causes Unemployment," *Capitalism Magazine*, November 14, 2005.

The No Child Left Behind Act of 2002, embodied at Public Law 107–110, 20 U.S.C. Section 630, mandated strict testing for children as young as the second grade. Kennedy backed the bill because of his belief it would help minority students and foster a better education for minorities. Kennedy distanced himself from the Act, especially amid scandals involving schools cheating on the test. Such accounts appear on the blogs in Atlanta, Georgia, and also such accounts have been relayed in a personal interview.

Finally, the text of the Immigration bills of 2005 and 2007 can be viewed in their entirety from the Library of Congress website. Reading the actual bills, rather than uninformed arguments about them, is well worthwhile.

Bibliography

Branch, Taylor. *Pillar of Fire: America in the King Years 1963–65*. New York: Simon & Schuster, 1998.

Brauer, Carl M. *John F. Kennedy and the Second Reconstruction*. New York: Columbia University Press, 1979.

Cannelos, Peter S. *Last Lion: The Fall and Rise of Ted Kennedy*. New York: Simon & Schuster, 2009.

Caro, Robert A. *The Years of Lyndon Johnson: Master of the Senate*. New York: Alfred A. Knopf, 2002.

Clymer, Adam. *Edward M. Kennedy: A Biography*. New York: Harper Perennial, 2000.

Collier, Peter, and David Horowitz. *The Kennedys: An American Drama*. New York: Warner Books, 1984.

Cowin, Andrew J. "A Campaign Finance Reform That Protects Incumbents." The Heritage Society, 1990, http://www.heritage.org/research/reports/1990/09/a-campaign-finance-reform-that-protects-incumbents.

Dalleck, Robert. *An Unfinished Life: John F. Kennedy 1917–1963*. Boston: Little, Brown, 2003.

David, Lester. *Ted Kennedy: Triumphs and Tragedies*. New York: Grossett & Dunlap, 1972.

Gillon, Steven M. *The Pact: Bill Clinton, Newt Gingrich and the Rivalry That Defined a Generation*. New York: Oxford University Press, 2008.

Goodwin, Doris Kearns. *The Fitzgeralds and Kennedys*. New York: St. Martin's, 1987.

Heilemann, John, and Mark Halperin. *Game Change*. New York: HarperCollins, 2010.

Herring, George C. *America's Longest War: The United States and Vietnam, 1950–1975*. New York: John Wiley & Sons, 1979.

Hersh, Burton. *The Education of Ted Kennedy*. New York: William Morrow, 1972.

Kennedy, Edward M. *America Back on Track*. New York: Penguin, 2007.

_____. *True Compass*. New York: Hachette Book Group, 2009.

Klein, Edward. *Ted Kennedy: The Dream That Never Died*. New York: Crown, 2009.

Lazarus, Edward. *Closed Chambers: The First Eyewitness Account of the Epic Struggles Inside The Supreme Court*. New York: Times Books, 1998.

Lippman, Theo, Jr. *Senator Ted Kennedy: The Career behind the Image*. New York: W.W. Norton, 1976.

McGinnis, Joe. *The Last Brother: The Rise and Fall of Teddy Kennedy*. New York: Simon & Schuster, 1993.

McGregor Burns, James. *Edward Kennedy and the Camelot Legend*. New York: W.W. Norton, 1976.

Patterson, James T. *Brown v. Board of Education: A Civil Rights Milestone and its Troubled Legacy*. New York: Oxford University Press, 2001.

_____. *The Dread Disease: Cancer and Modern American Culture*. Cambridge, MA: Harvard University Press, 1987.

_____. *Grand Expectations: The United*

States, 1945–1974. New York: Oxford University Press, 1996.

Peltason, J.W. *Fifty-Eight Lonely Men: Southern Federal Judges and School Desegregation*. Urbana: University of Illinois Press, 1978.

Schlesinger, Arthur, Jr. *A Thousand Days*. Boston: Houghton Mifflin, 1965.

Shesol, Jeff. *Mutual Contempt: Lyndon Johnson, Robert Kennedy and the Feud That Defined a Decade*. New York: W.W. Norton, 1997.

Sitkoff, Harvard. *The Struggle for Black Equality 1954–1980*. New York: Hall & Wang, 1981.

Thurston, Clarke. *Ask Not: The Inauguration of John F. Kennedy and the Speech That Changed America*. New York: Henry Holt, 2005.

_____. *The Last Campaign: Robert F. Kennedy and 82 Days That Inspired America*. New York: Henry Holt, 2008.

Toobin, Jeffery. *The Nine: Inside the Secret World of the Supreme Court*. New York: Doubleday, 2007.

Williams, Juan. *Eyes on the Prize: Americas Civil Rights Years 1954–1965*. New York: Penguin, 1988.

Woodward, Bob. *The Brethren: Inside the Supreme Court*. New York: Simon & Schuster, 1979.

Index